# MICROECONOMICS FOR BUSINESS DECISIONS

## THEORY AND APPLICATION

**John M. Heineke**

*University of Santa Clara*

PRENTICE-HALL, INC., *Englewood Cliffs, New Jersey*

*Library of Congress Cataloging in Publication Data*

HEINEKE, JOHN M  (date)
  Microeconomics for business decisions.

  1. Managerial economics.  2. Microeconomics.
I. Title.
HD58.5.H45        330'.02'4658        75–35748
ISBN  0–13–581389–1

Printed in the United States of America

10  9  8  7  6  5  4  3  2  1

PRENTICE-HALL INTERNATIONAL, INC., *London*
PRENTICE-HALL OF AUSTRALIA, PTY. LIMITED, *Sydney*
PRENTICE-HALL OF CANADA, LTD., *Toronto*
PRENTICE-HALL OF INDIA PRIVATE LIMITED, *New Delhi*
PRENTICE-HALL OF JAPAN, INC., *Tokyo*
PRENTICE-HALL OF SOUTHEAST ASIA PTE. LTD., *Singapore*

To my mother and father

# Contents

# Preface

In first courses in price theory students are usually introduced to the basic models of consumer and firm behavior, which are essential components in the tool kit of a practicing economist. Although these models constitute a "way of thinking" about real-world decision problems that is quite general and powerful, this is often not obvious to the student, it seems primarily due to the rather abstract nature of modern price theory.

It has been my intention in writing this book to make application of the various models an integral part of the learning process, thereby enhancing student understanding and appreciation of the theory. I have endeavored to accomplish this by adopting an exposition that on the one hand is solidly based in economic theory and on the other is constantly occupied with application of derived principles to problem solving. To give the book a unified theme, the exposition throughout is in terms of problems facing firm managers in the private sector.

My approach has been to develop most of the familiar models of microeconomics in sufficient detail to permit their utilization in solving common decision problems confronting managers. As concepts are defined and properties of demand, production, and cost functions are derived, I have tried to indicate why these ideas are of interest to decision makers both by discussing their meaning within the context of some related decision problem and by providing examples of their computation or use in a more or less "realistic" situation.

Features of this book that to my knowledge are not found elsewhere include a treatment of the firm's optimal production plan, which integrates classical production theory with modern process focused production theory in which production functions are no longer "smooth"; and an emphasis throughout on the information needed to solve decision problems and the conditions under which these problems can be simplified. (For example, under what conditions may the search for the optimal production plan be formulated as a linear-programming problem? Under what conditions is a "full-costing" pricing rule optimal? Or under what conditions may general problems of optimal product mix be simplified enough to make them readily solvable?) Finally, each chapter contains a set of problems of varying degrees of difficulty designed to test both the understanding of concepts and the application of these concepts to problem solving. Experience indicates that doing the problems pays off handsomely in increased understanding. Some problems are straightforward applications of the materials in the chapter; other problems amplify and extend the materials discussed; and a few problems present new topics.

The materials in this book have been used over a number of years in various forms both in an upper-division economics course and in the "micro" requirement in the MBA program here at the University of Santa Clara. I would expect that they could also be used profitably in upper-division business decision-making classes. Although no prior knowledge of economics has been assumed, previous courses in economics are bound to pay dividends in increased understanding.

As for a more detailed description of contents, Chapters 1 and 2 are concerned with demand functions. In particular, what information do demand functions contain and under what conditions may this information be extracted? Topics include relatively nontechnical discussions of estimation, predictive testing, and the identification problem. The Appendix to Chapter 1 focuses on the mathematical notions used in the text. Since differential calculus is the primary mathematical tool employed, a good part of the Appendix reviews topics from differential calculus. It should be emphasized that knowledge of the material in the Appendix is sufficient to understand *all* mathematical arguments in the text. Students rusty in the use of calculus should read this Appendix *before* beginning Chapter 1.

Chapter 3 begins a three-chapter discussion of production decisions by introducing basic concepts associated with the firm's production function. In Chapter 4 the problem of the optimal production plan is examined under different assumptions about firm technology and the availability of resources. The important concept of a "linear technology" is introduced as a possible means of substantially simplifying production decisions. Chapter 5 explores two applications of the linear technology model—the optimal product mix problem and the use of input-output analysis to forecast industry demand. Chapter 6 is devoted to production cost functions. The properties of cost functions and basic requirements for estimation are discussed. Topics include data requirements, adjusting for "changes in technology," the choice of functional form, and estimation of the cost function via estimation of the production function.

Chapter 7 forms the bridge between earlier chapters and the problem of optimal volume and pricing decisions, the topic of Chapters 8, 9, and 10. Basic concepts associated with firm revenue functions are introduced. Chapter 8 focuses on firms that, for various reasons, take the "current" market price as given. A primary concern of management in such firms is the determination of the optimal sales volume. This decision is carefully analyzed. The use of break-even charts for volume determination is discussed. A feature of this chapter, which to my knowledge is not available elsewhere, is a treatment of the volume decision problem for firms that possess market power but (a) are confronted with price controls or (b) have decided not to "rock the boat" by changing existing prices. Chapters 9 and 10 both deal with the pricing decision. Chapter 9 treats this decision for the case when management need not include the reaction of "other firms" in its pricing decision rule—"The Case of Pricing Autonomy." (Of course, industries in which firms possess pricing autonomy are comprised of firms in the traditional market structures of either monopoly or monopolistic competition.) Topics include pricing in multiple markets, break-even analysis for price determination, regulation of monopoly, and a discussion of the optimality of "full-cost" pricing. Chapter 10 covers "The Case of Pricing Interdependence" (oligopoly). The problems incurred in pricing in markets where firms are highly interdependent are explored in some detail, including an analytical treatment of "the problem of mutual interdependence" from a marketing perspective. The consequences of collusion among sellers on the firm's pricing decision are discussed, and several simple collusive pricing models are examined. Each chapter contains a number of examples illustrating calculation of concepts that have been introduced and use of theoretical principles that have been derived.

To allow more flexibility in the use of the book, I have starred those sections that may be omitted without loss of continuity. In many instances these sections contain more difficult materials that may be used at the discretion of the professor. Problems associated with these sections have also been starred.

In conclusion, I would like to thank several of my associates for their cooperation and thoughtful suggestions in reviewing the manuscript: Professor Mike Keenan of New York University; Professor Melvin C. Fredlund, California State University at Hayward; Professor William Alberts, University of Washington; Professor Jerome E. Hass, Cornell University; and Professor R. D. Peterson, Colorado State University.

# Demand Theory
# For Decision Makers

In this book we will be concerned primarily with business decisions of various types. The subject of this chapter, demand functions, is an essential ingredient in a number of areas of business decision making, including pricing, product mix determination, and sales policy decisions.

To an economist a demand function is the logical relation between quantity demanded of a commodity and the determinants of demand. Generally speaking, quantity demanded of a given product will depend upon the price of the product in question, the prices of related commodities, the level of advertising outlays, general business conditions, and perhaps other factors. Obviously the relationship between demand levels and prices, advertising outlays, business conditions, and any other determinants of demand is of considerable interest to firm managers. In this chapter and the next we will familiarize ourselves with the information content of demand functions and investigate the possibilities of extracting from these functions certain pieces of information for decision purposes.

## DEMAND THEORY FOR MANAGEMENT DECISIONS: AN OVERVIEW

Demand functions have been studied intensively in two areas of economics. The first area, microeconomic theory, is concerned with the theoretical basis of demand. Microeconomic theorists have studied the conditions under which demand functions exist, what in general can be said about the properties of these functions, and many other questions dealing with the logical foundations of demand. In the second area, econometrics, the problem of estimating economic functions in general and demand functions in particular is addressed. Powerful techniques have been developed which can often (but not always) yield valuable estimates of the functions in question. Although managers will have little direct interest in either microeconomic theory or econometrics, in this chapter and those that follow we will extract from these two highly technical areas of economic analysis a number of concepts and techniques that are of fundamental importance in business decision making. More specifically, the student will be acquainted with those portions of demand theory that are particularly useful for managerial decision making and also with the problems associated with getting numerical estimates of demand relationships.

### Factors that Influence the Level of Demand

To begin, we will need a systematic manner of displaying the relationship between demand and its determinants. With this in mind, we introduce the following notation:

$x_i \equiv$ the quantity of product $X_i$ demanded per unit of time
$P_i \equiv$ the price of $X_i$
$Y \equiv$ the "level of income"—an indicator of the level of consumer and/or business purchasing power
$A \equiv$ advertising outlays on $X_i$
$\alpha \equiv$ a portmanteau or "catchall" variable, which includes all other influences on demand

Using this notation, we will define

$$x_1 = f(P_1, P_2, \ldots, P_n, Y, A, \alpha) \qquad (1\text{-}1)$$

to be the demand function for product $X_1$. Notice that a lowercase $x_1$ denotes a *quantity* of commodity $X_1$. So, if $X_1$ represents Ford automobiles, then $x_1$ is the number of Fords demanded. Equation (1-1) tells us that the quantity of $X_1$ demanded depends upon its own price $P_1$, the prices of related commodities $P_2, P_3, \ldots, P_n$, the level of consumer and/or business purchasing power $Y$, the level of advertising outlays on $X_1$, $A$, and other influences $\alpha$ which will be specified whenever the need arises.

A few comments on the variable $Y$ are in order. If $X_1$ is a consumer good then $Y$ may be national income, consumer disposable income, or any other indicator of consumer purchasing power. For commodities sold to business and industry, the variable $Y$ may be national income, the "Index of Industrial Production," or any other indicator of the level of business activity. For example, if we were studying the demand for aluminum ingot, then the index of industrial production would be a good choice for $Y$, since refined aluminum is sold primarily to industrial users and the "Index" is an indicator of industrial activity.

The demand function we have written as equation (1-1) contains no surprises. In fact, if one were to stop an individual at random and inquire as to the influences that determine the demand for a commodity, most likely the reply would be "Price, prices of related goods, income, and advertising expenditures." So the only thing new thus far is the slightly technical way of depicting the demand relationship.

A key management concern is the sensitivity of demand to changes in the various determinants of demand. The question then arises as to the appropriate measure of demand sensitivity. Since partial derivatives measure the change in a dependent variable, due to a change in an independent variable, they would seem to be a likely candidate for a measure of demand sensitivity. And indeed they are. For example, the change in the quantity of $X_1$ demanded due *only* to a change in its own price is written $\partial x_1/\partial P_1$. The word "only" is emphasized because *partial* derivatives record the change in $x_1$ due to a change in $P_1$ alone, *given* a fixed set of values for each of the other variables in the demand function. (If one is interested in assessing the response of demand to a simultaneous change in several variables, additional calculations are required. This point is discussed below.)

Now let us write each of the partial derivatives of (1-1) to see what we know about their signs. First, we would expect $\partial x_1/\partial P_1 < 0$, since usually increases in sales will require decreases in price *for given values of the other variables* in the demand function. The sign of the other price derivatives $\partial x_1/\partial P_j$, $j \neq 1$, tells us whether $X_1$ and $X_j$ are *substitutes* or *complements*. Substitutes are competitive or rivals with $X_1$ and hence increases in the price of a competitive product will increase demand for $X_1$, while price decreases will decrease the demand for $X_1$. Therefore $\partial x_1/\partial P_j > 0$ if $X_1$ and $X_j$ are substitutes. The size of this derivative indicates how close a substitute $X_j$ is for $X_1$. For example, Hewlett Packard and Texas Instruments pocket calculators are close substitutes in the eyes of most buyers. Therefore $\partial x_1/\partial P_j$ will be large and positive if $X_1$ and $X_j$ represent these two calculators. Complements are commodities that are often used together. Therefore, if $X_1$ and $X_j$ are complements, a decrease in the price of $X_j$ leads to an increase in sales of $X_j$ (since $\partial X_j/\partial P_j < 0$), and since $X_1$ and $X_j$ are used together, also an increase in sales of $X_1$. Hence decreases in the price of a complement lead to increases in sales of both commodities, and an increase in price leads to a decrease in demand for both products. That is, $\partial x_1/\partial P_j < 0$ when $X_1$ and $X_j$ are complements. As with substitutes, the magnitude of the derivative indicates the closeness of the complementarity.

For most commodities increases in the level of income or business activity mean increased demand at constant prices, that is, $\partial x_1/\partial Y > 0$, but there is an important group of commodities for which rising incomes mean falling demand. We return to this topic later in the chapter. Finally, the response of demand to changes in advertising outlays will normally be positive, or at least not negative, $\partial x_1/\partial A \geq 0$. Of course we are not able to say anything about $\partial x_1/\partial \alpha$ until the variable $\alpha$ has been specified.

To illustrate the above discussion, assume that demand for $X_1$ is measured in thousands of units, prices are in dollars, and the demand function is a linear function that has been estimated to be[1]

$$x_1 = 9.1 - 2.1P_1 + 1.61P_2 - .11P_3 + 3.6Y + .0001A \qquad (1\text{-}2)$$

[1] The rationale for choosing a linear function to represent the demand function and the possibility of estimating the coefficients of such a function are the topics of the next chapter.

In this demand function, every dollar increase in price leads to a 2.1-thousand-unit decrease in demand, since $\partial x_1/\partial P_1 = -2.1$. Because $\partial x_1/\partial P_2 = 1.61$ is a positive number, we know that $X_2$ is a substitute or competitive product with $X_1$ and that the demand for $X_1$ will decline approximately 1,610 units for each dollar decrease in price of $X_2$. In other words, decreases in the price of $X_2$ result in the producer of $X_2$ capturing a portion of the market share previously held by the producer of $X_1$. At the same time, decreases in the price of $X_3$ lead to increases in demand for $X_1$. Commodities $X_3$ and $X_1$ are complements. The coefficient of $Y$ means that every unit increase in the "level of income" will be accompanied by a 3,600-unit increase in demand. The coefficient of the advertising variable may be interpreted in a similar manner.

### Graphing Demand Functions—The Necessary Condition

For a graphical analysis, we must collapse our multivariate demand function into a two-dimensional representation. More specifically, if the general demand function shown in equation (1-1) is written as

$$x_1 = f(P_1, P_2^0, P_3^0, \ldots, P_n^0, Y^0, A^0, \alpha^0)$$
$$= \bar{f}(P_1) \tag{1-1'}$$

where superscript "naughts" indicate that variables are fixed at given levels, then the $n + 4$ dimensional demand function ($n + 3$ independent variables and one dependent variable) becomes a two-dimensional function between $x_1$ and $P_1$ alone, *given* $P_2 = P_2^0, P_3 = P_3^0, \ldots, Y = Y^0$, and so forth. We have written this function as $x_1 = \bar{f}(P_1)$ in equation (1-1'). The variables $P_2, P_3, \ldots,$ $P_n, Y, A, \alpha$, which are fixed in equation (1-1'), are termed *parameters*. Generally, a parameter is a variable that is fixed in a particular model or for a particular purpose. As an example, if the price of $X_2$ is $2, that of $X_3$ is $9, the income variable is .8, and advertising expenditures are $21,000, then the linear demand function in equation (1-2) becomes

$$x_1 = 9.1 - 2.1P_1 + 1.61P_2^0 - .11P_3^0 + 3.6Y^0 + .0001A^0$$
$$= 16.31 - 2.1P_1 \tag{1-2'}$$

This is a particular case of the function we have called $\bar{f}(P_1)$ and is the relationship between demand for $X_1$ and its own price when $P_2 = \$2, P_3 = \$9,$ $Y = .8$, and $A = \$21,000$. Notice also that any other prices that might affect demand, except $P_2$ and $P_3$, and all other variables $\alpha$, were treated as parameters back in equation (1-2) and hence are included in the intercept term of *that* expression just as the influence of $P_2, P_3, Y$, and $A$ are included in the intercept of equation (1-2').

It should be clear that the procedure of treating some variables as parameters in an analysis in no way ignores these variables. Instead, the function formed when this is done (the function $\bar{f}$) is one of a *family* of functions in the sense that there is a different demand relationship for each set of values chosen for $P_2, P_3, \ldots, P_n$, $Y$, $A$, and $\alpha$. This point is illustrated in Figure 1-1 using the linear demand function given in equation (1-2'). If advertising expenditures were \$100,000 instead of \$21,000, but $P_2 = \$2$, $P_3 = \$9$, and $Y = .8$ as before, then $x_1 = 24.21 - 2.1P_1$ is another demand function in the family of demand functions obtained by treating all variables[2] as parameters except $P_1$. It is important to notice that changes in $P_1$ are *movements along* the function $\bar{f}(P_1) = 16.31 - 2.1P_1$, while a change in any other variable is a shift in the function $\bar{f}(P_1)$. The change in $A$ from \$21,000 to \$100,000 *shifted* $\bar{f}(P_1)$ to the right, as shown in Figure 1-1.

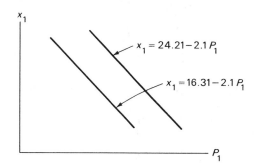

$x_1 = 24.21 - 2.1P_1$

$x_1 = 16.31 - 2.1P_1$

**FIGURE 1-1**

Two demand functions in a family of demand functions

## Demand Elasticities

We now return to the question of measuring the response of demand to a change in any one of the variables that affect demand. Instead of measuring the change in demand due to a change in $P_1$, all other variables constant, let us consider measuring the *percentage* change in demand due to a *percentage* change in $P_1$, all other variables constant. Since the relation between demand for product one and its price when all other variables are constant is given by $x_1 = \bar{f}(P_1)$, the quantity $dx_1/x_1$ is the *percentage* change[3] in demand when all variables are constant except $P_1$. In addition, $dP_1/P_1$ is a *percentage* change in $P_1$. Therefore

$$\frac{dx_1}{x_1} \bigg/ \frac{dP_1}{P_1} = \frac{dx_1}{dP_1}\left(\frac{P_1}{x_1}\right) \tag{1-3}$$

is the percentage change in demand for $X_1$ per (or due to) a percentage change in $P_1$. We may say "due to" a change in $P_1$ because demand for $X_1$ is a function of its price, and changes in price "cause" changes in quantity demanded. The quantity given as (1-3) is termed the *price elasticity of demand* for commodity one and will be denoted $\eta_{x_1 P_1}$, or $\eta_{11}$ for short. The price elasticity of demand, $\eta_{11}$, measures the percentage change in demand for $X_1$ due to a percentage change in $P_1$. By convention, if $\eta_{11} < -1$ the demand for $X_1$ is said to be

[2]Throughout the book "independent" variables will be placed on horizontal axes and "dependent" variables on vertical axes.

[3]The term $dx_1$ is read "the change in $x_1$" and therefore $dx_1/x_1$ is the change in $x_1$ divided by $x_1$, which by definition is a percentage change.

*elastic* or sensitive to price changes, and if $-1 < \eta_{11} < 0$ the demand for $X_1$ is said to be *inelastic* or insensitive to price changes.[4]

The formula for the price elasticity of demand given as (1-3) was derived using the two-dimensional demand function $\bar{f}(P_1)$. It is a simple matter to generalize (1-3) so as to make our definition of $\eta_{11}$ applicable to the general demand function $f(P_1, P_2, \ldots, \alpha)$. To do this notice that if $x_1 = \bar{f}(P_1)$, then $dx_1/dP_1$ is the change in demand due solely to a change in $P_1$. While if $x_1 = f(P_1, P_2, \ldots, \alpha)$, then $\partial x_1/\partial P_1$ performs precisely the same measurement. In other words, $\partial f/\partial P_1$ and $d\bar{f}/dP_1$ are the same measurement. Therefore, in general, the price elasticity of demand for $X_1$ is

$$\eta_{11} = \frac{\partial x_1}{\partial P_1} \frac{P_1}{x_1} \tag{1-4}$$

Analogously, the *cross-elasticity of demand between commodities* $X_1$ *and* $X_j$ is defined as

$$\eta_{1j} = \frac{\partial x_1}{\partial P_j} \frac{P_j}{x_1}, \qquad j \neq 1 \tag{1-5}$$

and the *income elasticity of demand for commodity* $X_1$ is defined as

$$\eta_{1Y} = \frac{\partial x_1}{\partial Y} \frac{Y}{x_1} \tag{1-6}$$

The calculation $\eta_{1j}$ measures the degree of substitutability (competitiveness), or complementarity, between commodity $X_1$ and commodity $X_j$. Notice that the magnitude of $\eta_{1j}$ is a convenient indicator of how closely the markets for $X_1$ and $X_j$ are related. In more detail, $\eta_{1j}$ measures the degree of market independence or autonomy enjoyed by the producer of $X_1$. If $\eta_{1j}$ is positive, the demand for $X_1$ and the price of $X_j$ move in the same direction; as we have seen, in this case $X_1$ and $X_j$ are termed *substitutes* and hence the producers of $X_1$ and $X_j$ are competitors. The larger is $\eta_{1j}$, the more competitive are $X_1$ and $X_j$. If $\eta_{1j}$ is negative, the demand for $X_1$ and the price of $X_j$ move in opposite directions, indicating that $X_1$ and $X_j$ are used together. Commodities $X_1$ and $X_j$ are *complements*; the smaller is $\eta_{1j}$, the more closely tied are the markets for $X_1$ and $X_j$. Therefore, *the amount that* $\eta_{1j}$ *deviates from zero* (*in either direction*) *is an indication of the extent to which the pricing policies of the producer of* $X_j$ *influence the market position of the producer of* $X_1$. The larger is $\eta_{1j}$ in absolute value, the more is the market for $X_1$ influenced by commodity $X_j$. Increases in the price of substitutes, or decreases in the price of complements, lead to increased volume for the producer of $X_1$, while decreases in substitute prices and increases in the price of complements have the opposite effect on sales of $X_1$. If $\eta_{1j} = 0$, then the markets for $X_1$ and $X_j$ are *independent*. So, in

---

[4]In general $\eta_{11}$ will be negative, since $dx_1/dP_1 < 0$. So if $\eta_{11} = -2$ demand is price *elastic*, since a 1 percent change in price leads to more than a 1 percent response of sales in the opposite direction of the price change. In particular, sales *increase* 2 percent for a 1 percent *decrease* in price and *decrease* 2 percent for a 1 percent *increase* in price.

general, the cross-elasticity of demand between commodity one and other commodities measures the sensitivity of the demand for $X_1$ to changes in the pricing policies of other sellers.

Calculation of an income elasticity yields a measurement of the sensitivity of demand to changes in the level of consumer income or business activity. If $\eta_{1y}$ is positive and high, then the firm producing $X_1$ will grow in an expanding economy—or at least has growth opportunities. At the same time, a high positive income elasticity is a warning that sales will fall off rapidly in recessionary periods. Sales of $X_1$ move with the business cycle. If $\eta_{1y}$ is small, then firm sales and profitability will not be sensitive to income levels or general business conditions. Sales of $X_1$ are relatively "recession proof." The producers of commodities with negative income elasticities will experience increasing sales at constant prices in recessionary periods and decreasing sales at constant prices in expansionary periods.

Commodities with positive income elasticities are termed *normal* commodities because "normally" sales increase, at constant prices, with the measure of income. In addition, normal commodities whose sales are very sensitive to changes in the level of income are often termed *luxuries*, merely because these items are the first to go in times of falling income; while normal commodities whose sales are relatively unaffected by changes in the level of income are usually termed *necessities*. These items are purchased in approximately constant quantities in periods of rising and falling income. They are in some sense "necessary."

Commodities with negative income elasticities are often called *inferior* commodities. Although this choice of words is unfortunate, the meaning of $\eta_{1Y} < 0$ is clear. The bottom items in most product lines, the least expensive cuts of meat, grocery items with "unheard-of labels," and so forth, are often bypassed as incomes increase and customers can afford more expensive substitutes. They are "inferior" goods.

The classification of a commodity as normal or inferior often changes over time. The normal commodity of one generation is often an inferior commodity to later generations, and sometimes vice versa. Can you think of any examples?

To illustrate our discussion, consider the following estimated demand function:

$$x_1 = 306.6 P_1^{-1.2} P_2^{.6} P_3^{-.9} Y^{2.5} A^{.09} \qquad (1\text{-}7)$$

This type of function is called a *power function* and is multiplicative in the independent variables, with each independent variable being raised to some power. We will be discussing functions of this type in much more detail later, but for now it is sufficient for us to know merely that the numbers in (1-7) have been estimated in some manner and that quantity demanded is measured in thousands of units of $X_1$, prices are all in dollars, advertising expenditures are in thousands of dollars, and the "business activity" variable, $Y$, is the Index of Industrial Production.

To calculate the price elasticity of demand for $X_1$, we need only partially differentiate (1-7) with respect to $P_1$ and then multiply the resulting expression by $P_1/x_1$. We then have

$$\partial x_1/\partial P_1 = (-1.2)306.6 P_1^{-2.2} P_2^{.6} P_3^{-.9} Y^{2.5} A^{.09}$$

and

$$\eta_{11} = \partial x_1/\partial P_1 (P_1/x_1) = \frac{(-1.2)306.6 P_1^{-2.2} P_2^{.6} P_3^{-.9} Y^{2.5} A^{.09}(P_1)}{x_1}$$

$$= -1.2$$

since by (1-7) the numerator of this expression is merely $-1.2x_1$. Using precisely the same procedure you should be able to show that

$$\eta_{12} = .6$$
$$\eta_{13} = -.9$$

and

$$\eta_{1Y} = 2.5$$

According to these calculations, a 1 percent increase in $P_1$ will bring about a 1.2 percent decrease in demand for $X_1$. We also see that commodity two is a substitute for commodity one and in particular that each percentage decrease in price of $X_2$ will reduce sales of $X_1$ by 0.6 percent. Finally note that $X_1$ and $X_3$ are complements and that $X_1$ is a "normal" commodity. (Interpret the meaning of the numbers $\eta_{13} = -.9$ and $\eta_{1Y} = 2.5$.) What is the meaning of the number .09 that is the exponent of $A$ in (1-7)?

### Measuring Demand Sensitivity—Derivatives or Elasticities?

The demand elasticities we have just defined measure the sensitivity of demand to changes in the various determinants of demand. Of course partial derivatives also measure demand responsiveness. The question then arises as to whether to use $\partial x_1/\partial P_1$ or $\eta_{11}$, $\partial x_1/\partial P_2$ or $\eta_{12}$, $\partial x_1/\partial Y$ or $\eta_{1Y}$, and so forth, to measure the sensitivity of demand to changes in the various determinants of demand. The answer to this question depends upon the ultimate use of the measurement. Although derivatives are perfectly legitimate measures, in some uses they do have a shortcoming—a shortcoming that stems from the fact that the value of a derivative depends upon the units of measurement. For example, if demand is measured in thousands of units of $X_1$ and price is in dollars, then $\partial x_1/\partial P_1 = -.21$ means that demand will fall $.21(1000) = 210$ units per dollar increase in the price of $X_1$. Since elasticities are percentage changes, their value does not depend upon the units of measurement. In comparing demand characteristics *across* markets, this difference can be significant, as the following example shows: Say we are interested in comparing the sensitivity of sales to changes in price in two different markets, the steel and color television set markets. Denote the demand for steel, in millions of tons, by $x_s$ and the demand for color television sets, in ten-thousand-set lots, as $x_T$. Then, say

$$\partial x_s/\partial P_s = -52$$

and

$$\partial x_T/\partial P_T = -4.75$$

The number 52 is, of course, 52 million tons, while 4.75 is 47,500 television sets, where the change in price in each case is a unit change. So, we know that a one-unit increase in the price of steel will decrease sales by 52 million tons, while a unit increase in the price of color television sets will decrease sales by 47,500 sets. Now consider the question, "Is the demand for steel more sensitive or less sensitive to price changes than the demand for color television sets?" That is, is 52 million tons of steel a "larger" or a "smaller" decrease in sales than 47,500 television sets? The question is, of course, nonsense and cannot be answered, since tons of steel and thousands of television sets cannot be compared. But if we had calculated, say, $\eta_{ss} = -.7$ and $\eta_{TT} = -1.8$ instead of the derivatives $-52$ and $-4.75$, the question is answered. It is answered because $\eta_{ss} = -.7$ means that a 1 percent price increase in the steel market will cause only a 0.7 percent decline in sales, while that same percentage price change in the color television set market will cause sales to drop 1.8 percent. The market for color television sets is much more sensitive to price changes than is the steel market.

### Further Remarks on Demand Elasticities

The demand elasticities we have been discussing are obviously of much interest to the business decision maker. For example, if $\eta_{11}$ could be estimated management would have an estimate of the sensitivity of sales to changes in the price of $X_1$, while, as we have seen, an estimate of $\eta_{1j}$ is an estimate of the decision-making autonomy possessed by the seller of $X_1$. To illustrate this last remark, assume $X_j$ is a substitute for $X_1$. *Then the estimate of $\eta_{1j}$ is an estimate of the change in the market share held by the producer of $X_1$ due to a change in pricing policy by the producer of $X_j$.* For example, if the price of $X_1$ and the price of $X_j$ are currently $P_1^0$ and $P_j^0$ and the producer of $X_j$ lowers price from $P_j^0$ to $P_j^*$, then $\eta_{1j}$ is the percentage drop in sales of $X_1$ *if the producer of $X_1$ does not retaliate by lowering price.* This situation is depicted graphically in Figure 1-2, where $\hat{f}(P_1)$ is the demand function for $X_1$ at the higher rival price, $P_j^0$, and $\bar{f}(P_1)$ is the demand function for $X_1$ after $P_j$ is lowered to $P_j^*$.

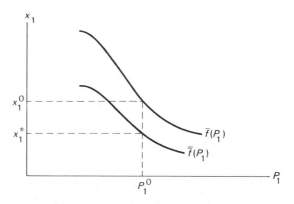

The loss in sales is $x_1^0 - x_1^*$, given the seller of $X_1$ does not lower price. Dividing $x_1^0 - x_1^*$ by $x_1^0$ yields the percentage of the market lost due to the change in $P_j$. The sales loss $x_1^0 - x_1^*$ is a prediction about the consequences of not responding to price cuts instigated by the producer of $X_j$.

Of course it will not pay to respond to all price cuts, since price changes are usually expensive due to the fact that new price lists must be printed, brochures and catalogs must be updated, and additional sales efforts may have to be undertaken to "explain" the change to established buyers. Whether a price change is called for obviously depends upon how large $x_1^0 - x_1^*$ is. An estimate of the demand function for $X_1$ would enable decision makers to make this calculation.

One important insight derives from this example: We do not always have to estimate the demand function for $X_1$ to be able to calculate an estimate of $\eta_{1j}$. Market observations on $x_1$ and $P_j$ may be sufficient. More precisely, observed values of $x_1$ and $P_j$ are sufficient for estimating $\eta_{1j}$ if *all* influences on the demand for $X_1$ except the price of $X_j$ were constant in the period under consideration. In this case

$$\eta_{1j} = \left(\frac{x_1^0 - x_1^*}{P_j^0 - P_j^*}\right)\left(\frac{P_j^0}{x_1^0}\right) = \frac{\Delta x_1}{\Delta P_j}\left(\frac{P_j^0}{x_1^0}\right)$$

To provide a numerical interpretation of this discussion, consider the linear demand function given above as equation (1-2). If the price of $X_2$ is \$2, the price of $X_3$ is \$9, $Y = .8$, and advertising expenditures are \$21,000, then $\bar{f}(P_1) = 16.31 - 2.1P_1$, as shown in Figure 1-3. Say the price of $X_1$ is currently \$1.90.

FIGURE 1-3

Loss of market share through a decrease in the price of a substitute: an example

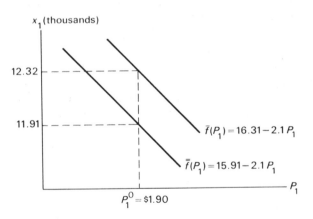

Sales are then 12,320 units. Now, if the producer of $X_2$ lowers price from \$2 to \$1.75 *and* the producer of $X_1$ does not respond, the demand function for $X_1$ will shift leftward to $\bar{f}(P_1) = 15.91 - 2.1P_1$ and at the current price of \$1.90, sales of $X_1$ drop to 11,918 units. Sales of 402 units[5] have been lost, which is $402/12,320 = 3.2$ percent of the market share of product $X_1$.

Since the percentage change in price of $X_2$ is $(\$2 - \$1.75)/\$2 = 12.5\%$, the cross-elasticity of demand under these market conditions is $3.2\%/12.5\% = .26$.

[5] The change in sales (402 units) could be divided by either 12,320 or 11,918 to get the percentage change in sales. For small changes in sales, the two numbers will be approximately equal. We will adopt the custom of always dividing by the original sales volume. Similar remarks hold for percentage changes in any variable. We will always use the original value of the variable in question as the divisor.

In other words, $\eta_{12} = .26$ when $P_1 = \$1.90$, $P_3 = \$9$, $Y = .8$, $A = \$21,000$, and the price of $X_2$ is changed from \$2 to \$1.75. The small cross-elasticity indicates that $X_2$ is a relatively poor substitute for commodity one under these conditions.

### Changes in Demand Due to Simultaneous Changes in Several Influences on Demand

Demand elasticities are percentage changes in demand due to a change in one and only one variable that affects demand. But often the decision maker will be confronted with a situation in which it would be desirable to be able to calculate the effect on demand when two or more of the variables influencing demand change simultaneously. For example, if there are indications that several rivals may be ready to change their prices, it would be of considerable interest to be able to estimate the net effect of these price changes on the demand for $X_1$. Or if only one rival, say, lowers price, what increase in advertising expenditures by the producer of $X_1$ would be needed to offset the influence of the price reduction? Or if $X_1$ is a normal commodity and the economy is entering a recession, what decrease in $P_1$ would leave volume unchanged? Each of these questions is of the sort, "What is the effect on demand of a simultaneous change in several of the variables that influence demand?"

To answer this question, write the differential of the general demand function $x_1 = f(P_1, P_2, \ldots, A, \alpha)$,

$$dx_1 = \frac{\partial x_1}{\partial P_1} dP_1 + \frac{\partial x_1}{\partial P_2} dP_2 + \cdots + \frac{\partial x_1}{\partial A} dA + \frac{\partial x_1}{\partial \alpha} d\alpha$$

In words, this expression merely tells us that the change in demand, due to a change in each of the influences on demand $dx_1$, is equal to the change in demand due solely to a one-unit decrease in $P_1$, $\partial x_1/\partial P_1$, times the size of the change in $P_1$, $dP_1$, plus the change in demand due to a one-unit change in $P_2$, $\partial x_1/\partial P_2$, times the size of the change in $P_2$, $dP_2$, and so forth, until each of the changes has been accounted for. Dividing both sides of the differential by $x_1$ converts it into a statement about *percentage* changes in demand. Finally, multiply the first term in the sum on the right-hand side by $P_1/P_1$, the second term by $P_2/P_2$, the term $(\partial x_1/\partial A) dA$ by $A/A$, and so forth. This procedure obviously changes nothing and yields the result we are interested in:

$$\frac{dx_1}{x_1} = \frac{\partial x_1}{\partial P_1}\left(\frac{P_1}{x_1}\right)\frac{dP_1}{P_1} + \frac{\partial x_1}{\partial P_2}\left(\frac{P_2}{x_1}\right)\frac{dP_2}{P_2} + \cdots + \frac{\partial x_1}{\partial A}\left(\frac{A}{x_1}\right)\frac{dA}{A} + \frac{\partial x_1}{\partial \alpha}\left(\frac{\alpha}{x_1}\right)\frac{d\alpha}{\alpha}$$

$$= \eta_{11}\frac{dP_1}{P_1} + \eta_{12}\frac{dP_2}{P_2} + \cdots + \eta_{1A}\frac{dA}{A} + \eta_{1\alpha}\frac{d\alpha}{\alpha}$$

(1-8)

*The percentage change in demand due to a percentage change in any number of the variables that influence demand is obtained merely by adding individual demand elasticities multiplied by the size of the percentage changes.* Therefore, once demand elasticities have been estimated, we are able to answer the questions posed at the beginning of this section. Any variable that is unchanged drops out of the sum, since if, say, $P_3$ is unchanged, then $dP_3 = 0$. So, if the price of $X_1$ and advertising expenditures are simultaneously varied and all other variables remain unchanged, the percentage response of demand is given by

$$\frac{dx_1}{x_1} = \eta_{11}\frac{dP_1}{P_1} + \eta_{1A}\frac{dA}{A}$$

The measure $\eta_{11}$ gives the response of demand to a 1 percent change in $P_1$. This measure is multiplied by $dP_1/P_1$, the actual percentage change in $P_1$. The result $\eta_{11}(dP_1/P_1)$ is the total demand response due to a percentage change in $P_1$ of size $dP_1/P_1$. The analogous interpretation holds for $\eta_{1A}(dA/A)$. As an example, assume $\eta_{11}$ has been estimated to be $-1.3$ and $\eta_{1A}$ is estimated to be .8 and that price and advertising expenditures are simultaneously increased by 5 and 10 percent, respectively. We then are able to calculate the predicted response of sales as

$$\frac{dx_1}{x_1} = -1.3(5) + .8(10) = 1.5$$

Based on these elasticity estimates, we see that increased advertising outlays more than make up for the increase in price, since sales will increase 1.5 percent if such a policy combination is undertaken. If each of the elasticities in the expression (1-8) is estimated, percentage demand changes may be predicted for any combination of policies. We will return to this important result again and again.

**PROBLEMS AND QUESTIONS**

1. Using your knowledge of demand functions and cross-elasticities of demand in particular, explain why power-generating utilities find it in their interest to promote sales of electric appliances.

2. Consider the problem of a firm whose product is losing an ongoing battle to retain its historic share of the market. In the last six months, 10 percent of the market has been lost to a rival commodity. In an attempt to rectify this situation, management decides to simultaneously lower price and increase advertising outlays. The marketing department estimates that sales will increase 1.3 percent for every percentage decrease in price and about 0.75 percent for every percentage increase in advertising outlays.

   a. If price is decreased 5 percent, what increase in advertising outlays will be needed to regain the lost share of the market? What assumption does your answer depend upon?

   b. If, instead, it is known that sales have dropped off 50,000 units in the last six months and that sales respond approximately 3,000 units per dollar drop in price and about 5,000 units per thousand dollar increase in advertising outlays, what increase in advertising will be necessary to regain the lost sales given that price is cut $7.50?

   c. Given that $x_1 = f(P_1, P_2, \ldots, P_n, Y, A)$, write a general expression for the change in demand as a function of changes in each of the influences

on demand. Interpret your result and notice that if all changes are zero
except for $P_1$ and $A$, you have the expression that you used either implicitly
or explicitly in answering part b.

3. The following data were gathered on the price of $X_1$ and the sales of $X_2$,
a competitive product of $X_1$.

| $X_2(1000)$ | 52.5 | 53.5 | 51.75 | 48 |
|---|---|---|---|---|
| $P_1(\$)$ | 3.5 | 4.0 | 3.0 | 1.5 |

Use these data to calculate an estimate of the cross-elasticity of demand between
$X_2$ and $X_1$ when $P_1 = \$3$. (You will have a choice of two values to use as your
estimate, use the average.) The validity of your calculations depends upon what
assumption?

4. Assume that you are employed by one of the four American automobile
manufacturers and are asked to reach a production decision for the next quarter.
One of the many pieces of information you have at your disposal to help reach
the decision is a demand forecast provided by a research and forecasting unit
at the main office. Their sales forecast is the following:

$$x_1 = 10.1 + 6.3P_1 + 3.7P_2 - 1.6P_3 + 2.7P_4 + 2.1Y$$

where $x_1$ represents the number of autos sold by firm 1 (your firm); $P_1$ is the
price of these automobiles; $P_2, P_3$, and $P_4$ are the prices of the other three
American competitors; and $Y$ is a measure of the level of national income.
After studying the sales forecast, you recommend that those responsible be
relieved of any further responsibilities. Based on the estimate given above, build
as strong a case as possible for your recommendation.

5. In September 1971 Videlectrix, a producer of microcircuits, lowered the
price of one of its items 2.5 percent. The following month, sales had increased
from 250,000 to 300,000 units. At the same time, another producer of microcircuits, Microcircuits, Inc., experienced a decline in sales of the affected item
from 450,000 to 395,000 units.
a. What is the price elasticity of demand for the Videlectrix microcircuit?
b. Calculate the cross-elasticity of demand between the Microcircuit, Inc.,
and the Videlectrix circuit. Are the two circuits close substitutes?
c. What assumption underpins your calculations in parts a and b? Is it likely
to be met in this case?
d. Interpret the numbers you have calculated in parts a and b.

## APPENDIX: MATHEMATICAL REVIEW

In this appendix we review topics from differential calculus that are used
in this book. Although coverage of the needed topics is both brief and heuristic,
knowledge of these materials is sufficient to understand all mathematical arguments used in the text. The time that should be allotted to this appendix will

of course depend upon the reader's training in the use of calculus. But even students who have recently taken a calculus course should skim the material to ensure familiarity with each of the included concepts.

Before we begin, one preliminary observation should be made: Paging through the text shows that many symbols have been used in the exposition. We hasten to point out that liberal use of symbols need not, and in this book does not, indicate a high level of mathematical sophistication. Rather, we have used symbols whenever clarity and brevity were served by so doing. In places the same purposes could have been accomplished using words alone, but at the price of a much longer and less concise treatment of the topics covered. But on other occasions there is just no relatively straightforward method of solving a problem except by using a little mathematics. To the uninitiated, this may be cold comfort. But we have made every effort throughout the book to interpret and explain symbolic and mathematical notation and results.

### Functions

When we say that one variable is a function of another variable, we mean that one magnitude depends upon another magnitude in such a manner that each value of the former determines a unique value of the latter. So if quantity demanded of a commodity is a function of price, this means that for each price there is a corresponding quantity demanded. More formally, the variable $y$ is a function of the variable $x$ if every value of $x$ determines a unique value of $y$. This is denoted as $y = f(x)$ and is read as "$y$ is (equals) a function of $x$." At the risk of being redundant, $y = f(x)$ means only that for every value of $x$ there is a unique corresponding value of $y$. In the expression $y = f(x)$, the specific function is not given and the letter $f$ is used to represent a general function. Of course, we may use any letter to denote a function.

We will often be concerned with two special types of functions—linear functions and power functions. The function $y = f(x)$ is called linear if

$$f(x) = a + bx \tag{1}$$

where $a$ and $b$ are constants that determine the particular form of the linear function. A particular linear function is obtained by substituting any two numbers for $a$ and $b$.

The function $y = g(x)$ is a power function if

$$g(x) = cx^d \tag{2}$$

Here $c$ and $d$ are constants that determine the particular form of the power function. A particular power function is determined by replacing $c$ and $d$ with any two numbers. The constants $a$ and $b$ in equation (1) and $c$ and $d$ in equation (2) are called *parameters*. In general, parameters are variables which are fixed or given in a particular function or model.

It is important to realize from the beginning that expressions such as equations (1) and (2) each represent infinitely many functions of a particular kind or class. For example, for a given value of $b$ we have a choice of an infinity of values for the constant $a$ in the linear function. Since an analogous statement holds for fixing the constant $a$ and varying the number $b$, we see that even the simple linear function when written as in (1) is quite general. We say that equations (1) and (2) represent classes or *families* of functions, since every choice of $a$ and $b$ (or $c$ and $d$) yields one function out of infinitely many with common characteristics—the common characteristic being that all functions in the family have the general functional form given by (1) and (2).

In Figures 1 and 2 we have graphed a specific linear function from the family of linear functions and a specific power function from the family of power functions. It is easy to see that $200 - .9x$ and $50x^{-.5}$ are functions, since given any value for $x$ we arrive at a unique value for $y$. For example, $f(100) = 110$ is the value of $y$ corresponding to the value $x = 100$ in the linear function, as $g(100) = 5$ is the value of $y$ corresponding to $x = 100$ in the power function.

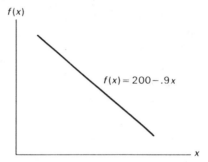

**FIGURE 1**
A linear
function

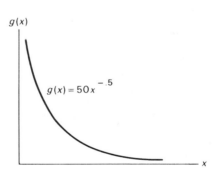

**FIGURE 2**
A power
function

There are of course innumerable other classes of functions which we shall not so much as mention. But before turning to a review of calculus, it is well to define one additional family of functions—polynomial functions. The function $h(x)$ is a *polynomial* function of *degree n* if

$$h(x) = a_0 + a_1x + a_2x^2 + a_3x^3 + \cdots + a_nx^n \tag{3}$$

where $a_0, a_1, a_2, \ldots, a_n$ are constants which determine the particular form of the polynomial. The cases where the degree of the polynomial is one, two, and three $(n = 1, 2, 3)$ are of special interest:

$$h(x) = a_0 + a_1 x \tag{4}$$
$$h(x) = a_0 + a_1 x + a_2 x^2 \tag{5}$$
$$h(x) = a_0 + a_1 x + a_2 x^2 + a_3 x^3 \tag{6}$$

We see by (4) that *linear* functions are a very special type of polynomial (first degree). The second- and third-degree polynomials given in (5) and (6) are called *quadratic* functions and *cubic* functions, respectively. Specification of the constants $a_0$, $a_1$, and $a_2$ in equation (5) or $a_0, a_1, a_2,$ and $a_3$ in equation (6) would determine a particular quadratic or cubic function from the family of these functions.

### Derivatives and Their Meaning

For many purposes it is important to be able to measure the *rate* at which one variable changes due to changes in another variable. This is the purpose of differential calculus. To be more specific, let $y$ be a function of $x$, that is, $y = f(x)$. Then the change in $y$ due to a change in $x$ is calculated by dividing the change in $y$ by the change in $x$. This is written as $\Delta y/\Delta x$, where $\Delta$ is read "the change in." Figure 3 illustrates this concept. In the figure consider the change in $y$ that accompanies a change in $x$ from $x^0$ to $x''$ along the function $f(x)$.

**FIGURE 3**

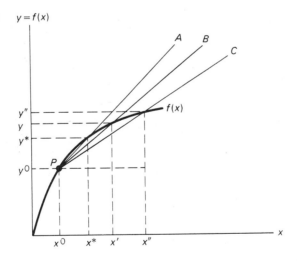

The change in $y$ is $y'' - y^0$. Therefore, $\Delta y/\Delta x$ is equal to $(y'' - y^0)/(x'' - x^0)$ and is merely the *slope* of the line $PC$ from the point $(x^0, y^0)$ to the point $(x'', y'')$.

Next consider a smaller change in $x$, say from $x^0$ to $x'$. In this case $\Delta y/\Delta x = (y' - y^0)/(x' - x^0)$ and $\Delta y/\Delta x$ is the slope of the line $PB$ which starts at point $(x^0, y^0)$ and passes through the point $(x', y')$. Comparing the slopes of $PC$ and $PB$ illustrates an important general concept—as the changes in $x$ become smaller, $\Delta y/\Delta x$ becomes closer and closer to the slope of $f(x)$ between the two points. The line $PC$ is the slope of the line between the points $(x^0, y^0)$ and $(x'', y'')$

and is very different from the slope of $f(x)$ at the point $(x^0, y^0)$. The line $PB$ is generated by a smaller change in $x$ and is a much closer approximation to the slope of $f(x)$. Finally, notice that a still smaller change in $x$ yields an even closer approximation to the slope of $f(x)$ at $(x^0, y^0)$ (see the line $PA$).

What we have seen is that as $\Delta x$ becomes increasingly small (as $\Delta x$ approaches zero), $\Delta y / \Delta x$ becomes a better and better approximation to the slope of $f(x)$ at a specific point. If $\Delta x$ is chosen sufficiently small $\Delta y / \Delta x$ *is* the slope of $f(x)$, and in this case $\Delta y / \Delta x$ is called the *derivative of $f(x)$ (or y) with respect to x*. The derivative is written $dy/dx$, or $df(x)/dx$, since $y = f(x)$. We can express this concept mathematically by writing

$$\lim_{\Delta x \to 0} \frac{\Delta y}{\Delta x} = \frac{dy}{dx} \qquad (7)$$

where $dy/dx$ is the slope of $f(x)$. In words, equation (7) says that the limit of $\Delta y / \Delta x$ as $\Delta x$ becomes increasingly small is the derivative of $y$ with respect to $x$. To find the slope of $f(x)$ at a *particular point* one need only evaluate the derivative at that point. In terms of Figure 3 if one evaluates $dy/dx$ at the point $(x^0, y^0)$, the result is the slope of function $f(x)$ at $(x^0, y^0)$. Likewise evaluating $dy/dx$ at any point along the function $f(x)$ yields the slope of $f(x)$ at that point.

We now know that derivatives are slopes of functions and that they measure the response of one variable to changes in another variable. This is all well and good, but why are derivatives of interest in an economics course? The answer to this question will become increasingly clear as we proceed. For now it is sufficient to note that the responsiveness of sales to changes in price, the response of cost to changes in the production rate, or the response of firm output to changes in the use of a certain factor of production are but several examples of common decision-making inputs which are nothing more than statements about derivatives.

### Differentiation Techniques

We know what a derivative is but as yet do not know how to actually calculate one. In this section we state without proof the rules of differentiation we use in the text.

i.  The derivative of the sum (or difference) of two functions is the sum (or difference) of the separate derivatives. That is, if $y = u(x) \pm v(x)$, then

$$\frac{dy}{dx} = \frac{du}{dx} \pm \frac{dv}{dx}$$

ii. The derivative of the product of two functions is equal to the first function times the derivative of the second function, plus the second function times the derivative of the first. That is, if $y = u(x) \cdot v(x)$,

$$\frac{dy}{dx} = u\frac{dv}{dx} + v\frac{du}{dx}$$

iii. The derivative of the quotient of two functions is equal to the denominator times the derivative of the numerator, minus the numerator times the derivative of the denominator, all divided by the denominator squared. That is, if $y = u(x)/v(x)$,

$$\frac{dy}{dx} = \frac{v\dfrac{du}{dx} - u\dfrac{dv}{dx}}{v^2}$$

iv. The derivative of a constant is zero. That is, if $y = k$ where $k$ is a constant,

$$\frac{dy}{dx} = 0$$

v. Finally, if $y = ax^b$, then

$$\frac{dy}{dx} = bax^{b-1}$$

The derivative of a power function is the power ($b$) times the function raised to one lower power ($b - 1$).

EXAMPLES

a. If $y = 50x^{-.5}$, then $\dfrac{dy}{dx} = -25x^{-1.5}$. (Rule v.)

b. If $y = 200 - .9x$, then $\dfrac{dy}{dx} = -.9$. (Rules i, ii, and iv.)

c. If $y = 10 + 12x + 15x^2 + 41x^3$, then $\dfrac{dy}{dx} = 12 + 30x + 123x^2$.
(Rules i, ii, iv, and v.)

Finally, it must be noted that all functions are not differentiable. Although the formal definition of differentiability is quite easy to comprehend, we will need only an intuitive understanding of this concept. To this end all one need do is graph the function $y = f(x)$. If the graph is continuous (has no "gaps") *and* has no "corners," the function $f(x)$ is differentiable. The functions graphed in Figures 4 and 5 are differentiable except at the points $x^0$ and $x'$. The function depicted in Figure 6 possesses derivatives at all points except at the "corners" $x^0$, $x'$, and $x''$.

**FIGURE 4**

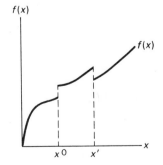

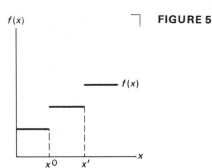

FIGURE 5

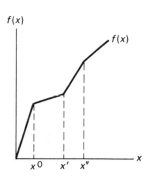

FIGURE 6

## Partial Derivatives

In our discussion of derivatives we have limited our attention to functions of only one independent variable. But in economics as well as in most other sciences, relationships between variables are much more complicated. One possible complication is that the behavior of one variable depends upon the values of several other variables. For example, sales of a commodity will in general depend not only upon price but also upon the prices of other related commodities, the firm's advertising outlays, and so forth. In other words, one variable is a function of several other variables, as in

$$y = f(x_1, x_2) \qquad (8)$$

Here $y$ is a function of the values of $x_1$ and $x_2$, which means that for every permissible pair of values of the *independent* variables $x_1$ and $x_2$, there is a unique value of the *dependent* variable $y$.

It is often of interest to inquire as to how the dependent variable responds to changes in *one* of the independent variables, the others being constant. For example, in reference to (8) we could ask how $y$ changes as $x_1$ changes *when the value of $x_2$ is fixed*. Symbolically, this statement may be expressed as

$$\left(\frac{\Delta y}{\Delta x_1}\right)_{x_2 = x_2^0} \qquad (9)$$

Expression (9) is read as "the change in $y$ due to a change in $x_1$ given $x_2$ is fixed at the value $x_2^0$," or equivalently, "the change in $y$ due *solely* to a change in $x_1$." The words "due solely" imply all influences on $y$ are constant except that

**19**

of $x_1$. As before, we will find it useful to consider this concept when $\Delta x_1$ becomes very small. And just as the limit of $\Delta y / \Delta x$ is equal to the derivative of $y$ with respect to $x$ when $y$ is a function only of $x$, so too is the limit of (9) equal to a derivative when $y$ is a function of more than one variable. This time the derivative is a *partial derivative* because not all influences on $y$ are being varied—only "part" of them are.

To more fully interpret the notion of a partial derivative, write equation (8) when the value of $x_2$ has been fixed at $x_2^0$. Then

$$y = f(x_1, x_2^0) \tag{8'}$$

and $y$ is a function only of $x_1$ for the given value of $x_2$. Equation (9) is then an approximation to the slope of the function given by (8'). As $\Delta x_1$ approaches zero, (9) becomes a better and better estimate of the slope of (8'), and in the limit (9) *is* the slope of (8') and is denoted by $\partial y / \partial x_1$—the *partial derivative* of $y$ with respect to $x_1$. What we have said may be written as the definition of a partial derivative

$$\lim_{\Delta x_1 \to 0} \left( \frac{\Delta y}{\Delta x_1} \right)_{x_2 = x_2^0} = \frac{\partial y}{\partial x_1} \tag{10}$$

Geometrically, $\partial y / \partial x_1$ is the slope of the function obtained by cutting the surface $f(x_1, x_2)$ at $x_2 = x_2^0$. The symbol $\partial$ is read as "partial," and $\partial y / \partial x_1$ is read as "partial $y$, partial $x_1$."

In general if $y = f(x_1, x_2, \ldots, x_n)$, then $\partial y / \partial x_2$ is the change in $y$ due solely to a change in $x_2$ *all other variables constant*. So we see that like regular derivatives, partial derivatives are also measures of responsiveness of one variable to changes in another but are measures tailored for use in functions with many variables. A partial derivative always measures the change in the dependent variable due to a change in one and only one independent variable.

The only question remaining is how one actually goes about calculating a partial derivative. Fortunately, the answer to this question requires nothing new. Calculation of a partial derivative is accomplished by using the same rules we used for finding derivatives of single variable functions. The only thing we need keep in mind in doing the calculations is that partial derivatives measure changes in one variable when all variables are constant except one. That is, all variables in the function to be partially differentiated are treated as constants except for one.

EXAMPLES

a.
$$y = 10 + 12x_1 x_2 + 24x_1^3 - 13x_2^2$$
$$\partial y / \partial x_1 = 12x_2 + 72x_1^2$$
$$\partial y / \partial x_2 = 12x_1 - 26x_2$$

In the derivative $\partial y / \partial x_1$, $x_2$ is a constant, so terms containing $x_2$ only drop out (Rule iv). In $\partial y / \partial x_2$ the variable $x_1$ is treated as a constant.

b. $y = ax_1^b x_2^c$; $a$, $b$, and $c$ are parameters. This is a power function with two independent variables. Its partial derivatives are

$$\partial y / \partial x_1 = bax_1^{b-1} x_2^c$$
$$\partial y / \partial x_2 = cax_1^b x_2^{c-1}$$

If the parameters $a$, $b$, and $c$ are found to be $a = .51$, $b = -.1$, $c = 1.7$, we have

$$y = .51x_1^{-.1} x_2^{1.7} \text{ and}$$
$$\partial y/\partial x_1 = -.051x_1^{-1.1} x_2^{1.7}$$
$$\partial y/\partial x_2 = .867x_1^{-.1} x_2^{.7}$$

These examples point out a further important characteristic of partial derivatives: In general a partial derivative is a function of all of the variables in the function that was differentiated. For instance, we see that $\partial y/\partial x_1$ in example (a) is a function of both $x_1$ and $x_2$. To graph this function in a two-dimensional graph, we choose different values of $x_2$ and graph $\partial y/\partial x_1$ as a function of $x_1$ for the different values of $x_2$. This is done in Figure 7 for three values of $x_2$.

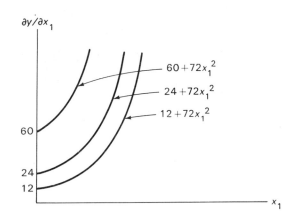

**FIGURE 7**

Three of the family of functions $\partial y/\partial x_1$

Notice that

$$\partial y/\partial x_1 = 12 + 72x_1^2 \qquad \text{when } x_2 = 1$$
$$\partial y/\partial x_1 = 24 + 72x_1^2 \qquad \text{when } x_2 = 2$$

and

$$\partial y/\partial x_1 = 60 + 72x_1^2 \qquad \text{when } x_2 = 5$$

### Derivatives of Composite Functions

One other technique of differentiation will be used occasionally. This technique is needed whenever one is confronted with the problem of differentiating a function which itself depends ultimately upon some other function. Such a situation arises if

$$y = f(x) \quad \text{and} \quad x = g(t) \tag{11}$$

Here the variable $y$ depends ultimately not upon $x$ but upon $t$, that is, $y = f[g(t)]$. The function $f[g(t)]$ is called a *composite* function.

Now, suppose one wanted to find the response of $y$ to a change in $t$. By (11), changes in $y$ are caused by changes in $x$, which in turn are caused by changes in $t$. Schematically, the causal connection between variables may be represented as

$$\Delta t \longrightarrow \Delta x \longrightarrow \Delta y$$

where the symbol $\longrightarrow$ is read "cause." The derivative of the function $f$ with respect to $t$ reflects this connection between variables and is the product of the derivative of $f$ with respect to $x$ and the derivative of $g$ with respect to $t$. Mathematically,

$$\frac{dy}{dt} = \frac{df(x)}{dx}\frac{dg(t)}{dt} \tag{12}$$

or

$$\frac{dy}{dt} = \frac{dy}{dx}\frac{dx}{dt} \tag{12'}$$

the latter equality holds, since $y = f(x)$ and $x = g(t)$. This formula for differentiation of a composite function is quite intuitive if we spend a moment thinking about it. The left-hand side of (12) or (12') asks us to find how $y$ responds to changes in $t$. The right-hand side provides the answer and may be roughly interpreted as in equation (13), where the arrow traces out the chain of reactions caused by a change in $t$:

$$\frac{dy}{dt} = \frac{d\!\uparrow\!y}{d\,\m13x}\left/\frac{d\,\mid x}{d\,\mid t}\right. \tag{13}$$

In words, changes in $t$ cause changes in $x$ (via $g(t)$), which in turn cause changes in $y$ (via $f(x)$). Equation (13) indicates that changes in $t$ are transmitted into changes in $y$ through $x$ by way of the function $x = g(t)$.

EXAMPLE.   Let $y = x^2 + 2x + 1$ and $x = \sqrt{t}$. Then

$$\frac{dy}{dt} = \frac{dy}{dx}\frac{dx}{dt}$$

$$= (2x + 2)(1/2\sqrt{t})$$

$$= (2\sqrt{t} + 2)(1/2\sqrt{t}) = \frac{1 + \sqrt{t}}{\sqrt{t}}$$

Now let us consider a more complicated case. Assume

$$y = f(x_1, x_2), \quad \text{but} \quad x_1 = g_1(t_1, t_2) \quad \text{and} \quad x_2 = g_2(t_1, t_2) \tag{14}$$

and say we want to find the response of $y$ due solely to a change in $t_1$. Looking at (14) we see that changes in $t_1$ cause both $x_1$ and $x_2$ to change, which in turn causes $y$ to change. The change in $y$ due solely to a change in $t_1$ is of course the partial derivative of the function $f$ with respect to $t_1$, $\partial y/\partial t_1$. The causal connection between changes in $t_1$ and changes in $y$ may be illustrated schematically as

(a)   $\Delta t_1 \longrightarrow \Delta x_1 \longrightarrow \Delta y$

and

(b)   $\Delta t_1 \longrightarrow \Delta x_2 \longrightarrow \Delta y$

The partial derivative $\partial y/\partial t_1$ is the sum of these two effects on $y$. Mathematically,

$$\frac{\partial y}{\partial t_1} = \frac{\partial f}{\partial x_1}\frac{\partial g_1}{\partial t_1} + \frac{\partial f}{\partial x_2}\frac{\partial g_2}{\partial t_1} \tag{15}$$

or from (14)

$$\frac{\partial y}{\partial t_1} = \frac{\partial y}{\partial x_1}\frac{\partial x_1}{\partial t_1} + \frac{\partial y}{\partial x_2}\frac{\partial x_2}{\partial t_1} \tag{15'}$$

The first term in (15) or (15') is the portion of the change in $y$ (due to the change in $t_1$) that has been transmitted through $x_1$. The portion of the change in $y$ (due to the change in $t_1$) that is transmitted through $x_2$ has not been accounted for. The second term in (15') does exactly this. The sum of the two separate effects is the response of $y$ to a change in $t_1$ when $t_2$ is constant. The rule for differentiation given as equation (15) or (15') is often called *the chain rule*.

EXAMPLE. Let $y = 12x_1x_2^3 + x_1^2$, $x_1 = 2t_1t_2$, and $x_2 = t_1 + t_2$. Then

$$\frac{\partial y}{\partial t_1} = \frac{\partial y}{\partial x_1}\frac{\partial x_1}{\partial t_1} + \frac{\partial y}{\partial x_2}\frac{\partial x_2}{\partial t_1}$$
$$= (12x_2^3 + 2x_1)(2t_2) + (36x_1x_2^2)(1)$$
$$= 12(t_1 + t_2)^3 + 2(2t_1t_2) + 36(2t_1t_2)(t_1 + t_2)^2$$

### Solving Quadratic Functions

On occasion we will find it necessary to solve a quadratic equation. Fortunately, as you may remember from high school algebra, this can always be done quite easily. As we saw above, a function $f(x)$ is a quadratic function if

$$f(x) = a_0 + a_1x + a_2x^2 \tag{16}$$

*Solving* a quadratic equation means nothing more than finding the values of $x$ that make $f(x) = 0$. This is a particularly simple task if (16) has recognizable factors. For example, if

$$f(x) = -15 + 2x + x^2 \tag{17}$$

then $x = -5$ and $x = 3$ are the solutions to $-15 + 2x + x^2 = 0$, since

$$-15 + 2x + x^2 = (x + 5)(x - 3)$$

and is equal to zero whenever $x = -5$ or $x = 3$.[1] If the factors of (16) are not recognizable, the following formula always yields the values of $x$ that satisfy $f(x) = 0$:

$$x = \frac{-a_1 \pm \sqrt{a_1^2 - 4a_0a_2}}{2a_2} \tag{18}$$

Let us try the formula out on the equation we just solved, $f(x) = -15 + 2x + x^2 = 0$. Then

$$x = \frac{-2 \pm \sqrt{4 - (-60)}}{2} = \frac{-2 \pm \sqrt{64}}{2} = 3, -5$$

the same answer we got by factoring. If $f(x) = 1.5 + 9x + x^2$, factors are not apparent, but the formula for solution given in (18) tells us that

$$x = \frac{-9 \pm \sqrt{81 - 6}}{2} = \frac{-9 \pm \sqrt{75}}{2} = -.17, -8.83$$

are the values of $x$ that satisfy $f(x) = 0$.

[1]This example brings out an important property of quadratic equations, viz., there are always two solutions. Similarly, it can be shown that cubic equations have three solutions, etc.

Many of the decision problems studied in this book are what operations researchers would call optimization problems.[2] Optimization problems are concerned with calculating the values of variables under the control of decision makers, which maximize or minimize certain functions. Common examples include finding sales volumes that maximize a firm's profit function or finding levels of resource utilization that minimize the cost of a project. If the function to be optimized is differentiable, calculus provides a simple method of finding maxima and minima.

To illustrate, consider the function $y = f(x)$ which is graphed in Figure 8.

**FIGURE 8**

Maxima and

minima of a

differentiable

function

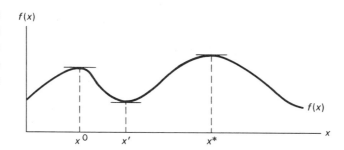

We would like a way of finding the points $x^0$, $x'$ and $x^*$ where the function $f(x)$ has either a maximum or a minimum. Note that $x^0$, $x'$, and $x^*$ have a common characteristic—the slope of $f(x)$ is zero at each of these points. Since the derivative of a function is the slope of the function at a point, we know that

$$\frac{df(x^0)}{dx} = \frac{df(x')}{dx} = \frac{df(x^*)}{dx} = 0 \qquad (19)$$

In (19) the derivative of $f(x)$ has been *evaluated* at the points $x^0$, $x'$, and $x^*$. We now have a way of finding maxima and minima: Calculate the derivative of the function, set the result equal to zero, and solve for $x$. In other words, for the function shown in Figure 8 the equation

$$\frac{df(x)}{dx} = 0 \qquad (20)$$

has three solutions, $x^0$, $x'$, and $x^*$, the maxima and minima of $f(x)$.

Our ability to find maxima and minima can be extended to functions of more than one variable by merely following the same general principle: Set *each* derivative of the function in question equal to zero and solve the resulting equations. Since we are speaking of functions of several variables, the derivatives

[2]The discussion of this section is concerned with maxima and minima that occur at *interior* points in the domain of independent variables. For example, if we are searching for the profit-maximizing sales volume, the techniques we develop will be adequate as long as the profit-maximizing volume is *not* zero. A sales volume of zero is a *boundary* point in this problem, since sales volumes can never be less than zero.

must be partial derivatives. So, if $y = f(x_1, x_2)$, solving the equations

$$\frac{\partial f(x_1, x_2)}{\partial x_1} = 0 \quad \text{and} \quad \frac{\partial f(x_1, x_2)}{\partial x_2} = 0 \tag{21}$$

will yield all maxima and minima of the function $f(x_1, x_2)$.

Before presenting examples it is important to put our discussion of maxima and minima into perspective. Modern optimization theory is a very sophisticated and interesting branch of applied mathematics. The material we have presented constitutes only the most rudimentary notions of this theory, and even at this level several important topics have been omitted. In particular, we have not worried about the fact that a solution to (20) or (21) could possibly be neither a maxima nor a minima, nor have we discussed how to determine whether the solutions to (20) or (21) are maxima, minima, or neither of the functions in question. If one were to continue the study of the decision problems presented in this book, these topics would have to be covered. But in the problems we will be discussing, we will always know enough about the "economic realities" of the functions involved to ensure that the solutions to equations (20) or (21) are maxima when the problem calls for maximizing and minima when minimization is called for. In this framework one need only be able to find the points where the appropriate derivatives are zero. In most cases there will be only one solution to these equations, and we will always know whether it is a maximum or a minimum.

EXAMPLE. First let us find the maxima and minima of the function

$$f(x) = 3x^3 + 7x^2 + x + 12 \tag{22}$$

Differentiation yields

$$\frac{df(x)}{dx} = 9x^2 + 14x + 1 \tag{23}$$

Equating (23) to zero and solving[3] yields $x = -.68$ and $x = -13.32$. Equation (22) is graphed as Figure 9, which shows that $x = -13.32$ is a maximum of (22) and $x = -.68$ is a minimum.

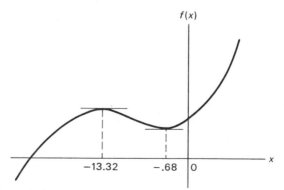

f(x)

−13.32        −.68   0        x

**FIGURE 9**

The function

$f(x) = 3x^3 + 7x^2 + x + 12$

[3] Use the formula for finding the solutions of a quadratic equation.

As a second example, consider the function

$$f(x_1, x_2) = 4x_1x_2 - x_1^2 - 9x_2^2 + 1040x_2 \tag{24}$$

Partially differentiating (24) with respect to $x_1$ and $x_2$ and setting the results equal to zero yields

$$\frac{\partial f}{\partial x_1} = 4x_2 - 2x_1 = 0$$
$$\frac{\partial f}{\partial x_2} = 4x_1 - 18x_2 + 1040 = 0 \tag{25}$$

To find the point that satisfies these two equations, solve the first equation and substitute the result into the second. We then have $x_1 = 2x_2$, which when substituted into the second equation yields $4(2x_2) - 18x_2 + 1040 = 0$. Solving for $x_2$ we find $x_2 = 104$, and hence $x_1 = 2(104) = 208$. There is only one point[4] that satisfies equations (25) and it is the point $x_1 = 208$, $x_2 = 104$. It can be shown that this point is the maximum of the function given in (24).

### Differentials

One additional concept from differential calculus will be used. This is the notion of the *differential* of a function. Differentials arise naturally if one were to inquire as to what would be the response of the dependent variable of a function if *all* independent variables were varied. To get right to the point, say we have the function

$$w = g(x, y) \tag{26}$$

and we wish to write an expression for the variation in $w$ due to variation in both $x$ and $y$. Let us write the answer and then see why it is true. The variation in $w$ is given by

$$\Delta w = \frac{\partial w}{\partial x}\Delta x + \frac{\partial w}{\partial y}\Delta y \tag{27}$$

In words, equation (27) says (roughly) that the change in $w$ ($\Delta w$) is equal to the change in $w$ *due solely* to a one-unit change in $x$ ($\partial w/\partial x$), times the size of the change in $x$ ($\Delta x$), plus the change in $w$ *due solely* to a one-unit change in $y$ ($\partial w/\partial y$), times the size of the change in $y$ ($\Delta y$). Of course this is precisely what we set out to obtain. Notice that individual terms in the differential measure the amount of the change in $w$ that is attributable to a change in one (and only one) of the independent variables. Hence $(\partial w/\partial x)/\Delta x$ is the portion of the change in $w$ that may be attributed solely to the change in $x$. If we consider only "small" changes in $x$ and $y$, we may replace $\Delta x$ and $\Delta y$ by $dx$ and $dy$ and $\Delta w$ by $dw$ as we did in equation (7) above when we first defined a derivative. Equation (27) may then be written as

$$dw = \frac{\partial w}{\partial x}dx + \frac{\partial w}{\partial y}dy \tag{27'}$$

---

[4]Remember that in this example we are in two-dimensional space, so each point has two coordinates $(x_1, x_2)$.

In this final section we introduce several definitions and some corresponding notation.

a.   A *set* is a collection of objects with a common characteristic or property. If we want a shorthand method of writing about, say, a set $T$ which is a collection of objects $A$ with a certain property $P$, we will write

$$T = \{\text{objects } A \mid A \text{ has property } P\}$$

This is read as "$T$ is the set (indicated by the braces { }) of objects $A$, such that (indicated by the vertical line) $A$ has property $P$.

Since functions are collections of points, we will often write functions as sets. For example, the function $y = 200 - .9x$ could be written as the set $S$:

$$S = \{(x, y) \mid y = 200 - .9x\}$$

In words, $S$ is the set of points $(x, y)$ such that $y = 200 - .9x$. The information on the left-hand side of the vertical line always tells what in general is contained in the set, while the information on the right-hand side of the line tells what specific property these objects possess. In reference to the set $S$, the left-hand side tells us $S$ is a set of points in two-dimensional space, while the right-hand side tells us exactly which points—the points satisfying $y = 200 - .9x$.

b.   A point that often seems to cause problems for students is the difference between identities and equations. An *equation* is a statement such as $x^2 = 4$, which is not always true. This equation holds only for the values $x = 2$ and $x = -2$. It is false (does not hold) for all other values of $x$.

An *identity* is a statement that is always true. Identities are the result of definitions. For example, if we call $R$ firm revenues and $C$ firm costs, then profits, $\Pi$, are defined as $R - C$ and denoted as $\Pi \equiv R - C$. The three horizontal lines are read as "identically equal to." So, profits are identically equal to (i.e., defined to be) revenues minus costs. The identity sign $\equiv$ indicates that this statement always holds. There are no values of $R$ and $C$ for which $R - C$ does not equal profits. In other words, $R - C$ *is the same as* $\Pi$. As another example, consider the statement $x^2 \equiv [(\sqrt[3]{x})^{3/2}]^4$. The identity symbol indicates that $x$ squared is the same as the cube root of $x$ to the three-halves power, all raised to the fourth power. This follows by definition from the rules for operating with exponents. There is no value of $x$ for which it does not hold.

In summary, equations hold only for specific values of the variables involved. To "solve an equation" means to find these values. Identities hold for every value of the variables involved. The quantity on the left-hand side of an identity is the same as the quantity on the right-hand side. Since the left-hand side and the right-hand side of identities are equal, it is permissible to use $=$ instead of $\equiv$ between them. The identity sign is used merely to emphasize the fact that the statement in question always holds.

# Empirical Demand Functions: Estimating Demand

Our discussion in Chapter 1 of demand functions, demand elasticities, and their meaning leaves no doubt as to the desirability of obtaining estimates of these quantities. The question is how one actually goes about estimating a demand function. The present chapter provides an introduction to the estimation problem and an overview of the difficulties and benefits associated with successful estimation.

The formal estimation problem consists of transforming data that are recorded by the firm (or should be recorded) into a function that is a good approximation of the actual but unknown demand function confronting the firm. To get a clear idea of this procedure, assume that data are available on the following variables for each of the past $T$ periods (perhaps quarters): sales of $X_1$, price of $X_1$, prices of all major substitutes and complements (say a total of $n - 1$), an index of business activity or consumer disposable income—whichever is appropriate, and advertising expenditures. If a $t$ subscript is used to denote the period of observation so that $P_{1t}$ is taken to mean the observed value of $P_1$ in period $t$, then the information needed to obtain an estimate of the demand function for $X_1$ is shown in Table 2-1. The table columns contain the values of

**TABLE 2-1**
Basic data requirements for estimating $f(P_1, P_2, \ldots, P_n, Y, A)$

| Period | $x_{1t}$ | $P_{1t}$ | $P_{2t}$ | $\cdots$ | $P_{nt}$ | $Y_t$ | $A_t$ |
|--------|----------|----------|----------|----------|----------|-------|-------|
| 1 | $x_{11}$ | $P_{11}$ | $P_{21}$ | $\cdot$ | $P_{n1}$ | $Y_1$ | $A_1$ |
| 2 | $x_{12}$ | $P_{12}$ | $P_{22}$ | $\cdot$ | $P_{n2}$ | $Y_2$ | $A_2$ |
| 3 | $x_{13}$ | $P_{13}$ | $P_{23}$ | $\cdot$ | $P_{n3}$ | $Y_3$ | $A_3$ |
| $\cdot$ | $\cdot$ | $\cdot$ | $\cdot$ | $\cdot$ | $\cdot$ | $\cdot$ | $\cdot$ |
| $\cdot$ | $\cdot$ | $\cdot$ | $\cdot$ | $\cdot$ | $\cdot$ | $\cdot$ | $\cdot$ |
| $\cdot$ | $\cdot$ | $\cdot$ | $\cdot$ | $\cdot$ | $\cdot$ | $\cdot$ | $\cdot$ |
| $T$ | $x_{1T}$ | $P_{1T}$ | $P_{2T}$ | $\cdot$ | $P_{nT}$ | $Y_T$ | $A_T$ |

a particular variable for each of the past $T$ periods, so $x_{11}, x_{12}, \ldots, x_{1T}$ are the recorded values of sales of $X_1$ for periods $1, 2, \ldots, T$. The rows in the table are the recorded values of demand and each of its determinants for a particular period. So row three $X_{13}, P_{13}, P_{23}, \ldots, P_{n3}, Y_3$, and $A_3$ are the values of these variables in period three. For convenience we have assumed there are no influences on demand other than those listed. If other influences are present, data on these variables will also be needed. Given the data listed in the table, the estimation problem is to utilize this information in such a manner that we obtain the best possible estimate of $f(P_1, P_2, \ldots, P_n, Y, A)$, the actual demand function facing the seller of $X_1$.

### Assumptions About the Form of the Demand Function

The first step in the direction of demand estimation must be an assumption about the functional form of the demand function to be estimated, since it is impossible to estimate a function that is specified as generally as $f(P_1, P_2, \ldots, P_n, Y, A)$. In our discussion of demand estimation, we will assume that demand functions are either *linear* functions or *power* functions. That is, we assume the demand function for $X_1$ is either of the form

$$x_1 = a_0 + a_1 P_1 + a_2 P_2 + \cdots + a_n P_n + a_{n+1} Y + a_{n+2} A \qquad (2\text{-}1)$$

a linear function, or of the form

$$x_1 = b_0 P_1^{b_1} P_2^{b_2} \ldots P_n^{b_n} Y^{b_{n+1}} A^{b_{n+2}} \qquad (2\text{-}1')$$

a power function. In (2-1), the "numbers" $a_0, a_1, a_2, \ldots, a_{n+2}$ are unknown constants (parameters), estimation of which is the object of the estimation process. In different words, once the values of these constants have been determined, equation (2-1) is ready for use in predicting the level of demand associated with various combinations of prices, business activity, and advertising outlays. Similar statements hold for the "numbers" $b_0, b_1, b_2, \ldots, b_{n+2}$, which are the unknown constants to be estimated if (2-1') is chosen to represent the demand function for $X_1$. So, in summary, the problem of estimating a demand function amounts to first choosing a class of functions to represent the demand function and then estimating the parameters of the chosen function (e.g., the parameters $\{a_i\}$ if the class of linear functions is chosen.)

We will call the functions given in (2-1) and (2-1') *empirical* demand functions to indicate that these are the functions to be estimated. Equations (2-1) and (2-1') are assumptions about the functional form of demand functions which are widely utilized in problems of demand estimation. Two factors are responsible for the widespread adoption of these particular empirical demand functions. First, the parameters (the constants $a_0, a_1, \ldots, a_{n+2}$ and $b_0, b_1, \ldots, b_{n+2}$) of these functions are relatively easy to estimate. Second, results based on years of estimation suggest that these functions provide reasonable approximations of demand functions in a great many market settings. Although our discussion of demand estimation will be in terms of the functions (2-1) and (2-1'), many alternative functions are possible but are not discussed so as not to needlessly complicate the exposition.

**Interpreting the Parameters of the Empirical Demand Functions**

With the assumption that demand functions have either the functional form given in equation (2-1) or (2-1′), the estimation problem becomes one of estimating the parameters of these functions, the $a_i$'s or $b_i$'s, so that the resulting function is "as close as possible" to the true demand function facing the firm. Another way of putting this is to define the estimation problem as the problem of finding the demand equation that "most likely" generated the observed sales and price data. In terms of Table 2-1, this means that we are searching for (via our estimation procedure) the demand function that is responsible for the data given in the table. Our assumption restricts our search to either the class of linear functions or the class of power functions.

Once the demand function has been estimated, the first question that must be asked is, "How good is the estimate?" One way of assessing how good the estimated demand function is, is to check the "reasonableness" of the parameters that have been estimated. Whether, for example, the estimate of $a_1$ or $b_3$ is "reasonable" depends upon what meaning these parameters have as far as the demand for $X_1$ is concerned. More specifically, what do these parameters measure? We should already have a pretty good idea as to the meaning of the parameters of equations (2-1) and (2-1′), since special cases of these demand functions were used as examples in the preceding chapter (see equations (1-2) and (1-7)).

First, consider equation (2-1), the linear demand equation. Clearly, the parameters of linear functions are the derivatives of the function with respect to each of its variables. That is,

$$\frac{\partial x_1}{\partial P_j} = a_j, \qquad j = 1, 2, \ldots, n, \tag{2-2}$$

$$\frac{\partial x_1}{\partial Y} = a_{n+1} \quad \text{and} \quad \frac{\partial x_1}{\partial A} = a_{n+2}$$

Therefore, the first property of a linear demand function that is of interest to us is that the response of demand to a change in any single variable is constant in a linear function and does not depend upon the values of other variables in the demand function. The percentage responses of demand to percentage changes in the different variables are then given by

$$\eta_{1j} = a_j(P_j/x_1) \qquad j = 1, 2, \ldots, n \tag{2-3}$$
$$\eta_{1Y} = a_{n+1}(Y/x_1) \quad \text{and} \quad \eta_{1A} = a_{n+2}(A/x_1)$$

Notice that demand elasticities are not constant in linear demand functions but will vary depending upon the point at which they are evaluated. Notice especially that $\eta_{11}$ approaches zero as $x_1$ gets larger.[1] So if we begin at the $x_1$ intercept of a

[1] Mathematically, $\partial \eta_{11}/\partial x_1 > 0$.

linear demand function, demand becomes continually more elastic as we move along the function. Draw a rough graph to make sure you understand this point.

The fact that demand elasticities are in general a function of all variables in the demand function and hence change when any one of these variables changes enables us to derive the effects of changes in market conditions on demand elasticities. As an example, consider the response of the price elasticity to changes in the different determinants of demand. Using equation (2-3) and substituting for $x_1$ we have

$$\eta_{11} = a_1 P_1/(a_0 + a_1 P_1 + a_2 P_2 + \cdots + a_{n+1} Y + a_{n+2} A)$$

Now, observe the effects on $\eta_{11}$ of changes in a rival's price, the level of business activity, or the level of advertising expenditure. If $X_j$ is a substitute for $X_1$, then $a_j > 0$ and increases in $P_j$ increase the denominator of $\eta_{11}$, implying that *increases in the price of substitutes make the demand for $X_1$ more inelastic.* Analogously, *decreases in the price of a substitute make the demand for $X_1$ more sensitive to changes in $P_1$.* That is, not only do price reductions by a rival cut into sales of $X_1$, but at the same time such actions reduce the pricing alternatives open to management by making demand for $X_1$ more sensitive to changes in the company's own price.

If $X_1$ is a normal good, then $a_{n+1} > 0$ and increases in the level of general business activity make demand less sensitive to price changes.[2] So, in times of rising business activity, sales not only will increase at constant prices but also will become less sensitive to price changes. In terms of the two-dimensional demand function $\bar{f}(P_1)$, increases in $Y$ shift $\bar{f}(P_1)$ to the right *and* make it more inelastic. What happens to $\eta_{11}$ during expansionary periods if $X_1$ is an inferior commodity? What effect do increased advertising expenditures have on the price elasticity of demand?

Now consider equation (2-1′), the power function. Once again, let us calculate the response of demand to a change in the various influences on demand. Since these derivatives are a little messier, we will formally calculate only the price derivatives. The function, however, is symmetric and the other derivatives follow immediately. The change in demand for $X_1$ due to a change in $P_j$ is given by

$$\frac{\partial x_1}{\partial P_j} = b_j[b_0 P_1^{b_1} P_2^{b_2} \ldots P_j^{b_j-1} \ldots P_n^{b_n} Y^{b_{n+1}} A^{b_{n+2}}], \qquad j = 1, 2, \ldots, n \qquad (2\text{-}4)$$

If power functions are used to represent demand functions, then, according to (2-4) and unlike the case of linear equations, the response of demand to a change in the price of $X_j$ will depend not only upon the level of $P_j$ but also upon the level of all other variables that influence demand. The *percentage* response of demand to a percentage change in $P_j$ is obtained merely by multiplying (2-4) by $P_j/x_1$, which gives

$$\eta_{1j} = \frac{\partial x_1}{\partial P_j}\left(\frac{P_j}{x_1}\right) = b_j, \qquad j = 1, 2, \ldots, n \qquad (2\text{-}5)$$

[2]Mathematically speaking, we have shown $\partial \eta_{11}/\partial P_j > 0$ if $X_1$ and $X_j$ are substitutes, and $\partial \eta_{11}/\partial Y > 0$ if $X_1$ is a normal commodity.

Price and cross-elasticities of demand *are* parameters of this function. Since analogous calculations hold for the other variables, we have now shown an important property of demand functions of this type: *The exponent of each variable in the demand function given by (2-1') is the elasticity of demand with respect to that variable.* Symbolically,

$$\eta_{1j} = b_j, \qquad j = 1, 2, \ldots, n \qquad (2\text{-}5')$$
$$\eta_{1Y} = b_{n+1} \quad \text{and} \quad \eta_{1A} = b_{n+2}$$

Finally, keep in mind that once the values of the sequences of parameters $\{a_i\}$ and $\{b_i\}$ have been estimated,[3] management has not only an estimate of elasticities but also an equation that can be used for predicting the sales volume associated with various pricing and advertising policies. In addition, sales predictions can be generated under different assumptions concerning the prices of competitors and the level of business activity, thereby giving decision makers valuable information for pricing purposes.

### Some Additional Considerations Prior to Estimation

One of the reasons that was given for choosing the functional forms (2-1) and (2-1') for empirical demand functions was that these forms were particularly easy to estimate. In fact, if one derives an estimation technique for estimating linear functions, the same technique suffices for estimating the parameters of power functions. The reason for this is that power functions are also linear if transformed into logarithms. That is, if the demand function is of the form given by equation (2-1'), then

$$\ln x_1 = \ln b_0 + b_1 \ln P_1 + b_2 \ln P_2 + \cdots + b_{n+1} \ln Y + b_{n+2} \ln A \qquad (2\text{-}6)$$

If we call $\ln x_1 = x_1'$, $\ln b_0 = b_0'$, $\ln P_i = P_i'$, and so forth, then equation (2-6) may be written as

$$x_1' = b_0' + b_1 P_1' + b_2 P_2' + \cdots b_{n+1} Y' + b_{n+2} A' \qquad (2\text{-}6')$$

Hence any technique for estimating the parameters $\{a_i\}$ will work equally well for estimating $\{b_i\}$. All that need be done is to transform each data point in Table 2-1 into its logarithm which yields the linear function (2-6'), and any technique that is capable of estimating the parameters of a linear function may also be used to estimate the parameters of a power function.

In the next section an actual technique for estimating the parameters $\{a_i\}$ or $\{b_i\}$ is developed and explained for the simplest possible demand function. The idea in presenting this material is *not* to turn the reader into an econometrician able to tackle tough estimation problems, but instead is intended to strip away some of the mysteriousness that often surrounds estimation by investigating at some length the link between the data gathered by a firm and an estimated demand function. If management is to be able to evaluate the quantitative

---

[3] The notation $\{a_i\}$ and $\{b_i\}$ is used to represent the sequence of parameters $a_0, a_1, \ldots, a_{n+2}$ and $b_0, b_1, \ldots, b_{n+2}$, respectively.

estimates that are being done with increasing frequency in research departments of large corporations, at least in the sense of knowing enough to ask the "right" questions, then some rudimentary knowledge of the estimation process will be required. At the very minimum, an overview that eliminates any elements of magic should be most helpful.

Since the purpose of our discussion of estimation is primarily descriptive, we will consider estimating the relationship between $x_1$ and $P_1$ alone. That is, we will examine the problem of estimating either $x_1 = a_0 + a_1 P_1$ or $x_1 = b_0 P_1^{b_1}$. *This will be permissible only when all variables in the demand function except $P_1$ are constant for the period in which data are available.* In other words, in our discussion of estimation we will assume that the only variable that actively influences demand over the $T$ observation periods is the price of $X_1$. By restricting the discussion to this case, we will be able to use a graphical exposition at several points. The results we obtain may be generalized in a straightforward manner, so as to permit estimation of the general empirical demand functions given in equations (2-1) and (2-1').[4]

Before estimation can begin, we must decide which of the two empirical demand functions should be estimated. We would like to estimate the one that best approximates the true, but unknown, relationship between demand and price. The simplest method of discriminating between the two alternative demand models is to plot sales against price and check the consistency of the resulting plot with the hypothesis of each model. The hypothesis of the linear model is that demand and price are linearly related for the $T$ periods in which data are available. This is indicated by writing $x_{1t} = a_0 + a_1 P_{1t}$, $t = 1, 2, \ldots$, $T$. If the plot of the $T$ points $(x_{1t}, P_{1t})$, $t = 1, 2, \ldots, T$ is approximately linear, as shown in Figure 2-1, then the linear model will probably be quite satisfactory.

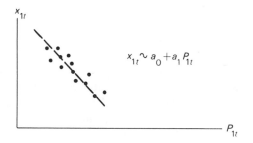

**FIGURE 2-1**
Plotting the
data on sales
and price

The hypothesis of the power function (log-linear) model is that demand and price are linearly related *if* they are expressed as logarithms. This hypothesis may be written as $x_{1t} = b_0 P_{1t}^{b_1}$ or $\ln x_{1t} = \ln b_0 + b_1 \ln P_{1t}$. If the plot of the $T$ points $(\ln x_{1t}, \ln P_{1t})$, $t = 1, 2, \ldots, T$ is approximately linear, as shown in Figure 2-2, then a power function should be estimated. Alternatively, if one plots the points $(x_{1t}, P_{1t})$ instead of $(\ln x_{1t}, \ln P_{1t})$ and the plot results in Figure 2-3, then the power function is the appropriate choice for the empirical demand

[4]A comprehensible exposition of the estimating procedure for the general empirical demand functions requires knowledge of matrix algebra.

**FIGURE 2-2**

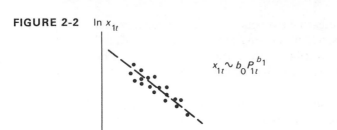

$$\ln x_{1t}$$

$$x_{1t} \sim b_0 P_{1t}^{b_1}$$

$$\ln P_{1t}$$

**FIGURE 2-3**

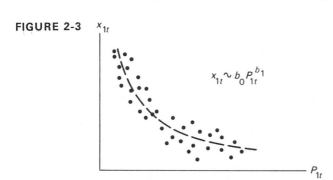

$$x_{1t}$$

$$x_{1t} \sim b_0 P_{1t}^{b_1}$$

$$P_{1t}$$

function. If the data are inconsistent with both of these hypotheses, further analysis is called for and a different demand model will probably be needed.

### Deriving Estimates of $a_0$ and $a_1$ (or $b_0$ and $b_1$)

Let us assume the linear demand model is chosen to be estimated. How does one go about actually utilizing the data in Table 2-1 to generate numerical estimates of $a_0$ and $a_1$? One possibility is to glance over the data and then *guess* the values of $a_0$ and $a_1$. But unless one is very perceptive, other estimation methods are preferable. Then how should $a_0$ and $a_1$ be chosen? Clearly, it would be desirable to use as estimates of $a_0$ and $a_1$ those numbers that yield the line that *best fits* the data available. To see exactly what is meant by this, call the estimated values of $a_0$ and $a_1$, $\hat{a}_0$ and $\hat{a}_1$ respectively, and call $\hat{x}_{1t}$ *predicted* demand (sales) in period $t$. Predicted sales in period $t$ are then given by $\hat{x}_{1t} = \hat{a}_0 + \hat{a}_1 P_{1t}$. (Given the estimates $\hat{a}_0$ and $\hat{a}_1$, $\hat{x}_{1t}$ is the level of sales predicted if price is $P_{1t}$.) *We will define the best-fitting line to be that line that minimizes the sales prediction error.* Since $x_{1t}$ is the actual value of sales in period $t$, $x_{1t} - \hat{x}_{1t}$ is the prediction error, say $e_t$, in period $t$, and $\sum_{t=1}^{T} (x_{1t} - \hat{x}_{1t})$ or $\sum_{t=1}^{T} e_t$ is the total prediction error over the $T$ periods in which data are available. The predicting equation $\hat{x}_{1t} = \hat{a}_0 + \hat{a}_1 P_{1t}$ is graphed in Figure 2-4 along with the actual values of price and sales for periods one and two. The prediction errors for these two periods, $x_{11} - \hat{x}_{11}$ and $x_{12} - \hat{x}_{12}$, are labeled $e_1$ and $e_2$ in the figure.

We have defined the demand equation that "best fits" the data as that demand equation that minimizes the sales prediction error. The problem with choosing $\hat{a}_0$ and $\hat{a}_1$ to minimize $\sum e_t$ is that some of the $e_t$ are positive and some are negative, which makes $\sum e_t$ a poor measure of how "close" the estimated line is to the actual sales values. The fit could be atrocious, but large positive and

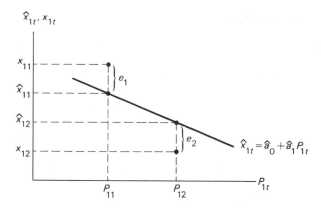

**FIGURE 2-4**

Prediction

errors

negative values of $e_t$ could render the sum approximately zero. This causes no particular problem, since all that needs to be done is to make sure positive and negative values do not cancel each other out. Minimizing the sum of *squared* prediction errors $\sum e_t^2$ accomplishes this objective. Every term in this sum is positive and hence the smaller the sum of squares, the closer the fit of the estimated equation to the data.

The problem of finding the best fitting line, then, amounts to no more than choosing $\hat{a}_0$ and $\hat{a}_1$ to minimize

$$\sum_{t=1}^{T} e_t^2 = \sum_{t=1}^{T} (x_{1t} - \hat{x}_{1t})^2 = \sum_{t=1}^{T} (x_{1t} - \hat{a}_0 - \hat{a}_1 P_{1t})^2$$

This is a simple calculus problem of finding a minimum in a two-variable function. If we calculate the two partial derivatives of this sum and then choose $\hat{a}_0$ and $\hat{a}_1$ such that these expressions are zero, we will have found the values of $\hat{a}_0$ and $\hat{a}_1$ that minimize the sum of squared sales prediction errors. Estimates of parameters found in this manner are called, strangely enough, *least squares estimates*. The derivatives are

$$\frac{\partial \sum e_t^2}{\partial \hat{a}_0} = 2 \sum_{1}^{T} (x_{1t} - \hat{a}_0 - \hat{a}_1 P_{1t})(-1) = 0$$

$$\frac{\partial \sum e_t^2}{\partial \hat{a}_1} = 2 \sum_{1}^{T} (x_{1t} - \hat{a}_0 - \hat{a}_1 P_{1t})(-P_{1t}) = 0$$

Notice that the two numbers we are looking for, $\hat{a}_0$ and $\hat{a}_1$, are functions only of the data available, $x_{1t}$ and $P_{1t}$. Solution of these two equations tells us how to use these data to calculate $\hat{a}_0$ and $\hat{a}_1$ so that prediction errors (squared) are minimized. Simplifying the first equation yields

$$\hat{a}_0 = \bar{x}_1 - \hat{a}_1 \bar{P}_1 \tag{2-7}$$

where $\bar{x}_1 = \sum_{t=1}^{T} x_{1t}/T$ and $\bar{P}_1 = \sum_{t=1}^{T} P_{1t}/T$ are the average values of sales and price over the $T$ periods. Summing the second equation gives

$$\sum x_{1t} P_{1t} - \hat{a}_0 \sum P_{1t} - \hat{a}_1 \sum P_{1t}^2 = 0$$

**35**

Substituting for $\hat{a}_0$ from (2-7) yields

$$\sum(x_{1t}P_{1t}) - (\bar{x}_1 - \hat{a}_1\bar{P}_1)\sum P_{1t} - \hat{a}_1\sum P_{1t}^2 = 0,$$

which upon rearranging yields

$$\hat{a}_1 = \frac{\sum x_{1t}P_{1t} - T\bar{x}_1\bar{P}_1}{\sum P_{1t}^2 - T\bar{P}_1^2} \tag{2-8}$$

The estimates $\hat{a}_0$ and $\hat{a}_1$ calculated according to these two formulas give the demand equation that minimizes the squared demand prediction error. The parameters of the log-linear demand function $x_{1t} = b_0 P_{1t}^{b_1}$ are calculated in the same manner, the only difference being that the data points $x_{1t}$ and $P_{1t}$ in Table 2-1 are replaced by $\ln x_{1t}$ and $\ln P_{1t}$.

As we noted above, a procedure analogous to the procedure we have used to calculate the two parameters of $x_{1t} = a_0 + a_1 P_{1t}$ may be used to calculate the $n + 3$ parameters of $x_{1t} = a_0 + a_1 P_{1t} + a_2 P_{2t} + \cdots + a_n P_{nt} + a_{n+1} Y_t + a_{n+2} A_t$ (or the $n + 3$ parameters of the general power function). The formulas for calculating the parameters of linear or log-linear equations are widely available as computer programs under the heading of *multiple regression analysis*.

An equation estimated in this manner is suitable for predicting demand as long as all variables that actively influence demand are included in the estimated equation. In our example only one variable, $P_1$, was assumed to actively influence demand. Such an estimate is useful for predicting the sales volume associated with various values of $P_1$ as long as all other influences on demand (which have not been included in the equation) are constant. In general $\hat{x}_{1t} = \hat{a}_0 + \hat{a}_1 P_{1t} + \cdots + \hat{a}_n P_{nt} + \hat{a}_{n+1} Y_t + \hat{a}_{n+2} A_t$ will be the estimated demand function, and it is valid to use this equation for predicting the level of demand associated with any combination of values of $P_1, P_2, \ldots, P_n, Y$, and $A$. *This equation will be valid only as long as there are no systematic influences on demand other than those included in the estimation.*[5] For example, changes in the interest rate brought about by a change in Federal Reserve policy will most likely affect the demand for automobiles, since most automobiles are purchased with loans. If interest rates have not been included in demand functions estimated for automobiles, then a change in interest rates will *shift* the estimated functions and invalidate their use.

• *Calculating the Least Squares Estimates—An Example.* In this section $\hat{a}_0$ and $\hat{a}_1$ are calculated based on six hypothetical observations on sales and price. The first two columns of Table 2-2 contain this information. The other columns contain the computations needed for calculating the estimates. The last numerical entry in each column is the sum of the elements in that column. These are the quantities required by the least squares formulas, (2-7) and (2-8). According

---

[5]It should be pointed out that demand parameters will generally change slowly over time due to the practical impossibility of including every systematic influence in any estimation procedure. Strictly speaking, if *all* influences were included in the estimated equation, one would never have to reestimate. But in practice one strives to include only "major" influences and then reestimates the equation periodically to update the estimate, thereby taking account of minor influences on demand which slowly shift the equation.

TABLE 2-2
Computation of
the least squares
estimates of $a_0$
and $a_1$

| $x_{1t}$ (1000) | $P_{1t}$ ($) | $x_{1t}P_{1t}$ | $P_{1t}^2$ |
|---|---|---|---|
| 6 | 2.5 | 15 | 6.25 |
| 5.5 | 3 | 16.5 | 9 |
| 7 | 2 | 14 | 4 |
| 4 | 4 | 16 | 16 |
| 6 | 2 | 12 | 4 |
| 5.5 | 3 | 16.5 | 9 |
| 34 | 16.5 | 90.0 | 48.25 |
| $\sum_{t=1}^{6} x_{1t}$ | $\sum_{t=1}^{6} P_{1t}$ | $\sum_{t=1}^{6} x_{1t}P_{1t}$ | $\sum_{t=1}^{6} P_{1t}^2$ |

$$\bar{x}_1 = \sum_{t=1}^{6} x_{1t}/6 = 34/6 = 5.66$$

$$\bar{P}_1 = \sum_{t=1}^{6} P_{1t}/6 = 16.5/6 = 2.75$$

$$\bar{x}_1\bar{P}_1 = 561/36 = 15.57$$

to these formulas:

$$\hat{a}_1 = \frac{90 - 93.42}{48.25 - 45.38} = -1.19$$

and

$$\hat{a}_0 = 5.66 - (-1.19)2.75 = 8.93$$

and the estimated demand function is

$$\hat{x}_{1t} = 8.93 - 1.19P_{1t} \qquad (2\text{-}9)$$

An estimate of the price elasticity of demand when price is, say, two dollars, is obtained by calculating predicted sales at this price and using this level of sales as the basis for the elasticity estimate. The sales prediction associated with a price of two dollars is

$$\hat{x}_{1t} = \hat{a}_0 + \hat{a}_1 P_{1t}$$
$$= 8.93 - 1.19(2)$$
$$= 6.55$$

So according to our estimated equation, at a price of two dollars 6550 units of $X_1$ will be demanded. Our *estimate* of $\eta_{11}$ is then

$$\hat{\eta}_{11} = -1.19\left(\frac{P_1}{\bar{x}_1}\right) = -1.19\left(\frac{2}{6.55}\right) = -.363$$

A 1 percent increase in price would result in a slightly more than 0.33 percent decline in sales. Demand is highly inelastic at this price.

• *Estimation: Additional Comments.*  The above example and the derivation of the least squares estimates that preceded it must now be put into perspective. Several points deserve emphasis:

  1.  One seldom, if ever, encounters a demand estimation problem where all influences on demand except price are constant over the estimation period. Usually, the level of demand will be jointly determined by a number of variables which, in

turn, must be included in the estimation problem. The basic requirement for successful estimation is that *all* systematic influences on demand be incorporated into the estimation process.

2.  Sales levels recorded by a firm are *jointly* determined by how much sellers are willing to sell and how much buyers are willing to buy. In practice this greatly complicates estimation—a point we will return to again in our discussion of the *identification* problem, often one of the most difficult obstacles confronting estimation.

3.  No mention has been made of testing procedures which would make it possible to assess the quality of the parameter estimates. In practice, one would subject estimates to testing before they are adopted for decision-making purposes. There are many tests that are designed to give the decision maker some idea of the worthiness of the estimates. Several of these tests are discussed in the next section.

4.  One of the problems with doing an estimation example of this kind is that it may give the reader a false sense of confidence concerning demand estimation. But lurking behind the mechanical computation of estimates are a number of formidable difficulties. Practitioners of estimation spend most of their time studying the firm and industry in question to learn as much as possible about the market in which the product or products are sold. The actual process of generating estimates is the last step of the estimation process and consumes very little time.

## EVALUATING THE ESTIMATED DEMAND FUNCTION

### Prediction Errors

Once a demand function has been estimated there will be one overriding concern on the part of management: How good is the estimate? In other words, is the estimated equation a good predictor of demand? One method of checking the predictive power of an estimated equation is to break up the available data into two parts with, say, $M$ observations in one group and the $T-M$ remaining observations in the second group. Use only $M$ of the data points to estimate the parameters of the demand function. Then, use the $T-M$ remaining data points to generate the *demand forecasts* $(\hat{x}_{1M+1}, \ldots, \hat{x}_{1T})$. The obvious test is to check to see if the prediction error $x_{1t} - \hat{x}_{1t}$ is sufficiently small for $t = M + 1$, $M + 2, \ldots, T$.

In more detail, this test consists of estimating the demand function with the first $M$ (out of $T$) observations, which yields

$$\hat{x}_{1t} = \hat{a}_0 + \hat{a}_1 P_{1t} + \hat{a}_2 P_{2t} + \cdots + \hat{a}_n P_{nt} + \hat{a}_{n+1} Y_t + \hat{a}_{n+2} A_t, \quad t = 1, 2, \ldots, M,$$

where $\hat{a}_0, \hat{a}_1, \ldots, \hat{a}_{n+2}$ are the estimated values of $a_0, a_1, \ldots, a_{n+2}$. Then, by substituting the values $P_{1t}, P_{2t}, \ldots, P_{nt}, Y_t, A_t$ for periods $M + 1, M + 2$, $\ldots, T$ into the estimated equation, the demand forecasts $\hat{x}_{1t}$, $t = M + 1$, $M + 2, \ldots, T$ are generated. One then compares $x_{1t}$ and $\hat{x}_{1t}$ for periods $M + 1$, $M + 2, \ldots, T$. If $x_{1t}$ is "close" to $\hat{x}_{1t}$, the estimated equation predicts satisfactorily.

The procedure we have described is illustrated in Table 2-3. The available data have been partitioned into two groups—one group to be used for estimating demand, the other group to be used for generating demand forecasts which will

| $x_{1t}$ | $P_{1t}$ | $P_{2t}$ | .... | $P_{nt}$ | $Y$ | $A$ | |
|---|---|---|---|---|---|---|---|
| $x_{11}$ | $P_{11}$ | $P_{21}$ | | $P_{n1}$ | $Y_1$ | $A_1$ | } $M$ observations to be used to estimate the demand equation. |
| $x_{12}$ | $P_{12}$ | $P_{22}$ | | $P_{n2}$ | $Y_2$ | $A_2$ | |
| . | . | . | | . | . | . | |
| . | . | . | | . | . | . | |
| . | . | . | | . | . | . | |
| $x_{1M}$ | $P_{1M}$ | $P_{2M}$ | | $P_{nM}$ | $Y_M$ | $A_M$ | |
| $x_{1,M+1}$ | $P_{1,M+1}$ | $P_{2,M+1}$ | | $P_{n,M+1}$ | $Y_{M+1}$ | $A_{M+1}$ | } $T-M$ observations which will be substituted into the estimated demand equation to generate demand forecasts for periods $M+1$, $M+2, \ldots , T$. These values are compared with actual demand levels in these periods (column one in the table). |
| . | . | . | | . | . | . | |
| . | . | . | | . | . | . | |
| . | . | . | | . | . | . | |
| . | . | . | | . | . | . | |
| . | . | . | | . | . | . | |
| . | . | . | | . | . | . | |
| . | . | . | | . | . | . | |
| . | . | . | | . | . | . | |
| $x_{1T}$ | $P_{1T}$ | $P_{2T}$ | | $P_{nT}$ | $Y_T$ | $A_T$ | |

**TABLE 2-3** Partitioning the available data for testing the estimated demand function

be checked against observed demands. If $\hat{x}_{1t}$ is "close" to $x_{1t}$ "most of the time," the estimated equation predicts satisfactorily.[6]

• *Prediction Errors: An Example.* For a numerical example of the above discussion, return for a moment to equation (2-9), the demand function we used to illustrate computation of $\hat{a}_0$ and $\hat{a}_1$, and assume that data from ten periods were available. Data for the first six periods were used for estimating $a_0$ and $a_1$ and were given in Table 2-2. The remaining four periods will be used for comparing predicted and actual sales. The observations from all ten periods, plus the four demand predictions and the associated errors, are presented in Table 2-4. We

| Period | $x_{1t}(1000)$ | $P_{1t}(\$)$ | $\hat{x}_{1t}(1000)$ | $x_{1t} - \hat{x}_{1t}$ | $\dfrac{x_{1t} - \hat{x}_{1t}}{x_{1t}}$ | |
|---|---|---|---|---|---|---|
| 1 | 6 | 2.5 | | | | $T = 10$, $M = 6$ Six observations used for estimating $a_0$ and $a_1$. |
| 2 | 5.5 | 3 | | | | |
| 3 | 7 | 2 | | | | |
| 4 | 4 | 4 | | | | |
| 5 | 6 | 2 | | | | |
| 6 | 5.5 | 3 | | | | |
| 7 | 4.9 | 3.25 | 5.06 | −.16 | −.03 | } Four observations used for predicting demand using the estimated function. |
| 8 | 5.0 | 3.00 | 5.36 | −.36 | −.07 | |
| 9 | 5.1 | 2.90 | 5.48 | −.38 | −.07 | |
| 10 | 5.5 | 2.75 | 5.66 | −.16 | −.03 | |

**TABLE 2-4** Data from ten quarters partitioned for estimation and predictive testing: an example

[6]Statistical tests are available which give quantitative meaning to this sentence.

saw that the first six observations on sales and price implied the predicting equation

$$\hat{x}_{1t} = 8.93 - 1.19 P_{1t} \qquad (2\text{-}10)$$

In column three of the table the four remaining observations on price are used to generate the sales forecasts presented in column four. The sales prediction errors for periods 7, 8, 9, and 10 are tabulated in the next to the last column. In period 7, for example, the predicted level of sales was .16 (1000) = 160 units higher than actual sales. And in fact predicted demand levels are "too high" in all four periods. As we'll soon see, this could indicate problems with the estimated equation. In general, whether the predictive ability of the estimated equation is "adequate" depends upon the accuracy of alternative means of forecasting. For example, if marketing managers can make "educated" guesses that are more accurate than the estimated equation, then obviously the former should be used to predict sales.

In evaluating predictions, it is often helpful to express prediction errors as a percentage of sales. This is done in the last column of Table 2-4. For the four periods in question, prediction errors range between 3 and 7 percent of sales.

• *Department of Commerce Demand Estimates.* In this section we reproduce several demand estimates that were done some time ago by the Department of Commerce. The first equation is a demand function for furniture, which was estimated using annual data for the years 1923–40.[7] Although several functional forms were tried, a power function was chosen as the empirical demand function. The estimate was[8]

$$x_t = .0036 P_t^{-.48} Y_t^{1.08} \alpha_t^{.16}$$

where $x$ = furniture expenditures per household, $P$ = the ratio of the furniture price index to the Consumer Price Index, $Y$ = disposable income per household, and $\alpha$ = the value of private residential construction per household.

Notice that the one price variable, $P$, actually incorporates both the price of furniture and other related prices. Since if $P$, say, increases, this means that the price of furniture is increasing *relative* to prices of substitutes and complements (which are picked up in a rough manner in the Consumer Price Index). The estimated price elasticity of demand is $-.48$. Intuition suggests that consumer disposable income should be an important influence on furniture demand, and indeed it is. Furniture demand is quite sensitive to the level of disposable income, with an income elasticity of 1.08. The variable $\alpha$, residential construction, was chosen to account for that substantial portion of furniture demand that derives directly from furnishing newly constructed homes.

As we have noted, the real test of an estimated equation is its ability to predict demand levels *outside* of the estimation period. This information is

---

[7] We have chosen to present these somewhat dated estimates primarily because of their simplicity. In recent years the level of estimation sophistication has increased so rapidly that it is difficult to find examples suitable for a text of this level.

[8] See *Survey of Current Business*, May 1950, p. 8. For obvious reasons these examples are of industry demand functions and not of demand functions confronting single firms. As you would expect, government agencies would not publish estimates of firm demand functions even when the necessary data are available to do the estimation.

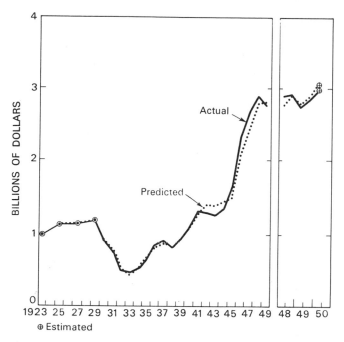

**FIGURE 2-5**
Actual versus
predicted
furniture sales:
1923–50

Source: *Survey of Current Business*, May 1950, p. 10.

shown in Figure 2-5, where instead of listing actual versus predicted furniture sales as we did in the last example (Table 2-4), we have plotted actual and predicted sales values. The plot encompasses the years 1923–50. Notice that for the years included in the sample (1923–40), the least squares procedure provides an estimated function that fits the data almost exactly. But it is more interesting to compare actual and forecast sales for the years 1941–50, since these data were not used in estimating the demand function. And beginning with 1941 the estimated demand function does remarkably well predicting actual sales rates. This is especially true in light of the fact that the events of the first half of this particular decade make it close to impossible to do accurate predictions. Normally one would not even attempt to predict demand levels in a period like 1941–46. The reason of course is that World War II was a major influence on the demand for most commodities—an influence that is difficult to successfully incorporate into any estimated equation.

We now take a look at a demand function for automobiles which was estimated using data from approximately the same period.[9] A study of the automobile market prior to estimation indicated that three variables played a major role in determining automobile demand: $P$ = the ratio of the automobile price index to the Consumer Price Index, $Y$ = disposable income per household, $\Delta Y$ = current household income as a percentage of the preceding year's income. In addition to these variables, a logarithmic time trend was introduced to account for a number of slowly moving factors which were felt to be influencing demand over the relatively long period from 1925 to 1940. Using $x$ to represent new car

[9]See *Survey of Current Business*, June 1950, p. 6.

registrations per thousand households,[10] the estimated function was

$$x_t = .00028 P_t^{-1.3} Y_t^{2.5} \Delta Y_t^{2.1} (.985)^t$$

Again, the price variable is a ratio that represents the price of automobiles relative to all other commodities and probably adequately accounts for the relation between the prices of autos and the prices of other commodities that compete for the consumer's budget. The price elasticity is quite large, indicating that changes in the relative price of automobiles bring about more than proportional responses in demand. Evidently both the *level* and the *rate of increase* of disposable income are important influences on auto demand, with the income elasticity being 2.5 and the elasticity relating demand to the rate of change of income being 2.1. The only other variable is the time trend, which tends to be rather unimportant, since if this estimate were 1.0 instead of .985 the trend would not affect the estimate.

In Figure 2-6 we have plotted actual automobile demand against the level of demand that was predicted using the estimated equation. This is done for

**FIGURE 2-6**

Actual versus predicted automobile sales: 1925–50

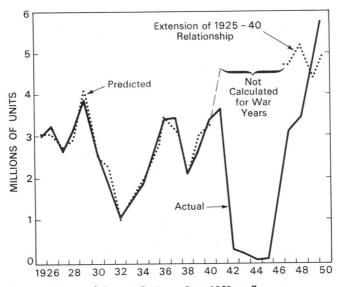

Source: *Survey of Current Business*, June 1950, p. 7.

the period 1925–50. Recall that the years 1925–40 were used for estimating the demand equation. The data from 1941 to 1950 are to be used for testing the predictive accuracy of the estimated equation. Examination of the figure for the years 1925–40 indicates that the least squares technique yields a function that is quite close to the actual data. Turning to the period 1941–50 we see from the figure that predictions for the war years 1941–46 were not made. This was done because of the feeling that war influences on the demand for autos would overwhelm all other factors. Examination of the predictions for the remaining years 1947–50 shows that the estimated equation is not a good predictor.

[10]"New car registrations" was used instead of "new car sales," since data were readily available on the former. Both variables measure the same thing.

One major weakness of this estimate is the use of a time trend to pick up slowly changing influences. This technique often works well under "normal" conditions but is entirely inadequate to account for changes of the magnitude of those that occurred during and after World War II. Analysis of the estimated function showed that prior to the war, the trend was picking up the slowly increasing age at which automobiles were scrapped (decreasing replacement demand). But during the war a huge pent-up demand had grown, which the trend, as a proxy for replacement demand, was entirely incapable of accounting for. If the demand function had been specified so as to include replacement demand explicitly as one of the active influences on new car demand, the postwar predictions would most likely have been much more accurate.

## ★ Testing the Predictive Ability of the Estimated Equation

In this section we examine several ideas developed by Professor Henri Theil for testing forecasting models. The first idea consists of plotting percentage changes in actual (observed) sales in periods $t = M + 1, M + 2, \ldots, T$ against percentage changes in forecast sales in the same periods. Call these two measures $R_t$ and $F_t$, where

$$R_t = \frac{x_{1t} - x_{1,t-1}}{x_{1t}} \quad \text{and} \quad F_t = \frac{\hat{x}_{1t} - \hat{x}_{1,t-1}}{\hat{x}_{1t}}$$

The location of points in $(R_t, F_t)$ space provides considerable information about the quality of the estimated demand equation. Three possibilities are illustrated in Figure 2-7. In these graphs, the 45-degree line passing through the origin contains those points where $R_t = F_t$ and hence points on this line are perfect forecasts.

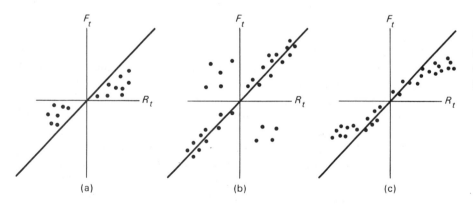

(a)          (b)          (c)

**FIGURE 2-7**

Percentage changes in actual and forecast demand

If the estimated equation generates the forecast sales changes shown in Figure 2-7a, we may draw two conclusions: First, we see that whenever $R_t$ is positive, $R_t$ is greater than $F_t$; and whenever $R_t$ is negative, $R_t$ is again larger than $F_t$ (in absolute value). The actual percentage change in demand is always greater than the predicted percentage change. That is, *the estimated demand model consistently understates the magnitude of actual changes in demand.*

Second, notice that $R_t$ and $F_t$ always have the same sign in Figure 2-7a. Hence if demand is increasing, $R_t > 0$, the forecast is for increased demand, $F_t > 0$. A similar statement holds for periods of decreasing demand. Therefore, we may infer that the *estimated model is successful in predicting "upturns" and "down-turns" in demand.* To illustrate, say that demand has been increasing for several quarters, but that in the next period demand falls. For the period in question, $R_t$ is negative, but in Figure 2-7a, $F_t$ would also be negative. The *turning point* is successfully predicted, although, as we have seen, it is somewhat underestimated.

Next, say that the estimated demand function generates values of $F_t$ that when plotted against $R_t$ look like Figure 2-7b. What conclusions can be drawn? According to the figure, when $R_t$ is positive $F_t$ is also usually positive and very close to $R_t$. But there are some exceptions in the lower-right quadrant where $R_t$ is positive and $F_t$ is negative. These points indicate that the forecast is for a decrease in demand ($F_t < 0$) but that actual demand has risen ($R_t > 0$). An analogous statement holds for negative $R_t$ and positive $F_t$. Decreases in demand are usually forecast very accurately, except for points in the upper-left quadrant. These points indicate that demand has fallen ($R_t < 0$), but the forecast is that demand will increase ($F_t > 0$). The *estimated model seems to predict well as long as the direction of movement does not change,* but fares poorly when it comes to predicting turning points.

In Figure 2-7c, turning points are adequately predicted and forecasts are quite accurate as long as demand changes are small. But changes of large magnitude are consistently underpredicted.

It should now be clear that the simple device of plotting actual demand changes against the demand changes predicted by the estimated model can be most helpful in evaluating the predictive performance of a model. If the forecasting equation is undistorted and effective, most of the points in the lower and upper portions of the diagram should be close to the 45-degree line, with a random scatter of points throughout the rest of the diagram. Figures 2-7a, 2-7b, and 2-7c point to problems with the estimated demand function and indicate that further market study followed by reestimation is probably necessary. Most likely, any additional information that is turned up in a market study will lead to an improvement in the forecasting accuracy of the model.

A second test, also suggested by Theil, is a method of evaluating the overall predictive ability of an estimated model. This test utilizes the values of $F_t$ and $R_t$ that were calculated above. As before, say that $T$ observations are available on the relevant variables and that $M$ of these observations are used to estimate the demand equation. The remaining $T-M$ observations are "saved" for calculating $F_{M+1}, F_{M+2}, \ldots, F_T$, which is to be compared with $R_{M+1}, R_{M+2}, \ldots, R_T$, according to the formula

$$I = \frac{\sum\limits_{t=M+1}^{T} (F_t - R_t)^2}{\sum\limits_{t=M+1}^{T} R_t^2}$$

Obviously, the smaller is $I$, the more accurate is the forecasting ability of the model. If the model forecasts perfectly, $R_t = F_t$ for periods $M + 1, M + 2,$

$\ldots, T$ and $I = 0$. One interesting test is to compare the predictive ability of the
estimated model with that of a *naive* model. For example, the simplest "naive"
forecasting model is $\hat{x}_{1,t+1} = \hat{x}_{1t}$, that is, demand in period $t + 1$ will be unchanged from demand in period $t$. This forecasting model implies $F_t = 0$ for
periods $M + 1, M + 2, \ldots, T$ and hence $I = 1$. We now have a cold objective
*minimum* standard against which the estimated model may be evaluated. A
minimum requirement as far as forecasting accuracy is concerned is that
forecasts done with the estimated model must do at least as well as forecasts
made by predicting that the "next" period will be the same as the "last" period.
That is, at the very least we must require $I < 1$ for forecasts made with the
estimated model. Admittedly this requirement is the very minimum we should
expect, but it is one test there will be little argument about: The predictive
ability of the estimated model must surpass that of a naive model which always
predicts "tomorrow" to be the same as "today." The model must pass this test
or be rejected.

## ★ IDENTIFYING DEMAND FUNCTIONS

We mentioned above that several perplexing problems lie hidden behind
the simple mechanical procedure of calculating parameter estimates. Very often
the most serious of these difficulties is what econometricians call the *identification
problem*. We introduce this problem with a paradigm which, in many cases, is
more fact than fancy: Suppose data are gathered on sales, price, and any other
variable that is deemed to be an important influence on demand. Regression
analysis is then used to estimate the demand function, and suppose it turns out
that $\hat{a}_1$ (or $\hat{b}_1$) is positive or that the coefficient on the price of a substitute is
negative or that the "income" coefficient is negative and it is known that the
commodity in question is a normal commodity. A check reveals that computations are correct. What has gone wrong?

The answer to this question requires an understanding of the process of
market price determination. Market prices are determined by the interaction of
demand and supply forces, the latter of which is the topic of the next few para-
graphs.

### Supply Functions—A Digression

Demand functions reflect the intention of buyers with respect to their pur-
chases of $X_1$. In particular, demand functions indicate the willingness of
customers to buy under various "conditions," that is, under various constella-
tions of prices, business conditions, advertising outlays, and so forth. Supply
functions reflect the willingness of firms to supply (produce) $X_1$. Generally, the
quantity supplied of $X_1$ will depend upon the price of $X_1$, the cost of producing
$X_1$, and perhaps other influences.

Symbolically, this relationship may be expressed as

$$x_1^S = g(P_1, w_1, w_2, \ldots, w_m, \beta) \qquad (2\text{-}11)$$

where

$x_1^S \equiv$ the quantity supplied of commodity $X_1$ per unit of time

$P_1 \equiv$ the price of $X_1$

$w_i \equiv$ the cost of the $i^{th}$ production input needed in the production of $X_1$ (as the supply function is written in equation (2-11), $m$ inputs are needed)

$\beta \equiv$ other factors that influence quantity supplied

Since increases in the price of $X_1$ will generally lead to an increased willingness on the part of firms to supply $X_1$, we would expect $\partial x_1^S/\partial P_1 > 0$. We also expect to find that $\partial x_1^S/\partial w_i \leq 0$, since increases in costs will usually cause decreased willingness to supply at any given price. Of course, nothing can be said about the derivative of the supply function with respect to $\beta$ until $\beta$ is specified.

If it were necessary to graph the supply function in $(x_1^S, P_1)$ space, we would write

$$x_1^S = g(P_1, w_1^0, w_2^0, \ldots, w_m^0, \beta^0)$$
$$= \bar{g}(P_1) \tag{2-11'}$$

The expression $x_1^S = \bar{g}(P_1)$ is the relationship between quantity supplied of $X_1$ and the price of $X_1$ when input costs are $w_1^0, w_2^0, \ldots, w_m^0$ and other influences on supply are constant. In terms of a graphical analysis, $\bar{g}(P_1)$ is a function in the two-dimensional space $(x_1^S, P_1)$ which will shift with a change in any influence on supply except $P_1$.

### The Identification Problem

To begin our discussion as simply as possible, consider the two-dimensional demand and supply functions:[11]

$$x_1^D = f(P_1, P_2^0, \ldots, P_n^0, Y^0, A^0, \alpha^0)$$
$$= \bar{f}(P_1)$$
$$x_1^S = g(P_1, w_1^0, \ldots, w_m^0, \beta^0)$$
$$= \bar{g}(P_1)$$

The demand function for $X_1$ reflects the willingness of buyers to purchase $X_1$ at various prices, while the supply function for $X_1$ reflects the willingness of producers to sell $X_1$ at various prices. It is important to understand that neither the willingness of buyers to purchase $X_1$ nor the willingness of producers to sell $X_1$, *alone* determines the price of $X_1$. It is the *interaction* of demand *and* supply forces that determines market price. For example, if sellers decide to set price at $P_1'$, as in Figure 2-8, then only $x_1''$ would be sold and sellers would be left holding $x_1' - x_1''$ more than they had planned. There is *excess supply* (unplanned inventory accumulation) of $x_1' - x_1''$ units at $P_1 = P_1'$. Hence, price would be lowered. If price were lowered to $P_1^*$, producers would quickly learn that buyers want more, $x_1^*$, than sellers are willing to sell, $x_1^{**}$, at that low price. There is *excess demand* of $x_1^* - x_1^{**}$ at this price (unplanned inventory depletion). Sellers would then raise price. Only at $P_1^0$ are the desires of sellers of $X_1$ consistent with those

[11]In this section we will use the superscripts $D$ and $S$ on $x_1$ to denote quantities demanded and supplied of $X_1$, respectively.

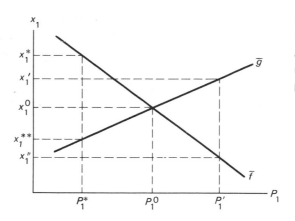

**FIGURE 2-8**

Excess demand
and supply at
nonequilibrium
prices

of buyers of $X_1$. $P_1^0$ is the equilibrium price that is established—very possibly through a trial-and-error procedure as we have sketched.

Mathematically, this discussion may be embodied in a simple three-equation model:

$$x_1^D = \tilde{f}(P_1)$$
$$x_1^S = \tilde{g}(P_1)$$

and

$$x_1^D = x_1^S \equiv x_1, \text{ the equilibrium quantity}[12]$$

In words, these three equations say nothing more than market price adjusts so as to make desires of buyers and sellers consistent with each other.

This model is only an approximation of actual market behavior in the world. To more accurately portray real-world market behavior we could write the third equation of the above model as $x_t^D - x_t^S = U_t$, where $U_t$ is a random term in period $t$. This change merely indicates that all transactions do not take place at $(x_1^0, P_1^0)$, as in Figure 2-8, but in general differ from this point by a stochastic amount $U$. The model may then be interpreted as depicting a *tendency* of prices and quantities to be "near" the equilibrium values. In this expanded model the quantities $x_1' - x_1''$ and $x_1^* - x_1^{**}$ in Figure 2-8 could be interpreted as representing the random differences between supply and demand in different periods. In the discussion that follows, we write the market model with $U = 0$ for simplicity, that is, with prices adjusting so that $x_1^D = x_1^S$.

The discussion and this simple model pinpoint the cause of the estimation pitfall we have labeled as the identification problem: Namely, *the observed quantity sold in period t, $x_{1t}$, is a point on both the demand function and the supply function* (observed sales rates are determined jointly by two equations, not just by the demand equation). For example, the statement that 100,000 units were sold means at one and the same time that suppliers sold 100,000 units and buyers bought 100,000 units. Therefore, our estimation technique had better be capable of "sorting out" the demand information in the sales data from the supply information. In other words, we need a means of "tracing out" the demand

[12]We will write that quantity of $X_1$ at which quantity demanded and supplied are equal as $x_1$, i.e., $x_1^D = x_1^S \equiv x_1$.

equation from the information contained in the available data. The following series of examples should help clarify this important point. In each case we assume that $T$ observations on $P_1$ and $x_1$ are available with which to estimate $\bar{f}(P_1)$.

CASE I.   In Figure 2-9 neither $\bar{f}$ nor $\bar{g}$ shifts during the period in which observations are available. The fact that neither the demand function nor the

**FIGURE 2-9**

Case I:

no estimation

is possible

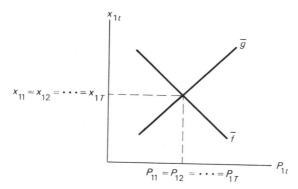

supply function shifts during the $T$ periods indicates that there were no active influences on demand or supply except $P_1$. (Make sure you understand this sentence before proceeding.) In such a case, all $T$ observations on sales and price are the same, and there is not sufficient information in the data to *identify* either the demand function or the supply function. Clearly, the data contain but one point which is not sufficient to estimate either $\bar{f}$ or $\bar{g}$. Therefore we may conclude that if the active influences on demand and supply are exactly the same (in this case $P_1$), then it will not be possible to estimate the demand function or for that matter the supply function. The reason is obvious: There is no variation that would allow the demand function, $\bar{f}$, to be "traced out."[13] In summary, the problem here is that the same variables that affect demand also affect supply, *and* these variables are the *only* variables that are active in the market.

To carry our analysis on to more complicated market situations, it is helpful to explicitly present the underlying market model. We will assume demand and supply functions are linear. In the case just investigated the model is

$$x_{1t}^D = a_0 + a_1 P_{1t}$$
$$x_{1t}^S = c_0 + c_1 P_{1t}$$
$$x_{1t}^D = x_{1t}^S \equiv x_{1t}$$

where lowercase $a$'s will be used to represent demand parameters and lowercase $c$'s to represent supply parameters. Demand and supply functions are "stationary" (in $(x_1, P_1)$ space), and the variation necessary to identify the demand function is absent.

---

[13] Or, if there is variation, it is not related specifically to demand or supply forces—it is random.

CASE II.  If demand and supply functions behave as depicted in Figure 2-10, then the underlying market model is

$$x_{1t}^D = a_0 + a_1 P_{1t} + a_2 Z_t$$
$$x_{1t}^S = c_0 + c_1 P_{1t}$$
$$x_{1t}^D = x_{1t}^S \equiv x_{1t}$$

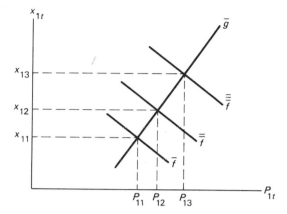

FIGURE 2-10
Case II:
estimation of
$\bar{g}(P_1)$ instead
of $\tilde{f}(P_1)$

where $Z_t$ is any variable that influences demand in period $t$ except $P_1$. Figure 2-10 indicates that a regression analysis using only observed sales and price information would yield an estimate of $\bar{g}$ instead of $\tilde{f}$.[14] That this is the case is evident from the fact that the data points $(x_{11}, P_{11})$, $(x_{12}, P_{12})$, and $(x_{13}, P_{13})$ are three points on the same supply function, $\bar{g}$, but "different" demand functions. So if we use the collected sales and price data to calculate estimates of $a_0$ and $a_1$ according to the formulas derived earlier, we will end up with estimates of $c_0$ and $c_1$, not $a_0$ and $a_1$ as we had intended. In fact, in this case the supply function is estimated perfectly. Unfortunately, the goal was to estimate the demand function.[15]

What went wrong? Figure 2-10 makes the answer to this question easy. The reason $\bar{g}$ was estimated by mistake instead of $\tilde{f}$ is that $\tilde{f}$ "shifted around" in the observation period and "traced out" $\bar{g}$, the supply function. What causes this behavior on the part of the demand function? Again, the answer is obvious. *The demand function will "shift around" in $(x_1, P_1)$ space and the supply function will remain stationary if there are influences on demand other than $P_1$ and no influences on supply other than $P_1$.* And this is precisely the role of the variable $Z$ which appears in the demand function but not in the supply function. Since $Z$ is the only variable except price that influences the market, the supply function is stationary in $(x_1, P_1)$ space while the demand function shifts with every change in $Z$, thereby *identifying* the supply function.

[14]We have graphed only three observations in Figure 2-10, the first three, to make this point very clear.

[15]In one sense management is fortunate in this case. The estimate of the "demand" function has a positive slope and would not be used. Things do not always work out this way, as we shall see.

CASE III.   Next, consider the model

$$x_{1t}^D = a_0 + a_1 P_{1t}$$
$$x_{1t}^S = c_0 + c_1 P_{1t} + c_2 V_t$$
$$x_{1t}^D = x_{1t}^S \equiv x_{1t}$$

The variable $V$ in the supply function represents any variable that influences supply except the price of $X_1$. This case is precisely analogous to the preceding one, only here regression analysis using observed data on sales and price will lead to proper estimation of the demand function; although it will be impossible to estimate the supply function. In $(x_1, P_1)$ space, the demand function is stationary and therefore changes in $V$ shift the supply function about, identifying the demand function. This situation is depicted graphically in Figure 2-11.

**FIGURE 2-11**

Case III:

identifying the

demand function

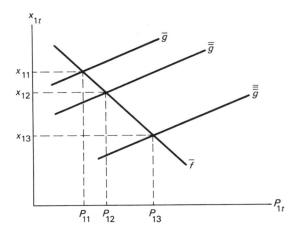

CASE IV.   It is now time to analyze the somewhat more complicated model obtained by combining the demand function of Case II with the supply function of Case III:

$$x_{1t}^D = a_0 + a_1 P_{1t} + a_2 Z_t$$
$$x_{1t}^S = c_0 + c_1 P_{1t} + c_2 V_t$$
$$x_{1t}^D = x_{1t}^S \equiv x_{1t}$$

We now wish to determine the outcome of an attempt to estimate demand when price and sales data alone are used to do the estimation and when in fact the market is as depicted in Case IV. Two possibilities are graphed in Figures 2-12a and 2-12b. (Again, only two observations on sales and price are shown for purposes of clarity.) Since both functions contain variables other than $x_1$ and $P_1$, both will shift about in $(x_1, P_1)$ space. In Figure 2-12, demand and supply functions have shifted in such a manner that if data on sales and price alone were used in a regression analysis of the sort we did above, the result would be the line $h$. This line is neither a demand function nor a supply function and contains no information of interest. Keep in mind that this "estimate" is generated when sales and price data are combined according to the formulas we

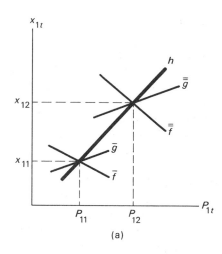
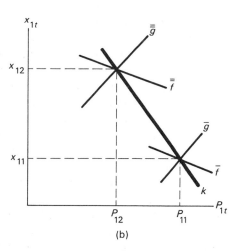

FIGURE 2-12
Omissions of
important
variables:
two cases

(a)                                              (b)

derived above. *The fundamental problem here is that there are influences on both demand and supply which have not been properly accounted for.* In practice, it is imperative that all active influences on both functions be accounted for in the estimation process. Which variables (influences) must be "accounted for" can be discovered only by careful study of the market in question.

If estimation led to a result as poor as that depicted in Figure 2-12a decision makers might be fortunate, since a demand estimate with a positive slope would never be used. But the world is not always so congenial. For example, if actual market forces are once again given as Case IV, but this time demand and supply functions shifted as shown in Figure 2-12b, then a simple regression analysis using price and sales data would yield the line $k$. This curve is nowhere close to the true demand function and, unfortunately, has a negative slope, which could be misleading. If management used this estimate without first testing its predictive capabilities, costly errors would be made. At the observed prices and quantities the estimated function is considerably more price elastic than is the true demand function. Hence a decision to increase price would probably not be made when price should be increased. According to the estimated function, price increases lead to "large" decreases in sales, but, in fact, such price increases have little impact on sales volume.

### A Summary of Cases I–IV

We have briefly examined four different market situations and, in each case, looked at the outcome of using price and sales data alone in accordance with some simple line-fitting mechanism like regression analysis. There were problems. Case I indicated that an essential ingredient of successful estimation is variation. If neither the demand nor the supply function shifts during the estimation period, no estimation is possible. Case II pointed out that the variation must be of a particular type. If market forces are as depicted in Case II, any attempt to estimate demand will fail, essentially because supply forces obscure the demand relationship. One ends up with an estimate of the supply function when one is attempting to estimate demand. In Case III, the appropriate type of variation occurs. A shifting supply function combined with a stationary demand function allows a demand estimate to be obtained.

Up to this point, intuition might seem to be an accurate guide for determining whether or not the demand equation can be estimated. And for the most part it is. (A shifting supply function implies an estimable demand function, etc.) But Case IV raises some questions, because in Case IV *both the demand and supply functions may be estimated, if the appropriate techinques are used.* This is not the place to prove this assertion. Instead, I will indicate "intuitively" why it is so and then attempt to give an overview of what we should have learned from our analysis of these cases.

First, why is it possible to estimate both demand and supply functions in Case IV? We saw that omitting important influences in each equation led to estimation of the lines *h* or *k* in Figure 2-12a and 2-12b, lines that do not contain the desired market information. The crucial point is that in this case these omitted influences (the variables $Z$ and $V$) contain sufficient information to identify (estimate) both the demand and supply functions (if the appropriate techniques are used). To see why this is so, consider the three-dimensional space $(x_1, P_1, Z)$ instead of $(x_1, P_1)$ space we have been using. Since the demand function in Case IV is $x_1^D = a_0 + a_1 P_1 + a_2 Z$, it is stationary in $(x_1, P_1, Z)$ space. In this space, every change in the supply variable, $V$, will shift the supply function, and, as with model III, the shifting supply function will "trace out," or identify, the stationary demand function. In fact, this argument is precisely analogous to that used to show that the demand function was estimable in Case III; only here we are dealing with one more variable in the demand function.

Any attempt to summarize our discussion must include the following key points: *First, observed sales and price data that are used to estimate the demand function are points on both a demand function and a supply function.* This is due to the fact that the observation "100 million units were sold in period *t*" is at one and the same time a statement about the amount supplied and the amount purchased in period *t*. That is, the observed sales rate is the rate at which "demand equals supply." The effects of demand and supply must be disentangled, that is, identified, in the estimation process. *Second,* a consideration intimately related to identifying the demand equation is that *all active influences on both demand and supply functions must be included in the estimation process.* In each of the models we have looked at, it was necessary to know which variables are in the demand function and which are in the supply function. Thus the first step in successful estimation is a thorough, thoughtful study of the market designed to determine as well as possible which variables are active in the underlying demand and supply functions.

### An Overview of Demand Identification

Our discussion has not been intended to be a guide to doing actual estimation. Instead, it was intended to be a parable of sorts in which several problems inherent in demand estimation were highlighted. This would seem to be a

necessary procedure, because the benefits of successful demand estimation have
a tendency to overshadow the complicated nature of the problem. This final
section on demand estimation attempts to summarize the more important
aspects of the identification problem from the perspective of a sales manager
faced with the decision of whether or not to use an estimated demand function.
In particular, we will be looking for general conditions, which if *not* met, imply
that the estimated function need be considered no further as a method of
forecasting demand.

First, recall that even if data were obtainable on all relevant variables, they
would be of no avail in an attempt to estimate demand if market forces were as
depicted in Cases I and II. The demand function cannot be estimated in these
cases. Although we did not show how to actually perform the estimation of
demand in Cases III and IV, we did indicate why it is possible if market forces
are as depicted in these cases. Contrasting Cases I and II with Cases III and IV
makes clear the condition necessary for successful demand estimation: *The
supply function must contain at least one active influence (variable) that does not
affect the demand function.*[16] Notice that this is precisely the condition present
in Cases III and IV but absent in Cases I and II.

The condition just stated obviously depends upon knowing what the
influences on demand and supply are—what the forces at work in the market
are. In other words, successful demand estimation requires knowing which
variables influence quantity demanded and which variables influence quantity
supplied. This statement should not be misunderstood. Demand estimation
does not require quantitative knowledge of *how* different variables influence
demand but instead requires merely what the different influences on demand are.
(Ascertaining the quantitative influence of different variables on demand is the
purpose of estimation.) How does one find out what the influences on demand
and supply are? There is only one way—by "knowing" the market, either
through a market study or through "experience" in the market. Both are methods
of observing market behavior, one indirect, one direct.[17]

Since managers are the individuals who are given (with increasing frequency)
estimated forecasting equations but seldom are the ones doing the actual estimation, can any guiding principles be gleaned from our discussion which might be
helpful to managers in evaluating estimates? There are at least two. First, have
all known active influences on demand and supply been accounted for in the
estimation procedure? If the answer to this question is negative, it is unnecessary to further test the equation—the estimate is probably worthless. But even
if all influences have been properly included, the estimated equation may be
worthless. The second hurdle that must be cleared before the estimated equation
can be seriously considered as a candidate for forecasting demand is whether
there is an active influence on supply that does not affect demand. If the answer
to this question is also yes, it is probably worthwhile to allocate some time and

[16]This influence is the variable or variables that "shift" the supply function, thereby
"tracing out" the demand function.

[17]For example, years of selling in a given market will give any marketing manager worth
his salt a very accurate notion as to what the important influences on demand are.

money to testing the predictive capabilities of the model. It still may not predict, but at least the estimated equation *could* be a demand function. If the answer to this question is no, the estimated equation could not be a demand function.

Finally, an operational remark: Due to the complexity of the estimation problem, it will usually be necessary, in all but the simplest cases, to hire specialists to do the actual estimation. The point of interest to managers is that in a number of situations, it is possible to get reliable estimates of the demand function. Appropriate use of the estimated equation is explored when optimal pricing and volume policies are analyzed in Chapters 8, 9, and 10.

## ★ ESTIMATING SHORT-TERM AND LONG-TERM DEMAND ELASTICITIES: A POSTSCRIPT

The problem of accounting for all influences on demand in the estimation procedure is exacerbated if demand for $X_1$ in period $t$ depends not only on $P_{1t}$ but also on the past, say $k$, pricing decisions, $P_{1,t-1}, P_{1,t-2}, \ldots, P_{1,t-k}$. In this case, the demand function becomes

$$x_{1t} = f(P_{1t}, P_{1,t-1}, \ldots, P_{1,t-k}, P_{2t}, \ldots, P_{nt}, Y_t, A_t, \alpha_t) \qquad (2\text{-}12)$$

To focus attention on the role of past prices on present sales, we treat all variables except $P_1$ as parameters over the estimation period. The demand function may then be written as

$$x_{1t} = \tilde{f}(P_{1t}, P_{1,t-1}, \ldots, P_{1,t-k}) \qquad (2\text{-}12')$$

Dropping the "one" subscript on the demand and price variables and assuming demand to be approximately linear in past prices, we may write (2-12′) as

$$x_t = a_0 + a_1 P_t + a_2 P_{t-1} + \cdots + a_{k+1} P_{t-k} \qquad (2\text{-}12'')$$

Equation (2-12″) says that present demand depends upon the pricing decisions of the last $k$ periods for any given level of rival prices, business conditions, and advertising expenditures. A valid concern would be to estimate the parameters $\{a_i\}$ using the $T$ available observations on sales and prices.

The demand function shown in equation (2-12″) suggests two particularly interesting questions: First, what will be the *immediate* response of demand to a change in price, say, in period $t$? And second, if price is changed and left unaltered after period $t$, what will be the *eventual* effect on sales? The immediate, or "short-run," response to a price change in period $t$ is

$$\frac{\partial x_t}{\partial P_t} = a_1$$

The eventual, or "long-run," response of demand to a change in price in period $t$ is given by adding up *all* responses of demand to the change in price in period $t$. Keep in mind that a price change in period $t$ will affect demand for $k$ periods into the future. We then have

$$\frac{\partial x_t}{\partial P_t} + \frac{\partial x_{t+1}}{\partial P_t} + \frac{\partial x_{t+2}}{\partial P_t} + \cdots + \frac{\partial x_{t+k}}{\partial P_t} = a_1 + a_2 + a_3 + \cdots + a_{k+1}$$

The "long-run" response of sales to a price change in period $t$ is the sum of the effect on sales in periods $t, t+1, t+2, \ldots, t+k$. If the parameters of equation (2-12″) were estimated to be the numbers $\hat{a}_0, \hat{a}_1, \ldots, \hat{a}_{k+1}$, the resulting forecasting equation

$$\hat{x}_t = \hat{a}_0 + \hat{a}_1 P_t + \hat{a}_2 P_{t-1} + \cdots + \hat{a}_{k+1} P_{t-k}$$

could be used to estimate the short- and long-term price elasticities of demand at any new price level management might be considering. If a change in price to, say, $P^*$ is being contemplated, it is of considerable interest to have an estimate of the immediate and long-term response of sales volume. In percentages, $\hat{a}_1(P^*/\hat{x}^*)$ is the *short-term price elasticity of demand* at the price $P^*$; where $\hat{x}^*$ is the sales volume predicted by the estimated demand function when price $P^*$. An estimate of the *long-term price elasticity of demand* at the price $P^*$ is given by $(\hat{a}_1 + \hat{a}_2 + \cdots + \hat{a}_{k+1})(P^*/\hat{x}^*)$.

1. The following demand function for urban rapid transit was estimated a few years ago in a large urban area in the eastern United States:

$$x_T = P_T^{-.13} P_a^{.05} Y^{-.2} W^{-.6} Z^{.91}$$

where

$x_T$ = number of transit trips demanded
$P_T$ = transit fare
$P_a$ = cost of driving
$Y$ = average income in transit area
$W$ = walk time to transit terminal
$Z$ = index of population in area of terminal

a. Calculate and interpret the price and income elasticities of demand for rapid transit.
b. Use the estimates of $\eta_{T_a}$ and $\eta_{TY}$ to explain some of the difficulties urban transit systems have had in the area of public acceptance.
c. A new parking tax will increase the cost of driving to the central business district by 10 percent. What will be the effect of the tax on the demand for transit trips to this area?
d. What increase in income would offset the influence on transit demand of the parking tax?

2. A number of years ago a detailed analysis of the steel industry in the United States led R. H. Whitman to conclude that the demand for steel, $x_s$ (millions of tons), depended upon the price of steel, $P_s$ (cents per lb.), upon the rate of change of price over time, $dP_s/dt$, and upon the level of national production, $Y$ (the index of industrial production). He also concluded that the demand

function for steel could be adequately approximated with a linear function. Based upon his study, he estimated the following demand function:

$$x_s = 1.49 - 1.27P_s + 6.27\frac{dP_s}{dt} + 4.64Y$$

a. If the index of industrial production is estimated to be 130 for the coming quarter and price will remain unchanged from the last quarter at eighty cents per lb., what level of sales does the demand function predict?

b. What is the price elasticity of demand predicted for the next quarter? Interpret this number.

c. Do the same calculation if the index of industrial production is 150, and compare the price elasticity computed in each case. Can you make a general statement about how changes in $Y$ affect $\eta_{ss}$? Interpret this result in terms of the amount of discretion management will be able to exercise in pricing steel in periods of increasing business activity.

d. Briefly interpret the coefficient of $dP_s/dt$ using the fact that the demand for steel is highly speculative.

3. Just after World War II, R. Stone estimated the demand function for beer in the United Kingdom to be

$$x_B = 1.06P_B^{-.73}P_0^{.91}Y^{.14}g^{.82}$$

where

$x_B$ = quantity of beer sold
$P_B$ = price of beer
$P_0$ = average retail price level of all other commodities
$Y$ = aggregate real income
$g$ = an index of alcohol content

a. Interpret in your own words the meaning of each of the parameters estimated (exclude 1.06).

b. What is the response of beer sales to a simultaneous 1 percent increase in
(1) The price and alcohol content of beer?
(2) The retail price level and the level of aggregate income?

c. What would you predict about sales in part b (2) if the price of beer were also raised 1 percent?

4. Several years ago in a period of rising steel and aluminum prices, it was noted that steel sales were also increasing. A certain financial columnist concluded from this that the demand function for steel was positively sloped, at least in a limited region. Based on the above information, may this conclusion be drawn? Show why or why not.

5. In the face of an increasingly aggressive advertising campaign on the part of a competitor, the marketing department of Unico. Inc., is instructed to come up with some policy recommendations that would regain the 10 percent of Unico's market that has recently been lost. As a first step, price is reduced 4 percent from the present level of $10 and a consulting firm is hired to estimate the demand function for the besieged product. The estimate is

$$x = 99.1 P_X^{-1.2} P_Y^{1.6} A_X^{1.4} A_Y^{-2.0} B^{1.0}$$

where

$P_X$ = price of Unico's product, $X$
$P_Y$ = price of the rival commodity
$A_X$ = Unico's advertising outlay on $X$
$A_Y$ = advertising outlay on the rival commodity
$B$ = an indicator of "business activity" in the market

a. Interpret the coefficient of $A_Y$.

b. What increase in advertising outlays by Unico, when combined with the 4 percent reduction in the price of $X$, will regain Unico's lost market? Upon what assumption does your calculation depend? Presently, $P_Y = \$10.50$, $A_X = \$100,000$, $B = 1000$, and best estimates give $A_Y = \$200,000$. What is the new price and the new level of advertising?

c. Say that management of the firm that sells $Y$ is determined not to give up its newly acquired share of the market and responds to the Unico policy calculated in part b by lowering the price of $Y$ enough to retain its share of Unico's market. What will be the new price of $Y$?

6. Some time ago a prominent business periodical had several members of its research staff estimate the price elasticity of demand for scotch whiskey. The research staff gathered monthly data on quantities of scotch sold and prices of scotch for a two-year period. Their result was $\eta_{xx} = .82$, where $x$ is quantity of scotch sold. Is this result satisfactory? Explain.

* 7. In our discussion of the identification problem, four cases were analyzed. For the market depicted as Case IV, it was asserted that both the demand and supply functions could be estimated. A brief argument was then presented that indicated the demand function could be estimated. Use an analogous argument to show that it is also possible to estimate the supply function in this case.

* 8. In the first case we studied in the section on the identification problem (Figure 2-9), we saw that if neither the demand function nor the supply function shifted over the estimation period it would be impossible to estimate *either* function. Prove this statement by trying to calculate $\hat{a}_1$ in the demand equation $x_{1t}^D = \hat{a}_0 + \hat{a}_1 P_{1t}$. Use the fact that $P_{11} = P_{12} = \cdots = P_{1T} = \bar{P}_1$ and $x_{11} = x_{12} = \cdots = x_{1T} = \bar{x}_1$.

9. Suppose we observe that a 10 percent increase in the price of $X$ leads to a 15 percent increase in the sales of $X$. What conclusions may be drawn about the demand function for commodity $X$?

*10. The following data on sales and prices are available for the past five quarters:

| Sales (100s) | Price |
| --- | --- |
| 1.46 | 9.00 |
| 1.53 | 8.50 |
| 1.60 | 8.00 |
| 1.67 | 7.50 |
| 1.75 | 7.25 |

The supply function has been estimated to be

$$x^S = 110 + 4P + 9t$$

where $x^S$ is quantity supplied, $P$ is price, and $t$ represents "time." This variable ("time") was assigned the values 0, 1, 2, 3, 4 in the regression analysis.

a.  Plot the "family" of supply functions in $(x^S, P)$ space. Can you think of a reason for including the variable $t$ in the supply equation?

b.  Plot the data in the table on the same graph as the supply functions and draw a line that approximately "fits" the data.

c.  Under what conditions is the line that you have drawn an approximation to the demand function for $X$? (Hint: Reread Cases II and III in the section on the identification problem.)

*11.  For certain types of appliances it has been observed that price changes have an effect on sales for up to three quarters after the change. In an attempt to measure this effect, the function $x_t = a_0 + a_1 P_t + a_2 P_{t-1} + a_3 P_{t-2} + a_4 P_{t-3} + a_5 Y_t$ is estimated using quarterly data on sales, price and $Y$. ($x_t$ is the number of appliances, in thousands, sold in period $t$; $Y_t$ is an index measuring the level of consumer disposable income in period $t$; and $P_t$ is the dollar price of the appliances in period $t$.)

The estimates are $a_0 = 13{,}101.1$, $a_1 = -31.1$, $a_2 = -29.2$, $a_3 = -17.7$, $a_4 = -3.1$, and $a_5 = 53.4$. (a) On the basis of these estimates, calculate the short-term and the long-term price elasticity of demand at a price of $60, assuming that the index of disposable income remains approximately constant at 100 and that price has been $60 for over a year. Interpret these two numbers. (b) If the price of these appliances were lowered to $50, calculate the short-term and the long-term price elasticity of demand at the new price, assuming price was established four quarters ago.

*12.  In a 1969 study of the domestic lead-refining industry (Heineke, "Demand for Refined Lead," *Review of Economics and Statistics*, August 1969), the demand function for refined lead was estimated. If we call $x_t$ the demand for refined lead (in thousands of tons) in period $t$, $P_t$ the price of lead (in cents per lb.) in period $t$, and $Y_t$ the value of the index of industrial production in period $t$, a simplified form of the estimated equation is

$$x_t = a_0 + a_1 \sum_{i=0}^{\infty} (\lambda_1)^i P_{t-i} + a_2 \sum_{i=0}^{\infty} (\lambda_2)^i Y_{t-i}$$

where $a_0$, $a_1$, $a_2$ are familiar parameters, and $\lambda_1$ and $\lambda_2$ are two additional parameters which must take on values between zero and one. The basic hypothesis of this model is that demand at any point in time depends upon all past pricing policies of sellers. The estimates were $a_0 = 513.80$, $a_1 = -2.14$, $a_2 = 1.46$, $\lambda_1 = .97$, and $\lambda_2 = .86$.

a.  By writing out the coefficients of $P_t$, $P_{t-1}$, $P_{t-2}$, and $P_{t-3}$, can you state the basic relationship between the responsiveness of demand in period $t$ to changes in price in past periods? In particular, what happens to the demand responsiveness in period $t$ as the time between period $t$ and the price change increases?

b. Calculate the "immediate" and "eventual" response of sales to a change in the price of lead of one cent per lb. in period $t$. (Hint: You will have to remember your high school formula for summing a geometric series.)

c. At the price of sixteen cents per lb., calculate the short- and long-term price elasticities of demand. Assume the index of industrial production is equal to 103.

d. Calculate the short- and long-term income elasticities of demand for the same value of price and the index of industrial production. Interpret your results.

13. The following figure appears in *Resources and Man*, a publication of the Natural Academy of Sciences.[18] Being as precise as possible, comment on the first sentence in the note under the figure.

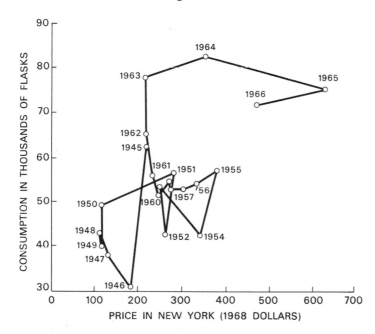

Note: Consumption of mercury in the United States is not related to price. The jointed line traces U.S. consumption of mercury and corresponding price from 1945 to 1966. (Data are annual averages from the U.S. Bureau of Mines Minerals Yearbooks.)

[18]From *Resources and Man*, Committee on Resources and Man, National Academy of Sciences—National Research Council (San Francisco: W. H. Freeman, 1969).

# Production Theory:
# Preliminary Concepts

CHAPTER

3

In Chapter 4 we will be concerned with management's problem of organizing the resources under its control in the most efficient manner possible, a problem that will be solved under a number of different assumptions about the firm's production technology and the availability of resources. The present chapter provides a framework within which this problem can be analyzed. Most of our attention will be focused on the firm's production function and closely related concepts which play a fundamental role in determination of the "most efficient" production plan.

In our investigation of firm decisions we will use the terms *factor of production* and *input* interchangeably to mean any commodity used in a production process. Broadly speaking, inputs may be classified as *land* (non-man-made resources), *labor* (physical and mental), and *capital* (man-made resources). Notice that the latter category does not include financial capital. Inputs will be classified as being either *fixed* or *variable*, depending upon whether or not their utilization can be varied in a given production period. For example, in a reasonably short decision period, man-hours of labor and the quantity of many raw materials are variable factors, while "plant" and heavy equipment will be fixed factors. The fixed factor–variable factor distinction is purely temporal, and as the planning period is lengthened, all factors become variable factors. We will term planning periods within which at least one input is fixed as the *short run*. Decisions taken in such periods are *short-run decisions*. On the other hand, decisions taken when all inputs are variable will be termed *long-run decisions*.

### The Production Function

The firm's production function is the mathematical expression of the transformation between quantities of inputs used and quantities of outputs produced.

60

The concept of a production function is completely general and may be a point,
a set of points, an equation, or a set of equations and is defined with respect
to a given technology and way of doing things. If a firm produces only one
commodity (a product or a service), say $X_1$, with $m$ inputs, $V_1, V_2, \ldots, V_m$, we
may noncommittally write the production function as

$$x_1 = f(v_1, v_2, \ldots, v_m) \tag{3-1}$$

where

$x_1 \equiv$ the *quantity* of $X_1$ produced per unit time
$v_i \equiv$ the *quantity* of variable input $V_i$ needed to produce $x_1$ units of $X_1$

Equation (3-1) tells us that the quantity of $X_1$ produced depends upon the quantity of each of the inputs used. In (3-1) variable inputs are represented explicitly,
while fixed inputs (the "type of plant") are implicit in the particular type of
function $f$ happens to be. In other words, the production function shown as
(3-1) contains fixed inputs at predetermined levels along with the $m$ variable
inputs. Management is unable to alter the availability of the fixed inputs during
the time period for which (3-1) is defined. In addition, (3-1) is defined only for
nonnegative values of $x_1, v_1, v_2, \ldots$ and $v_m$.

It is important to distinguish between the firm's *technology* and its *production function*. The former is more general and encompasses all technical information concerning how much of each input is needed to produce the firm's
output. Often the technology will be such that a single combination of inputs
can be utilized in several different ways and hence yield several different output
levels. The production function differs from the technology in that it presumes
technical efficiency and gives the *maximum* amount of output possible from each
input combination. So if one input combination yields several different output
levels depending on how the inputs are utilized, the firm's production function
contains only that method of utilization yielding maximal output.

If the firm produces $n$ products $X_1, X_2, \ldots, X_n$ with $m$ inputs, the production function must be written in what is called *implicit* form. The implicit form
of the production function in equation (3-1) is

$$F(x_1, v_1, v_2, \ldots, v_m) = 0 \tag{3-1'}$$

and is accomplished merely by writing (3-1) as $x_1 - f(v_1, v_2, \ldots, v_m) = 0$ and
calling the entire expression on the left-hand side, $F$. Analogously, the production function for the $n$ output, $m$ input firm is

$$F(x_1, x_2, \ldots, x_n, v_1, v_2, \ldots, v_m) = 0 \tag{3-2}$$

Equation (3-2) says nothing more than that the inputs and products of the firm
are related in some manner, the particular relation of course varies from firm
to firm and is given by the particular form of $F$. For example, if the production
function given in equation (3-2) is for a hospital, then the $x_i$ represent the
various types of medical services produced by a hospital and the $v_i$ represent
the variable inputs going into the production of these services (primarily labor

inputs of varying skills, i.e., doctors, nurses, orderlies, maintenance men, etc.). We will return to the formulation of the production function given in (3-2) on several occasions when analyzing the decisions of multiproduct, multi-input firms.

Finally it should be noted that if a firm produces environmental pollution along with products $X_1, X_2, \ldots, X_n$, one or more of the variable factors may be environmental control inputs which are necessary to bring pollution levels to legal standards. Only a few years ago one seldom if ever found inputs of this type in firm production functions. Now environmental control expenditures are increasingly common.

Two special cases of the general production function given in (3-2) are of interest:

$$F(x_1, x_2, v_1) = 0 \qquad (3\text{-}2')$$

and

$$F(x_1, v_1, v_2) = 0 \qquad (3\text{-}2'')$$

We are interested in (3-2') and (3-2'') primarily because these production functions depend upon only three variables and hence may be used in graphical expositions of production problems. The production function given in equation (3-2') represents a firm producing two products with one variable input (say labor) and any number of fixed inputs. An interesting set of problems that may be studied with a production function of this type, are problems of optimal product mix. Problems of optimal product mix are concerned with choosing the most satisfactory production and sales volumes for each of the products in a product line. The production function given in (3-2'') represents a firm producing one product with two variable inputs and any number of fixed inputs. With a production function of this type, one can study, among other things, problems concerned with most efficient use of factors of production.

We shall investigate both types of problem in the course of our study, beginning with problems of efficient factor use. In this case the firm's production function, (3-2''), may be written *explicitly* as

$$x = f(v_1, v_2) \qquad (3\text{-}1'')$$

where the subscript on $x$ has been dropped, a practice we will continue whenever no confusion arises. Equation (3-1'') is the relation between the quantity of product or service $X$ produced, the fixed factors available, and the quantities of variable inputs $V_1$ and $V_2$ used. As we noticed previously, (3-1'') is defined only for nonnegative values of $x, v_1, v_2$. Although we will often present material in terms of a three-dimensional production function, all results are readily extended to more general cases.

### Productivity Functions

From the firm's production function one can easily derive total, average, and marginal product functions which tend to be quite useful in analyzing production decisions.[1]

---

[1] Recall that capital letters $X_i$ and $V_i$ denote the product or factor itself, while lowercase letters $x_i$ and $v_i$ represent *quantities* of products and factors.

**The Total Product Function for Factor $V_1$** (the total product of $V_1$)—the level of output of $X$ resulting from an input of $v_1$ units of $V_1$, the use of $V_2$ being constant at $v_2^0$.

Hence, $x = f(v_1, v_2^0)$ is the total product function for factor one when $v_2 = v_2^0$ and is merely the relationship between firm output and the level of use of $V_1$ when use of $V_2$ is fixed. Geometrically the total product function of $V_1$ is a "slice" of the production function parallel to the $v_1$ axis at $v_2 = v_2^0$. Figure 3-1 depicts two of a *family* of total product functions defined by the production function $x = f(v_1, v_2)$.

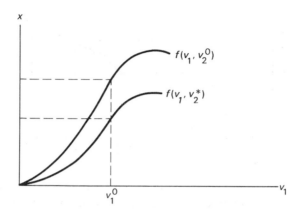

**FIGURE 3-1**

Two total

product functions

We as yet know little about the "shape" of production functions so, in Figure 3-1, we have drawn what would seem to be a "reasonable" set of total product functions. These functions are "reasonable" in the sense that given some level of utilization of $V_2$, increasing the use of $V_1$ increases output first at an increasing rate, then at a constant rate, and finally at a decreasing rate. The properties of production functions will soon be investigated more thoroughly.

**The Average Product Function for Factor $V_1$** (the average product of $V_1$)—the output per unit of $V_1$ used, the use of $V_2$ being constant at $v_2^0$.

Hence, $x/v_1 = f(v_1, v_2^0)/v_1$ is the average product function of $V_1$ when $V_2$ is being utilized at level $v_2^0$. Average product functions measure the output per unit of some input, given fixed levels of utilization of other inputs.

**The Marginal Product Function for Factor $V_1$** (the marginal product of $V_1$)—the change in output due to a change in the use of $V_1$, given $V_2$ is being utilized at level $v_2^0$.

If the production function is differentiable, then $\partial x/\partial v_1$ is the marginal product function of $V_1$; if not, $\Delta x/\Delta v_1$ is the marginal product function of $V_1$. In writing $\Delta x/\Delta v_1$ remember that this represents $\Delta f(v_1, v_2^0)/\Delta v_1$ and not $\Delta f(v_1, v_2)/\Delta v_1$, since $v_2$ is fixed by definition.

In each of these definitions, all factor usage is constant except for one. Hence productivity functions are two-dimensional families of functions, and a different productivity function will exist for each given level of "other" factor usage. We will often use $TP_i$, $AP_i$, and $MP_i$ to denote the total, average, and marginal product functions of factor $V_i$.

Since total, average, and marginal product functions are all derived from the production function, they are obviously intimately related. We now briefly indicate these relationships. In Figure 3-2 calculation of the average product of $V_1$ from the total product function is illustrated. For example, the average productivity of $v_1^*$ units of $V_1$, when employed with $v_2^0$ units of $V_2$, is $x^*/v_1^*$.

**FIGURE 3-2**

Calculation of

average product

from total

product

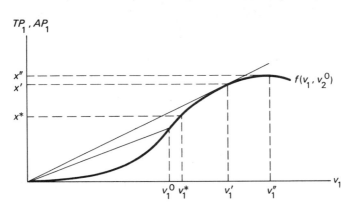

Notice that $x^*/v_1^*$ is the slope of a ray from the origin to the point $(v_1^*, x^*)$ on the total product function. In general, average product is maximum where this ray has maximum slope. In the figure, this occurs at $v_1'$.

In Figure 3-3 the relationship between marginal product and average product functions is illustrated. The principle is simple. If marginal product is above average product, average product must be rising. If marginal product equals average product, average product must be constant; and if marginal product is below average product, then average product must be falling. The points $v_1^0$, $v_1'$, and $v_1''$ represent the same points in each figure. Could you prove this?

**FIGURE 3-3**

Marginal and

average product

functions

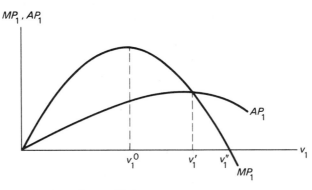

## Diminishing Factor Returns

We now present a principle that has been utilized regularly in economics since the time of Adam Smith—the *law of diminishing factor returns*. Simply put, this classical principle states that the marginal product of any factor of production must *eventually* fall. Since the definition of a marginal product function requires that all factors be fixed except for one, this "law" says that increasing the use of the variable factor *alone* must eventually cause output to increase at a diminishing rate.[2] Note that the definition states only that marginal product functions must eventually decline and hence does not imply a region of negative marginal productivity, nor is a region of increasing marginal productivity ruled out. The principle of diminishing factor returns is termed a "law" only because we cannot imagine a world in which it would not hold. Figure 3-4 illustrates several different marginal product functions that are consistent with diminishing factor returns.

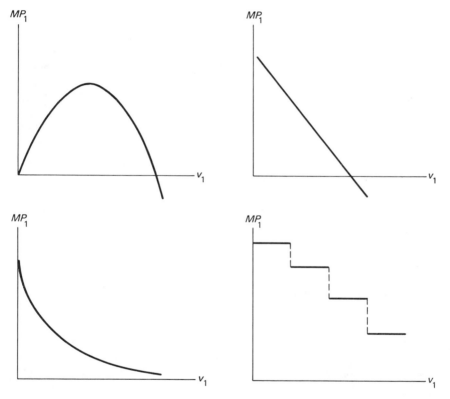

**FIGURE 3-4**

Marginal
product
functions that
are consistent
with the law of
diminishing
returns

In our study of the theory of production, we will take the law of diminishing returns to be operative. More formally, our analysis will be based upon the following two assumptions:

Assumption I: The law of diminishing returns is operative for all factors.

Now, Assumption I alone is not sufficient for a theory of production. In addition, an assumption is needed concerning the manner in which factors of production are organized in the production process. A very general assumption is

Assumption II: The firm attempts to use inputs as efficiently as possible.

[2] Clearly, diminishing factor returns is closely akin to intuitive notions of capacity limitations.

We will soon define "efficient input use" rigorously, but for the present it suffices to say that firms that use inputs efficiently strive to get as much output as possible from any expenditure. This assumption does *not* imply profit maximization. In fact, it should be noted that Assumption II is ideologically neutral. Whether one is a Maoist factory manager, a Socialist bureaucrat, or an American capitalist, adherence to Assumption II is usually taken for granted. The efficiency conditions of Assumption II are logical antecedents to the primary ideological differences of how much to produce (and consequently the level of prices) and how production is to be distributed.[3]

Obviously, Assumption II prevents production from occurring in the region where marginal products are negative. In such a region, output may be *increased* merely by using *less* of the variable factor. This is not to be confused with the case where marginal productivity is low and using *less* of the variable input *decreases* output, but not by much. In the world we seldom, if ever, observe firms operating in the region of the production function where marginal products are negative. This is clear from an example. Say that the marginal product of the last one hundred laborers hired by a profit-maximizing firm is negative, and say that these laborers are under contract for a year and cannot be fired. It would not only be in the firm's interest to require these laborers to stay home but it would also be in the firm's interest to pay them to stay home. Just how much the firm would be willing to pay would depend on "how negative" was productivity. Therefore one property of any reasonable production function is that the marginal product of every input be positive. Production functions, or regions of production functions, in which marginal products are zero or negative are inconsistent with efficient factor use (Assumption II).

### Output Elasticities and Returns to Scale

As in our study of demand, we will again often be interested in the responsiveness of one variable to changes in other variables. And as before, it will be convenient to measure responsiveness in percentages. We have already defined the responsiveness of output to changes in the use of one input, since marginal product functions give us precisely this information. To transform marginal product functions into measures of percentage changes in output, define:

**The Output Elasticity of Factor** $V_1$, $\varepsilon_1$—the percentage change in output due to a percentage change in the use of $V_1$, for a given utilization of $V_2$.

Symbolically,

$$\varepsilon_1 = \frac{\partial x}{\partial v_1}\left(\frac{v_1}{x}\right)$$

[3] Although this efficiency criterion is quite general, under certain circumstances it will not be in the interest of the firm to adhere to it. A classic example occurs with government contracts in which the contractor's payment is the direct cost of the order plus a percentage of costs to cover profits and overhead. If one were asked to design a contracting procedure that would provide incentives to minimize firm efficiency, it would be difficult to do much better than having profits depend only on the level of costs.

where $\partial x / \partial v_1$ is the marginal product of $V_1$. Analogous to the case of demand elasticities, multiplication of $\partial x / \partial v_1$ by $v_1 / x$ turns the marginal productivity function for $V_1$ into a measure of percentage changes. Notice that $\varepsilon_1$ is the marginal product of $V_1$ divided by the average product of $V_1$, $\varepsilon_1 = MP_1 / AP_1$.

Output elasticities are of considerable interest, both theoretically and practically. Later we will be examining estimates of both output elasticities and marginal product functions. It is important to notice that, in general, output elasticities like marginal product functions are *functions* and not merely numbers, since $\varepsilon_i$ and the marginal product of $V_i$ will usually vary depending upon fixed factor availability and the level of usage of $V_i$. Assumption II implies $\varepsilon_i > 0$.

The concept of "returns to scale" is closely allied to that of output elasticities. We denote our measure of returns to scale by $\varepsilon$ and define $\varepsilon$ as follows:

**Returns to Scale, $\varepsilon$**—the percentage response of output due to an *equal* percentage change in the use of *all* inputs.[4]

Three distinctions are often made:

If $\varepsilon < 1$, the production function is said to exhibit *decreasing returns to scale*.
If $\varepsilon = 1$, the production function is said to exhibit *constant returns to scale*.
If $\varepsilon > 1$, the production function is said to exhibit *increasing returns to scale*.

For example, if $\varepsilon = .6$, a 1 percent increase in the use of all inputs leads to a 0.6 percent increase in output. The production process exhibits decreasing returns to scale.

The choice of $\varepsilon$ to represent our measure of returns to scale and $\varepsilon_i$ to represent the output elasticity of factor $V_i$ was made to give the student a hint that returns to scale and output elasticities are intimately related. The next result provides a means of calculating returns to scale from output elasticities and thereby establishes the logical link between the two concepts.

As a first step, calculate the response of output to a change in use of *all* factors, that is, write the differential of the production function:

$$
\begin{aligned}
dx &= \frac{\partial x}{\partial v_1}\, dv_1 + \frac{\partial x}{\partial v_2}\, dv_2 \\
&= MP_1 dv_1 + MP_2 dv_2
\end{aligned}
\tag{3-3}
$$

Intuitively, the change in output, $dx$, resulting from a change in the use of both factors is the change in $x$ *due solely* to a one-unit change in the use of $V_1$, $(MP_1)$, times the size of the change in $V_1$, $dv_1$, plus the change in $x$ due solely to a one-unit change in use of $V_2$, $(MP_2)$, times the size of the change in $V_2$, $dv_2$. These two terms summed yield the total response of output to a change in the use of $V_1$ and $V_2$. We are interested here in obtaining an analytical expression for $\varepsilon$. Keep in mind that $\varepsilon$ is to measure *percentage* changes in output due to *percentage* changes in input usage. To transform (3-3) into a statement about percentage

[4]Here returns to scale are computed holding all fixed inputs constant, since $V_1$ and $V_2$ are variable factors by definition (see equation (3-1)). Later we will have cause to calculate $\varepsilon$ when all factors are allowed to vary.

changes in input usage, multiply the first term on the right-hand side of equation (3-3) by $v_1/v_1$ and the second term by $v_2/v_2$ (which obviously changes nothing). We then have

$$dx = v_1 MP_1(dv_1/v_1) + v_2 MP_2(dv_2/v_2) \qquad (3\text{-}4)$$

Equation (3-4) tells us how percentage changes in $v_1$ and $v_2$ affect output. If we are to end up with a statement about returns to scale, (3-4) must be transformed into a statement about percentage changes in output. This is accomplished by dividing both sides of (3-4) by $x$. The percentage change in $x$ due to variations in $v_1$ and $v_2$ is then[5]

$$dx/x = (v_1/x)MP_1(dv_1/v_1) + (v_2/x)MP_2(dv_2/v_2)$$
$$= \varepsilon_1\,(dv_1/v_1) + \varepsilon_2(dv_2/v_2) \qquad (3\text{-}4')$$

To turn (3-4') into a statement about returns to scale, $\varepsilon$, all that is lacking is the requirement that factors be varied in the same percentage (reread the definition of $\varepsilon$). In symbols this condition implies that $dv_1/v_1 = dv_2/v_2$ must hold. Call this equal percentage change in $V_1$ and $V_2$, $\beta$. That is, $dv_1/v_1 = dv_2/v_2 \equiv \beta$. Factoring $\beta$ from (3-4') we have

$$dx/x = \beta(\varepsilon_1 + \varepsilon_2) \qquad (3\text{-}5)$$

Dividing by $\beta$ yields

$$\frac{dx/x}{\beta} = \varepsilon_1 + \varepsilon_2 \qquad (3\text{-}5')$$

But $(dx/x)/\beta$ is the percentage response of $x$ due to an equal percentage change in the use of *all* inputs, the definition of returns to scale. Hence

$$\varepsilon = \varepsilon_1 + \varepsilon_2 \qquad (3\text{-}6)$$

Equation (3-6) tells us that returns to scale may be calculated merely by adding up output elasticities and generalizes immediately to the case of an $m$ factor firm. Since output elasticities are in general functions of $v_1$ and $v_2$, returns to scale will usually vary depending upon the level of input use.

EXAMPLE. Let $x = 20v_1v_2 - 2v_1^2 - v_2^2$ be a production function. This is a production function of the general form $x = av_1v_2 + bv_1^2 + cv_2^2$ in which the three parameters $a$, $b$, and $c$ have been estimated to be 20, $-2$, and $-1$, respectively. Marginal product functions are given by the partial derivatives of the production function with respect to $v_1$ and $v_2$ and are $20v_2 - 4v_1$ and $20v_1 - 2v_2$, respectively. If $v_2 = 10$, the marginal product function for factor one becomes $200 - 4v_1$ and is one of a family of marginal product functions all with slope $-4$. If the firm is currently utilizing 20 units of $V_1$ and 10 units of $V_2$, then $\varepsilon_1 = 120(20/3100) = 24/31 = .77, \varepsilon_2 = 380(10/3100) = 38/31 = 1.22$, and $\varepsilon = .77 + 1.22 = 1.99$. At the input rate $v_1 = 20, v_2 = 10$, a 1 percent increase

[5]Note that the following expression is a precise analog of equation (1-8), Chapter 1. In equation (1-8), we were talking about percentage changes in demand due to percentage changes in the determinants of demand; here percentage changes in production are related to percentage changes in input usage.

in the use of both factors will cause output to increase almost 2 percent. The production function exhibits increasing returns to scale *in this range.* Notice that a different input combination will yield different marginal product functions, output elasticities, and returns to scale. The marginal product function of $V_1$ for $v_2 = 10$ and several points on the output elasticity function for $V_1$ when $v_2 = 10$ are graphed in Figures 3-5 and 3-6, respectively.

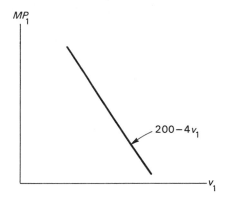

**FIGURE 3-5**
Marginal
product
function for
factor one
when $v_2 = 10$

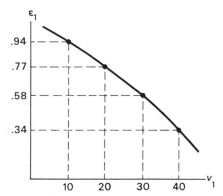

**FIGURE 3-6**
Points on the
output elasticity
function for
factor one
when $v_2 = 10$

**Graphing the Production Function: The Isoquant Map**

By Assumption II inputs are to be used as efficiently as possible. What is the most efficient combination of $V_1$ and $V_2$? Among other things, the answer to this question depends upon the firm's production function. If we are to analyze the problem of efficient factor use graphically, the production function must be graphed. To this end define an

**Isoquant**—$\{(v_1, v_2) \mid f(v_1, v_2) = x^0\}$, where $x^0$ is a constant—a parameter—for a given isoquant.

An isoquant is, then, the locus of all input combinations that yield production level $x^0$ and hence gives the relation between inputs and one particular production level. In other words, an isoquant is a list of all the possible ways of producing an order of a given size. If we desire to represent *all* production levels, the entire production function, an isoquant for each possible production level will be needed. The collection of all isoquants is called

> **The Isoquant Map**—$\{(v_1, v_2) \mid f(v_1, v_2) = x^i\}$, where $x^i$ is the constant production level along the $i^{th}$ isoquant. (The superscript $i$ is an indexing variable which changes from isoquant to isoquant.)

An isoquant map is the collection of all isoquants and gives the relationship between inputs and every possible output. Hence the isoquant map *is* the production function, and since isoquants are a function of only $v_1$ and $v_2$ for a given production level, the isoquant map is a way of graphing the three-dimensional production function in two space.

In more detail, the production function $x = f(v_1, v_2)$ is a surface in three space, possibly as shown in Figure 3-7. The "slices" of $f(v_1, v_2)$ parallel to the

**FIGURE 3-7**

Two isoquants in the production function

$x = f(v_1, v_2)$

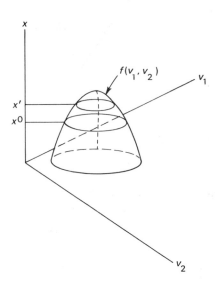

$v_1, v_2$ axis at $x^0$ and $x'$ are by definition isoquants. The isoquant map is the collection of isoquants associated with every point along the $x$ axis.

If the isoquant $x^0$ is graphed in $(v_1, v_2)$ space, a curve similar to that shown in Figure 3-8 is obtained. At this point we know very little about the "shape" of isoquants except that we must ensure they are consistent with the require-

**FIGURE 3-8**

The isoquant $x^0$

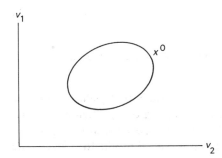

ment that marginal productivities of each input be positive. Therefore, *only those portions of isoquants that imply positive marginal productivities for each factor will be of interest.* To see the implications of this condition, notice that the definition of an isoquant requires output to be constant along any isoquant. Therefore, since output does not change as one moves along an isoquant, an alternative definition of an isoquant is

**Isoquant**—$\{(v_1, v_2) | dx = 0\}$.

This definition tells us that isoquants pertain only to those input combinations that leave output unchanged. And since by equation (3-3) we know

$$dx = MP_1 dv_1 + MP_2 dv_2,$$

the condition $dx \equiv 0$ implies $MP_1 dv_1 + MP_2 dv_2 \equiv 0$, or

$$\frac{dv_1}{dv_2} \equiv -MP_2/MP_1 \qquad (3\text{-}7)$$

The expression $dv_1/dv_2$ is the slope of the isoquant (in $v_1, v_2$ space), and by equation (3-7) we see that the slope of an isoquant is always equal to the negative of the ratio of marginal productivities. But since we know that marginal productivities of each factor are positive by Assumption II, we may conclude from equation (3-7) that isoquants *must* have negative slopes. Those portions of the isoquant $x^0$ (Figure 3-8) that are inconsistent with positive marginal product functions are shown crosshatched in Figure 3-9.[6] We have now shown that only negatively sloping isoquants are consistent with efficient input use. Intuitively, negatively sloped isoquants mean that as more of one input is used in the production of a given output, less of the other is needed.

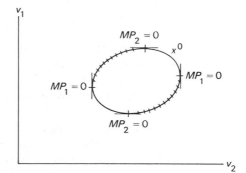

**FIGURE 3-9**

An isoquant
with certain
inconsistent
portions
crosshatched

• *More on Properties of Isoquants.* We have seen that positively sloping portions of isoquants are not consistent with properties of real-world production functions and for this reason have eliminated from further consideration these portions of isoquants. But the fact that an isoquant is negatively sloping does

[6]Points in the figure where "crosshatching" begins and ends are points of zero marginal product for one of the two inputs. These points are obtained by noting that since $dv_1/dv_2 = -MP_2/MP_1$, $dv_1/dv_2 = 0$ implies $MP_2 = 0$, and $dv_1/dv_2 = \infty$ implies $MP_1 = 0$.

not guarantee that the associated marginal product functions are positive, since equation (3-7) is also negative whenever *both* marginal productivities are negative. We now explore the implications of this fact.

First note that positive marginal productivities imply $\varepsilon > 0$, and hence increases in the use of all inputs must increase output in the production region of interest. So, at least for "small" input combinations, isoquants farther from the origin imply higher outputs than those close to the origin. The modifying phrase "At least for 'small' input combinations" is needed because it may be possible to so overutilize a given plant that marginal productivities are zero, or even negative, and further increases in input use leave output unchanged or lower. With this in mind, consider region $A$ in Figure 3-10.

**FIGURE 3-10**

Two isoquants

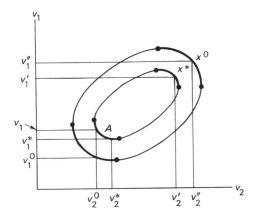

In region $A$ the marginal product of each factor is positive, since increasing the use of either factor will increase output. For example, production level $x^0$ may be produced by using the input combination $(v_1^0, v_2^0)$. Increasing the use of $V_1$ from $v_1^0$ to $\bar{v}_1$ will increase output from $x^0$ to $x^*$. This represents an increase in the use of $V_1$ with the level of $V_2$ constant and, as is evident from Figure 3-10, brings about an increase in production. That is, the marginal product of $V_1$ is positive in region $A$. Similarly, it can be shown that the marginal product of $V_2$ is also positive in region $A$.

Now beginning at input combination $(v_1^0, v_2^0)$ in Figure 3-10, increase the use of both $V_1$ and $V_2$ to the input combination $(v_1^*, v_2^*)$. Production increases to $x^*$. Next, consider the consequences of greatly increasing the use of both $V_1$ and $V_2$, to say $(v_1', v_2')$. The production level associated with this input combination is still only $x^*$! Again, increase the use of both inputs, this time to $(v_1'', v_2'')$. Production *falls* from $x^*$ to $x^0$. (Remember output is constant along an isoquant, so if $x^* > x^0$ at one point, the same relation holds at all points.) Increased use of $V_1$ and $V_2$ led to a fall in output. Obviously at least one marginal product is negative. But since the slope of the isoquant in this region is negative, we have from equation (3-7) that both marginal products must be of the same sign and hence *both are negative*. This region may also be crosshatched. It is not consistent with the minimal properties a realistic production function must have—namely, that marginal productivities be positive.

We are now in a position to make a general statement about the "shape" of isoquants if they are to be consistent with minimal properties of real-world production functions: *Isoquants must be negatively sloped and not be concave to the origin.* In graphical terms isoquants must have the *general* shape of region *A*, as reproduced in Figure 3-11a, with limiting cases depicted in Figures 3-11b and 3-11c. Combinations of these figures will also be admissible as long as the

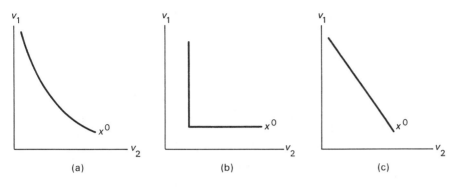

**FIGURE 3-11**
Admissible
isoquants

(a)    (b)    (c)

result is negatively sloped and nonconcave.[7] A particular isoquant which we will look at more closely in the next chapter is the combination of Figures 3-11b and 3-11c, shown in Figure 3-12. Production functions that generate isoquants that "look like" Figure 3-12 are closely allied to production functions that arise in a linear-programming model of the firm. Our interest in production functions of this type stems from the fact that under certain conditions extremely complex production decision problems can be solved very rapidly and accurately via linear programming. This topic will be investigated in more detail in Chapters 4 and 5.

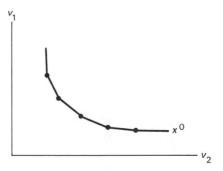

**FIGURE 3-12**
Another
admissible
isoquant

### Factor Substitutability

In our study of production decisions we will find it convenient to have a concept that summarizes the technical information concerning input substitutability in the production of a given order. Such a concept is

**The Rate of Technical Substitution of $V_1$ for $V_2$ ($RTS_{12}$)**—the reduction in units of $V_1$ necessary to permit use of one more unit of $V_2$, given a constant output level.

[7]Figure 3-11b is the limiting case between negatively and positively sloped isoquants, while 3-11c is the limiting case between concave and convex isoquants.

The word "technical" refers to the fact that $RTS_{12}$ is strictly a technical relation between factors one and two, which is given by the firm's production function. The rate of technical substitution indicates the degree to which factor one can be substituted for factor two in the production of a given order.

We are already familiar with the rate of technical substitution but have not as yet given it a name. To see this, note that in Figure 3-13 if $v_2' - v_2^0 = 1$,

**FIGURE 3-13**

The

substitutability

of $v_1$ for $v_2$:

the rate of

technical

substitution

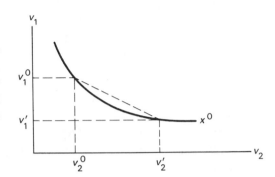

then $v_1^0 - v_1'$ is the reduction in units of $V_1$ necessary to permit the use of one unit of $V_2$ given output is $x^0$. The ratio $(v_1^0 - v_1')/(v_2^0 - v_2')$ is the change in $v_1$ per unit change in the use of $V_2$ and is nothing more than the slope of the chord between $(v_1^0, v_2^0)$ and $(v_1', v_2')$. As such, it is an approximation of the slope of the isoquant between these points. For small changes in $v_1$ and $v_2$ this becomes $dv_1/dv_2$, which is the slope of the isoquant. But notice that $dv_1/dv_2 \neq RTS_{12}$, since the rate of technical substitution must be a nonnegative number (to see this reread the definition), while $dv_1/dv_2$ is always less than, or in the limit equal to, zero. This problem is easily remedied by using the function $-dv_1/dv_2$ as the analytical representation of the rate of technical substitution. That is,

$$RTS_{12} \equiv -dv_1/dv_2 \tag{3-8}$$

and since $-dv_1/dv_2 \equiv MP_2/MP_1$ from equation (3-7),

$$RTS_{12} \equiv MP_2/MP_1 \tag{3-8'}$$

The rate of technical substitution may be expressed either as the negative of the slope of the isoquant or as the ratio of marginal product functions.

EXAMPLE. As an example of this concept recall the production function $x = 20v_1v_2 - 2v_1^2 - v_2^2$, which we used above to illustrate computation of marginal product functions and output elasticities. To calculate $RTS_{12}$ using definition (3-8'), merely calculate the two marginal product functions by partially differentiating the production function with respect to $v_1$ and $v_2$. Then

$$MP_1 = 20v_2 - 4v_1 \text{ and } MP_2 = 20v_1 - 2v_2 \tag{3-9}$$

The rate of technical substitution is given by the ratio of these functions:

$$RTS_{12} \equiv (20v_1 - 2v_2)/(20v_2 - 4v_1) \tag{3-10}$$

Notice that the value of the rate of technical substitution depends upon how much of each factor is being used.

If $v_1$ and $v_2$ represent, say, hours of unskilled and skilled labor going into the production of some product $X$, and if at present $v_1 = 2000$ and $v_2 = 1100$, then

$$RTS_{12} = 37,800/14,000 = 2.7 \qquad (3\text{-}10')$$

This calculation indicates that skilled labor is 2.7 times as productive at the margin as unskilled labor (given 2000 hours of unskilled labor and 1100 hours of skilled labor are being used). Different labor combinations will usually imply different rates of technical substitution.

One final point: The fact that $RTS_{12} = 2.7$ by itself says nothing about whether "too much" or "too little" skilled labor is being utilized. Clearly, we must know something about relative wage rates before such questions can be analyzed. The role of relative costs and productivities in the determination of the most efficient production plan is the topic of the next chapter.

1.  Given that $x = 3011\sqrt{v_1 v_2}$ is a production function:
a.  Graph the marginal product function of factor one when $v_2 = 10$. When $v_2 = 100$.
b.  Graph the marginal product function of factor two when $v_1 = 100$. When $v_1 = 400$.
c.  Briefly discuss the differences between $MP_1$ and $MP_2$. Are these marginal product functions consistent with our two assumptions?
d.  Graph the output elasticities for several values of $v_1$ and $v_2$. Interpret your findings.
e.  Calculate the rate of technical substitution when $v_1 = 250$, $v_2 = 400$ and compare this with the analogous calculation when $v_1 = 250$, $v_2 = 500$. Interpret what has occurred as the usage of $v_2$ was increased from 400 units to 500 units.
f.  Could you graph this production function in two space, i.e., could you draw the isoquant map? Draw the isoquant for $x = 1000$.

2.  If $x = .5v_1 + .7v_2$ is a production function:
a.  Calculate marginal product functions.
b.  Calculate output elasticities.
c.  Calculate returns to scale.
d.  Calculate the rate of technical substitution of $V_1$ for $V_2$.
e.  Contrast these calculations with the analogous ones in problem 1.
f.  Interpret your calculation for $RTS_{12}$.
g.  What do isoquants look like? Draw the isoquant for $x = 100,000$.

3.  Imagine you are hired as a production analyst by a large firm and are interested in trying out some of the concepts you have learned. When you inquire about the nature of the firm's production function you are met with bewildered

looks and told that the only relationship between inputs and output that exists is the daily production record. Given this record you manage to construct the following table:

Daily production of $X$ (1000s of units)

| 5 | 142 | 200 | 242 | 278 | 310 |
|---|-----|-----|-----|-----|-----|
| 4 | 130 | 180 | 218 | 250 | 278 |
| 3 | 114 | 156 | 190 | 218 | 242 |
| 2 | 94 | 130 | 156 | 180 | 200 |
| 1 | 70 | 94 | 114 | 130 | 142 |
| $v_1$ \\ $v_2$ | 1 | 2 | 3 | 4 | 5 |

a. What is this table?
b. Graph the family of total product functions associated with factor one. The families of average and marginal product functions.
c. Are marginal product functions for factor one consistent with the two axioms we have adopted?
d. Calculate the output elasticity of factor one when three units of factor two are being used.

# Efficient Resource Use

In this chapter we begin our analysis of an important class of production decisions confronting management, those decisions concerned with utilizing the resources under control of the firm in the "most efficient" manner possible. Two elements jointly determine the "most efficient" production plan—factor productivities and factor costs. Although the rate of technical substitution provides the productivity information needed for efficient production decisions, factor prices may not adequately account for factor costs. For this reason we begin with a discussion of factor costs.

### Cost as Opportunity Forgone

Suppose you are told a firm earned $18 million in the past year and, on the basis of this information, are asked to evaluate the firm's performance. What is your response? If it is that you must know the return to investment, that figure is implied by the $18 million. Say it is 9 percent. Has the firm done well? If you think for a moment or two you will realize that the answer to this question depends upon what the firm's invested capital could have earned elsewhere, in other alternatives. If other firms with similar resources and in similar risk situations earned 14 percent, then the firm has done poorly indeed. Since we will often be concerned with evaluating firm performance, it is helpful to have a concept of profit that takes into account earnings in alternative but similar situations. With this in mind, we define

**The Opportunity Cost of a Decision**—the benefit forgone by taking the decision.

In other words, what is given up is the cost of taking an action. For example, the cost of keeping one's life's savings in one's mattress is the amount that could have been earned in a savings account, in bonds, or whatever the best alternative might be. As a second example, consider a successful doctor who claims he can't afford a vacation. The doctor doesn't mean he can't afford plane fares and hotel bills. Instead, he knows that the true cost of his vacation is these direct expenses *plus* earnings forgone. (Note that the cost of his vacation is a function of his fee.)

As we begin to analyze particular firm decision problems, it is helpful to keep in mind that decision problems are, in general, cost-benefit problems in which one takes an action whenever projected benefits from taking the action are greater than projected costs, and vice versa. It is evident that one must have a reasonable assessment not only of benefits but also of costs if the decision process is to yield the desired outcome. It is with this in mind that we define

**The Opportunity Cost of Using an Input**—the return an input could earn in its best alternative use.
**The Direct Cost of Using an Input**—the costs incurred in purchasing an input.
**The Total Cost of Using an Input**—the sum of direct and opportunity costs.

For example, the total cost of using a piece of equipment developed "in house" by an R and D unit is not only the direct cost associated with operating and maintaining the equipment but also what it would bring if marketed (its opportunity cost). The next two definitions relate opportunity costs to profits.

**Accounting Profit**—revenue minus direct costs.
**Economic Profit**—accounting profit minus opportunity costs.

It is total costs, the way we have defined them, that are relevant for optimal decision making. There can be no argument that opportunity costs are, at times, hard to estimate.[1] But they must be estimated, since if not, they have been estimated by default to be zero, and few factors have no alternative uses. Indeed, we will see that failure to include *all* costs in total costs will lead the profit-maximizing firm to "underprice" its products.

A couple of examples will clarify the issues involved:

Say a small businessman earned $18,000 one year and that the best alternative use of his time and money is the stock market, in which he could have earned $10,000 (discounted for risk). Accounting profits are $18,000. But notice that this figure alone is insufficient to tell us whether or not the businessman earned a "good" return. Since $10,000 was "given up" by not investing in securities, economic profits are $18,000 − $10,000 = $8,000. Economic profits of $8,000 indicate that inputs (including management) in that business for that year earned $8,000 more than they could have earned in any other alternative. The concept of economic profit provides a straightforward means of evaluating market performance.

Next, consider a self-employed chemist who earns around $4,000 per year. Say that in industry, a chemist of similar background and experience earns about $14,000. The chemist's accounting profits are $4,000, while economic profits are −$10,000. The chemist is earning $10,000 less than he could in his best alternative. Or, alternatively, the cost of being self-employed is $10,000. This need not say the

---

[1]Although for any input for which an active market exists, the opportunity cost of using the input is merely the return (net) the input could earn if sold.

chemist is "irrational," since "benefits" from self-employment may be worth more than $10,000.

## The Input Cost Function

Two assumptions underpin production theory, the "law" of diminishing returns and the assumption that firms use inputs as efficiently as possible. It is now time to interpret this second assumption. We interpret efficient input use to mean that decision makers choose input combinations (production plans) so as to make the output from any given expenditure on inputs as large as possible.[2] That is, our second assumption implies production decisions are taken so as to maximize the output associated with any expenditure on inputs. To "get as much as possible" from an expenditure would seem to be precisely what one would term efficient input use. We now set up this maximization problem formally and solve it, obtaining a decision rule for finding the most efficient input combination.

As we have noted previously, two "pieces of information" jointly determine the most efficient production plan—the firm's production function and the cost of inputs. To begin, we will assume that the total cost per unit of each input is independent of the amount of the input used. That is, we assume that there are no quantity discounts, nor are there inputs whose price increases with the firm's order size.[3] If we call $w_i$ the total cost per unit of factor $V_i$, then $w_1 = w_1^0$ and $w_2 = w_2^0$ where $w_1^0$ and $w_2^0$ are parameters as far as the firm is concerned. Input cost functions under these conditions are shown in Figure 4-1. Total input costs are then given by $C = w_1^0 v_1 + w_2^0 v_2 + b$, where $b$ represents costs that do not vary with input use levels—fixed costs.

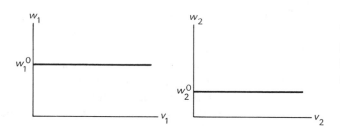

**FIGURE 4-1**
The cost of inputs as a function of quantity used

To facilitate a graphical solution of the firm's economizing problem, define

**The Isocost Function**—$\{(v_1, v_2) \mid w_1^0 v_1 + w_2^0 v_2 + b = C^0\}$.

An isocost function is a "list" of all possible combinations of $v_1$ and $v_2$ that could be purchased for an outlay of $C^0$ (say $1,000). By Assumption II, we are interested only in those production plans that are most efficient, that is, those that produce the maximum output for an outlay of $C^0$. Plotting the isocost

---

[2] A production plan is a particular way of producing an order, i.e., a particular combination of inputs.

[3] The analysis to be presented can easily accommodate factor costs that vary with the amount purchased. The student is asked to think about aspects of this problem in an exercise at the end of the chapter.

function in input space allows a geometrical solution to this problem. To aid in interpretation of the results, express the isocost function in slope-intercept form, $v_1 = (C^0 - b)/w_1^0 - (w_2^0/w_1^0)v_2$, and plot. This is done in Figure 4-2. Note that the slope of the isocost function is $-w_2^0/w_1^0$, the negative of the ratio of factor costs. So for example if $-w_2^0/w_1^0 = -4$, input two is four times as costly to use as is input one.

**FIGURE 4-2**

The isocost

function

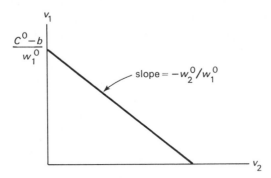

The isocost function *partitions* input space (all possible input combinations) into three mutually exclusive regions: (i) those input combinations above the isocost function which are termed *nonfeasible* combinations, since none of these combinations can be purchased for an outlay of $C^0$; (ii) those input combinations below the isocost function which are also termed nonfeasible, since these combinations are also inconsistent with an outlay of $C^0$; and (iii) those input combinations lying along the isocost line which are called *feasible* combinations, since these are the only points in the input space that are consistent with the expenditure level $C^0$. The collection of points along the isocost function is the *feasible region* of the input space. The solution to the output maximization problem will always lie in the feasible region.

Technically, the problem we have outlined here is a *mathematical programming problem*. In general, mathematical programming problems are maximization or minimization problems whose solutions must satisfy certain side conditions, or *constraints*. Our problem here is to find the production plan that maximizes output subject to the condition (the constraint) that the level of expenditure is only $C^0$. In terms of this more general description, the feasible region for any mathematical programming problem is comprised of those solutions to the problem that satisfy all constraints.

At this point we break our discussion into two cases: The output maximizing problem of firms whose production functions are "smooth" (differentiable) and generate isoquants like those pictured in Figure 3-11a in the preceding chapter. Once this is accomplished, we consider the same problem again, but this time for firms whose production functions are composed of linear segments (piecewise linear). Production functions of this latter type generate isoquants like those shown in Figures 3-11b, 3-11c, and 3-12. As we proceed, the interpretation of these two types of production functions and their meaning in terms of the firm's optimal production plan will become increasingly clear.

### Output Maximization

A geometric solution to the problem of efficient factor use may be obtained by plotting the firm's production function (isoquant map) in input space along with the isocost function which specifies the given available level of expenditure. This is done in Figure 4-3. The output-maximizing production plan is found by

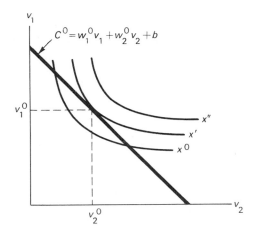

**FIGURE 4-3**

The most efficient production plan: output maximization

moving along the isocost function (the set of feasible production plans) and stopping when the highest isoquant is reached. This occurs at the point $(v_1^0, v_2^0)$. The production plan $(v_1^0, v_2^0)$ yields the maximum amount of production for the expenditure $C^0$. The maximum output for this expenditure is $x'$. No other combination of inputs yields an output as large as $x'$. As is clear from the figure, cost information alone is not sufficient to establish the most efficient production plan. Both factor costs and factor productivity information are needed: Isocost functions contain the former and isoquants the latter.

All production plans in the feasible region except $(v_1^0, v_2^0)$ are termed *nonoptimal*, since output could be increased at any such point merely by using a different plan. The word *optimal* is used to denote that input combination that maximizes output subject to the expenditure constraint. More generally, an optimal policy, or an optimal decision, is a policy or decision that achieves the objectives of the firm. As we saw above, points in *nonfeasible* regions need not be considered, since the production levels associated with these points are either less than or more than can be achieved with an expenditure of $C^0$. They are not feasible. Therefore, only points on the isocost line can be solutions to the maximization problem. Inspection of the point $(v_1^0, v_2^0)$ reveals that any movement away from $(v_1^0, v_2^0)$ along the isocost function leads to a point on a lower isoquant. Hence $(v_1^0, v_2^0)$ is the output-maximizing input combination, given the expenditure level $C^0$.

At the point $(v_1^0, v_2^0)$, the slope of the isoquant is equal to the slope of the isocost function. Since the slope of an isoquant is $dv_1/dv_2$ and the slope of an isocost function is $-w_2^0/w_1^0$, at the most efficient input combination

$$dv_1/dv_2 = -w_2^0/w_1^0$$

or

(4-1)

$$-dv_1/dv_2 = w_2^0/w_1^0$$

But, since $-dv_1/dv_2 \equiv RTS_{12}$, we may write equation (4-1) as

$$RTS_{12} = w_2^0/w_1^0 \qquad (4\text{-}1')$$

We also know that the rate of technical substitution of factor one for factor two is the ratio of the marginal products of the two factors (see equation (3-8′)), so an alternative way of expressing equation (4-1′) is

$$MP_2/MP_1 = w_2^0/w_1^0$$

or

(4-1″)

$$MP_1/w_1^0 = MP_2/w_2^0$$

Exactly what does equation (4-1′) or (4-1″) tell us? They tell us that if production decision makers use inputs as efficiently as possible, then factor use decisions are made *as if* $v_1$ and $v_2$ were chosen to satisfy either equation (4-1′) or (4-1″). In other words, output-maximizing behavior implies that factor one be substituted for factor two until the rate of technical substitution of $V_1$ for $V_2$ is equal to the ratio of factor prices. Or, in terms of equation (4-1″), factor one is substituted for factor two until the marginal productivity *per dollar* of expenditure is equal in each use. It would be difficult to imagine a more intuitive interpretation of efficient input use than the "equal productivity per dollar" rule of equation (4-1″). Equations (4-1′) and (4-1″) reemphasize a point mentioned above: *Factor costs and productivity jointly determine optimal factor use.* The fact that one machine is merely less expensive than another is not sufficient information to draw any conclusion about which machine is "best" for the firm. Why?

As an example of the decision rule displayed in equation (4-1′), say that at the present level of factor usage, $RTS_{12} = 5$ and that input two is twice as expensive as input one. Since $RTS_{12} \neq 2$, inputs could be used more efficiently. To see this note that $RTS_{12} = 5$ means that at current factor utilizations one unit of $V_2$ will replace five units of $V_1$ in production. But $V_2$ costs only twice as much as $V_1$. Therefore, use of $V_2$ should be increased and use of $V_1$ cut back until $RTS_{12} = 2$, the point where $RTS_{12} = w_2^0/w_1^0$.

The same example could be phrased in terms of the decision rule shown in equation (4-1″). Since $RTS_{12} > w_2^0/w_1^0$ (i.e., $5 > 2$) it follows that $MP_1/w_1^0 < MP_2/w_2^0$. This latter inequality indicates that at the existing input combination, "productivity per dollar" spent on factor two is higher than that for factor one. Again we may conclude that more $V_2$ and less $V_1$ should be used. The rate of technical substitution (or $MP_2/MP_1$) tells the decision maker the rate at which $V_1$ can be substituted for $V_2$ in *production*, while $w_2^0/w_1^0$ gives the input substitution rate in *purchasing*. Efficient factor use demands that substitution be done until the two rates are equal.

## Cost Minimization

Somewhat more formally, the problem that we have been discussing is one of choosing $v_1$ and $v_2$ so as to maximize $x$ subject to the condition that the level of expenditure is $C^0$. (Call this problem 1.)

The solution to this problem was a production plan $(v_1^0, v_2^0)$, which yielded a production level of $x'$ units (Figure 4-3). We now pose a closely related question: If it were desired to produce an order of $x'$ units at the lowest possible cost, what combination of $v_1$ and $v_2$ should be used? In other words, find a rule for combining factors such that if the rule is adhered to, the cost of producing a *given* order is minimum. Analytically, this problem is one of choosing $v_1$ and $v_2$ so as to minimize $C$ subject to the condition that $x'$ units must be produced. (Call this problem 2.) Comparing problems 1 and 2 shows they are inverses of one another. Problem 1 is a maximization problem, and problem 2 is a minimization problem. The maximization objective in problem 1 is the constraint in problem 2, and the minimization objective in problem 2 is the constraint in problem 1. The problems are obviously related. The exact nature of the relationship is brought out next.

For problem 2 the *nonfeasible* region of input space is those production plans above and below the isoquant $x'$. The *feasible* region is composed of all input combinations on the isoquant $x'$, those that satisfy the condition (the constraint) that $x'$ units be produced. The solution to this problem is presented graphically in Figure 4-4 and is obtained by graphing all isocost functions and

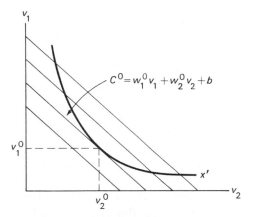

**FIGURE 4-4**

The most efficient production plan: cost minimization

then moving along the isoquant $x'$ (the list of feasible production plans) until the *lowest* possible isocost function is reached. In other words, the objective here is to choose the production plan as close to the origin as possible and still be consistent with a production level of $x'$ units. This production plan minimizes the cost of producing $x'$ units. In the figure the lowest isocost function consistent with $x'$ units of production is $C^0$ and yields the optimal production plan

$(v_1^0, v_2^0)$. Notice that any movement away from $(v_1^0, v_2^0)$ along the isoquant $x'$ leads to higher cost input combinations. The input combination $(v_1^0, v_2^0)$ will produce the order of $x'$ units at the lowest possible cost.

It is not a coincidence that we labeled the optimal production plan in the output-maximization problem $(v_1^0, v_2^0)$ (see Figure 4-3) and used the same notation for the optimal production plan in the cost-minimization problem. *Both problems yield exactly the same solution!* In somewhat more detail, this important result is as follows:

> *If the factor combination $(v_1^0, v_2^0)$ minimizes the cost of producing an order of $x'$ units (say minimum cost is $C^0$), then the same factor combination maximizes the output from an outlay of $C^0$ (maximum output will be $x'$). Minimizing the cost of producing a given output is the same problem as maximizing the output from a given outlay.*

It should be clear from Figure 4-4 that the decision rule for choosing the cost minimizing production plan is the same as the rule for choosing the output maximizing production plan and is given in equation (4-1′) or (4-1″).

• *Efficient Production Plans: Additional Constraints.* The decision rule we have derived for calculating efficient production plans assumes that all necessary inputs are available in unlimited amounts. More specifically, no constraints were placed upon the availability of each factor of production. In the world this is often not the case. Certain kinds of specialized labor are regularly in short supply and must be replaced with less productive (skilled) substitutes; stocks of some raw materials may be limited in a given production period, forcing the firm to use "second best" alternatives; and of course physical reality places upper bounds upon utilization rates of labor and equipment. The fact that there are but twenty-four hours in a day places an absolute limit on the intensity with which these factors can be used, a limit that is likely to be much lower in practice. We now take a look at how such constraints affect the firm's optimal production plan.

Assume that inputs one and two are available in amounts $\bar{v}_1$ and $\bar{v}_2$, respectively, and consider the problem of minimizing the cost of producing an order of $x'$ units. We have represented this graphically in Figure 4-5. As with prior problems, the method of solution amounts to no more than finding the feasible region of input space and then moving in this region to the minimum cost production plan. The feasible region is that region where *all* constraints on the firm's production problem are satisfied and is shown as a heavy black line in Figure 4-5.

If input $v_1$ were available in larger quantities, the efficient plan would be $(v_1^0, v_2^0)$ as before. But $v_1^0 > \bar{v}_1$, and hence this plan is inconsistent with factor availability. The most efficient plan is the input combination $(\bar{v}_1, v_2^*)$ and is obtained by moving along the feasible region to the lowest cost production plan, as shown. This plan produces the order of $x'$ units at lower cost than any other feasible plan. At this point $v_1$ is being utilized to capacity while $v_2$ is not. We say that the constraint on $v_1$ is *binding* while that on $v_2$ is not binding.

Notice that if *relative* factor costs fell enough (the cost of $v_2$ falls *or* the cost of $v_1$ increases), we get the same type of solution we had before these constraints

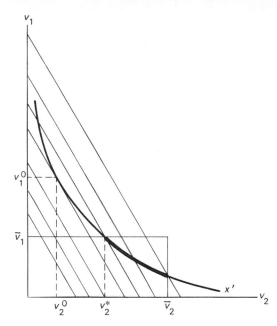

**FIGURE 4-5**

The most
efficient
production plan
with constraints
on factor
availability

were introduced. That is, in this case the most efficient plan is *within* the feasible region (not on the boundary as in Figure 4-5), and neither input availability constraint is binding. Hence the original problem we solved (Figure 4-3 or 4-4) is a special case of the problem we have investigated here. An example should clarify a number of points raised in this and prior sections.

EXAMPLE. Earlier we used the production function $x = f(v_1, v_2) = 20v_1v_2 - 2v_1^2 - v_2^2$ to illustrate calculation of marginal product functions and output elasticities. Here we will use the same production function to illustrate computation of the most efficient input combination. For concreteness, say that

$v_1$ = hours of unskilled labor (thousands)
$v_2$ = hours of skilled labor (thousands)

Assume unskilled labor earns four dollars an hour, and skilled labor receives eight dollars an hour.

This production function is differentiable (smooth), and as we have seen is of the general form $x = av_1v_2 + bv_1^2 + cv_2^2$. The parameters have thus been estimated to be $a = 20$, $b = -2$, and $c = -1$. The fact that the production function is "smooth" and does not have "corners" means that skilled labor and unskilled labor are completely substitutable in the sense that an order could be produced by using all skilled labor, all unskilled labor, or any combination of the two. Presumably, skilled laborers are more "productive" than unskilled laborers, but they are also more expensive. Hence we have a typical "economizing" problem—finding the most economical combination of inputs.

Let us assume the firm receives an order for 1,000 units of $X$ and wants to choose its labor inputs to minimize the cost of producing this order. How much of the two types of labor should be used? At this point, we break our analysis into two cases. First we solve the problem just posed and then reconsider the same problem when the maximum amount of unskilled labor available is 5,000 hours and only 15,000 hours of skilled labor is available.

CASE I. We have seen that $v_1$ and $v_2$ must be chosen so that $RTS_{12} = w_2^0/w_1^0$ and $20v_1v_2 - 2v_1^2 - v_2^2 = 1000$. The last requirement is the equation of the isoquant $x = 1000$ and ensures that the chosen labor combination will indeed produce 1,000 units.

Since

$$RTS_{12} \equiv MP_2/MP_1$$

and

$$MP_1 = \partial x/\partial v_1 = 20v_2 - 4v_1$$
$$MP_2 = \partial x/\partial v_2 = 20v_1 - 2v_2$$
$$RTS_{12} \equiv \frac{20v_1 - 2v_2}{20v_2 - 4v_1}$$

The decision rule for cost minimization is $RTS_{12} = w_2^0/w_1^0$, which in this case is

$$\frac{20v_1 - 2v_2}{20v_2 - 4v_1} = \$8/\$4, \text{ which implies } v_1^0 = 1.5v_2^0$$

Here, superscript "naughts" have been placed on $v_1$ and $v_2$ to indicate that given $w_2^0/w_1^0 = 2$, the *optimal* input proportion is to use $V_1$ one and one-half times more intensively than $V_2$. Notice that solving $RTS_{12} = w_2^0/w_1^0$ yields only the optimal factor *proportion* and does not give the *level* of factor use. This is illustrated in Figure 4-6. The equation $v_1^0 = 1.5v_2^0$ tells the decision maker that $v_1$ and $v_2$ will be used in this *proportion* whatever the order size happens to be, as long as $w_2^0/w_1^0 = 2$. By introducing order size information, the optimal *level* of $v_1$ and $v_2$ can be determined.

**FIGURE 4-6**

The set of
efficient
production
plans

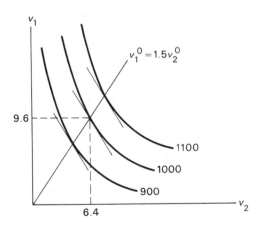

Analytically, calculation of the level of utilization of $v_1$ and $v_2$ requires using the equation of the isoquant associated with the 1,000-unit order. This equation is $1000 = 20v_1v_2 - 2v_1^2 - v_2^2$. The optimal factor combination is determined by finding the point along this isoquant where $v_1 = 1.5v_2$. Substituting $v_1 = 1.5v_2$ into the isoquant equation accomplishes this and yields

$$1000 = 20(1.5v_2)v_2 - 2(1.5v_2)^2 - v_2^2$$
$$= 30v_2^2 - 4.5v_2^2 - v_2^2$$
$$= 24.5v_2^2 \text{ and } v_2^2 = 40.8$$

Hence $v_2^0 = 6.4$, and since

$$v_1^0 = 1.5v_2^0$$
$$v_1^0 = 1.5(6.4)$$
$$v_1^0 = 9.6$$

Using 6,400 hours of skilled labor and 9,600 hours of unskilled labor is the least expensive way of producing the 1,000-unit order. (Recall that $V_1$ and $V_2$ were measured in thousands of hours.)

At this factor combination, the marginal product of unskilled labor is $MP_1 = 20(6.4) - 4(9.6) = 89.6$, and the marginal product of skilled labor is $MP_2 = 20(9.6) - 2(6.4) = 179.2$. An additional hour of skilled labor will produce just twice the output of an additional hour of unskilled labor. Notice that this is the condition required by (4-1'') above.

The cost of this order is $C = \$4(9,600) + \$8(6,400) = \$89,600$ plus overhead charges. Any labor combination other than (9.6, 6.4) would produce the order at higher costs.

In an exercise at the chapter's end you are asked to consider the problem of allocating $89,600 to production, with the charge to produce as many units of output as possible with that outlay. Solution of this problem would tell the decision maker to use 9,600 hours of unskilled labor and 6,400 hours of skilled labor. This combination of unskilled and skilled labor would produce 1,000 units of output for the expenditure of $89,600. Any other labor combination would produce less output for this expenditure. Of course this is the same answer we arrived at in the cost minimization we just finished and illustrates the relationship between cost minimization and output maximization we discussed above.

CASE II. If the availability of skilled and unskilled labor in the present production period is limited to 15,000 hours and 5,000 hours, respectively, the result we obtained previously is not a feasible solution to the production problem. In other words, the production plan $v_1 = 9,600$ hours and $v_2 = 6,400$ hours does not lie in the feasible region of the input space. This is illustrated in Figure 4-7, where we have again used a heavy line to denote the feasible region.

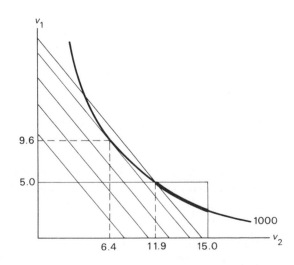

**FIGURE 4-7**

The optimal production plan when $v_1 \leq$ 5,000 hours and $v_2 \leq 15,000$ hours

As before, to solve this problem we need only move along the feasible portion of the isoquant $x = 1000$ until we reach the minimum cost combination. In the figure this input combination is the production plan that calls for using all 5,000 available hours of unskilled labor and 11,900 hours of skilled labor to produce the order. No other production plan produces 1,000 units at lower cost with the given availability of labor. Notice that the shortage of unskilled labor has driven the cost of the order up from $89,600 plus overhead to

$$C = \$4(5000) + \$8(11,900) + b$$
$$= \$115,200 + b$$

Costs have increased by approximately $25,000. This shows up in Figure 4-7 by the fact that the efficient production plan under these constraints is on a higher isocost function than the plan (9.6, 6.4).

To arrive at the solution we just gave, one first solves the problem without the constraints and finds that the production plan (9.6, 6.4) is inconsistent with the given availabilities of resources. In particular $V_1$ is in short supply, while $V_2$ seems to be abundant enough. If this is true, it will pay to use all of the unskilled labor available, "making up the difference" by using skilled labor. Mathematically, the problem is simple: We know the feasible region is given by that portion of the isoquant $x = 1000$ where $v_1 \leq 5$ and $v_2 \leq 15$. We also know that $V_1$ will be used to capacity (see Figure 4-7), so we want to find that point on the isoquant $x = 1000$ that corresponds to $v_1 = 5$. This is obtained by plugging $v_1 = 5$ into the equation of the isoquant

$$1000 = 20(5)v_2 - 2(5)^2 - v_2^2$$

which upon rearrangement becomes

$$v_2^2 - 100v_2 + 1050 = 0$$

Recalling the formula for solving a quadratic equation, we have[4]

$$v_2 = \frac{100 \pm \sqrt{(-100)^2 - 4(1050)}}{2}$$
$$= 11.9 \text{ and } 88.1$$

Quadratic equations always have two solutions, so we will be forced to choose between the two. To see why we chose 11.9 instead of 88.1, calculate the marginal productivity of skilled labor when 5,000 hours of unskilled labor and 88,100 hours of skilled labor are used to produce the order. Your answer shows that the production plan (5, 88.1) is inconsistent with Assumption II, Chapter 3, which underpins our production theory.

In summary, the optimal production plan is to use all 5,000 hours of unskilled labor that are available, with 11,900 hours of skilled labor. This plan is much more costly than the unconstrained plan (9.6, 6.4) but is the best that can be done under the circumstances.

[4]In case you have forgotten, see the Appendix to Chapter 1.

The production function $x = T v_1^a v_2^b$ is widely used in applied work and has been estimated countless times over many years. Because the first extensive estimation of this function was done in the 1930s by Professors C. W. Cobb and Paul Douglas, production functions of this type are usually called Cobb-Douglas production functions.

The student might legitimately inquire as to why this particular functional form—a power function—was chosen to represent the production function. The answer is primarily pragmatic: It is relatively easy to estimate functions of this type. But of course this fact alone cannot justify the choice. In addition, years of estimating Cobb-Douglas production functions have shown that this particular type of function adequately approximates a wide variety of production processes. Because Cobb-Douglas production functions are widely used, it is worth spending a little time investigating their properties.

The constants $T$, $a$, and $b$ are parameters which must be estimated and whose values completely determine the characteristics of production. The parameter $T$ is a technological parameter which "picks up" the state of technology in the firm or industry in question. Of course, $T$ must be positive. (Why?) In addition, "increases in technology" will generally increase the value of $T$, which means that given levels of use of $V_1$ and $V_2$ are capable of producing more output after the "increase." The parameters $a$ and $b$ measure the productivity of $V_1$ and $V_2$, respectively.

The marginal productivity functions of $V_1$ and $V_2$ are given by

$$\partial x/\partial v_1 = a\, T\, v_1^{a-1} v_2^b$$

and

$$\partial x/\partial v_2 = b\, T\, v_1^a v_2^{b-1}$$

(4-2)

Output elasticities are of an especially simple form.

$$\varepsilon_1 = (\partial x/\partial v_1)(v_1/x) = a$$

and

$$\varepsilon_2 = (\partial x/\partial v_2)(v_2/x) = b$$

(4-3)

Since $T > 0$ and $v_1, v_2 \geq 0$, examination of equation (4-2) reveals that marginal product functions will be positive as long as output elasticities are positive. Of course, production would never be undertaken if $\varepsilon_1$ or $\varepsilon_2$ were negative. So we see that functions of this type have at least the general features we require of a realistic production function. Also, note that the marginal productivity of each factor will, in general, depend upon the level of usage of both inputs, although output elasticities are constant and hence do not depend on the levels of $V_1$, $V_2$ use.

Since returns to scale are measured by summing output elasticities, in Cobb-Douglas production functions we have

$$\varepsilon = \varepsilon_1 + \varepsilon_2$$
$$= a + b$$

(4-4)

Returns to scale are the same throughout the feasible production region and are obtained by merely adding the coefficients of the estimated function. Regions of, say, increasing returns, followed by decreasing returns, are not possible with production functions of this type. In many cases this will do no serious harm; in other cases some other production function in which $\varepsilon$ is not a constant must be used.

Given the marginal product functions expressed above, we can derive another property of Cobb-Douglas production functions. Since

$$RTS_{12} \equiv MP_2/MP_1 = (b\,T\,v_1v_2^{b-1})/(a\,T\,v_1^{a-1}v_2^b)$$

we have

$$RTS_{12} = bv_1/av_2$$

The rate of technical substitution depends only on the *proportion* of $V_1$ to $V_2$ used, not on the absolute amount of $V_1$ and $V_2$ used. Therefore $RTS_{12}$ will be the same when $v_1 = 10$, $v_2 = 30$ as when, say, $v_1 = 100$, $v_2 = 300$. Substitutability between $V_1$ and $V_2$ in production depends only upon factor proportions, not on the level of output being produced. Whether or not this property is reasonable depends upon the firm in question. But before estimation can begin, a judgment must be made as to whether input substitutability depends primarily on factor proportions or whether it also depends upon the *scale* of operation. If the latter is the case some other production function should probably be estimated.

Since $RTS_{12} = bv_1/av_2$, the rule for efficient factor use is

$$\frac{bv_1}{av_2} = \frac{w_2^0}{w_1^0} \tag{4-5}$$

Cost minimization or output maximization, therefore, demands that $V_1$ and $V_2$ be used in the proportion

$$v_1 = (aw_2^0/bw_1^0)v_2 \tag{4-5'}$$

So once the parameters $a$ and $b$ are estimated (the output elasticities), one only needs input costs to find the most efficient production plan. As is evident from (4-5) or (4-5'), the optimal production plan depends upon the responsiveness of output to changes in the use of $V_1$ and $V_2$, $a$ and $b$, and on relative factor prices. As always, "productivity" and "costs" determine efficient factor use.

## EFFICIENT FACTOR USE: THE CASE OF PIECEWISE LINEAR PRODUCTION FUNCTIONS[5]

Let us now consider a production function that generates isoquants like those depicted in Figure 4-8. Production functions of this type have several notable properties: First, the only efficient points are the "corners" $(v_1^0, v_2^0)$, $(v_1', v_2')$, and $(v_1'', v_2'')$. This follows from the fact that efficient points are points of tangency between isoquants and isocost functions and that since factor prices

---

[5]These production functions have nondifferentiable regions ("corners") unlike the "smooth" production functions we have studied up to this point.

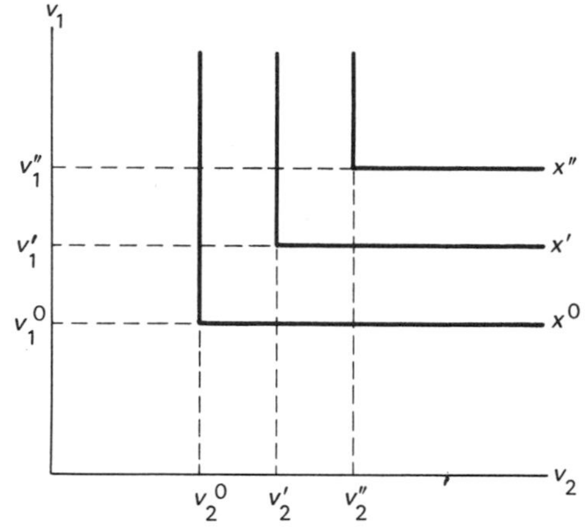

**FIGURE 4-8**

A "one-process" production function

are always positive and finite, tangency cannot occur where $RTS_{12}$ is zero or infinite (i.e., on the horizontal or vertical portions of the isoquant). This means that the decision problem of minimizing the cost of producing an order always leads to the same solution, *no matter what factor prices might be*. In Figure 4-8 the most efficient way of producing $x^0$ is always $(v_1^0, v_2^0)$ *regardless* of the prices of $V_1$ and $V_2$. This statement does not take into account the fact that some factor prices will lead the firm to decide not to produce the order at all. But if the decision is made to produce the order, then the given combination of factors will always be used.

Why is the solution to the cost-minimization problem always the same? The answer is simple. For production processes like that depicted in Figure 4-8, there is but *one way* of producing the product. And one production process means that factor *proportions* are fixed for all order sizes. In terms of Figure 4-8, $v_1^0/v_2^0 = v_1'/v_2' = v_1''/v_2''$, and so forth. The optimal factor *proportion* associated with producing an order of size $x^0$, $x'$, and $x''$ is always the same. Although the proportion of $V_1$ to $V_2$ used is the same no matter what the order size may be, of course the *amount* of $V_1$ and $V_2$ used increases with the order size. Obviously, if there is but one way of producing $X$, then all orders are produced by utilizing the single production process more or less intensively.

It is evident that the entire production function in this case of fixed input proportions may be exhibited as a single ray from the origin of input space with slope $v_1^0/v_2^0$. That is, Figure 4-8 may be replaced by Figure 4-9, where each point on the ray corresponds to a particular production level, $x$. Figure 4-9 makes it obvious that the production function we have been discussing is a single *process* production function. There is only one production process in the firm, and hence the ray is the entire isoquant map.

Clearly, production functions of this kind do not pose decision problems of the type we have been analyzing, since the optimal production plan is always the same: The order is produced with the single available process. But, in most firms, there will be more than one way of producing the product. That is, if an order for $x^0$ units is received and the decision is made to produce the order, then a number of different *processes* (ways of producing) are available with

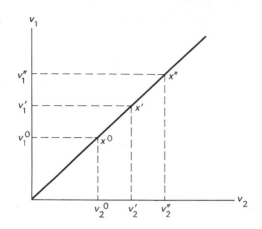

**FIGURE 4-9**
The
isoquant map
for a "one-
process"
production
function

which to produce the order. Formally, a *production process* is any production activity in which factor proportions are constant. Therefore, we can always represent a production process as a ray from the origin into input space. The slope of the ray is the proportion of $V_1$ to $V_2$ that is utilized in the process.

Figure 4-10 depicts a firm with four available production processes. Process I is the most $V_1$ intensive process, process II is a little less $V_1$ intensive, and process III is still less $V_1$ intensive (and consequently more $V_2$ intensive). Finally, Process IV is the most $V_2$ intensive process. The decision problem is to choose the process that produces $x^0$ units at minimum cost. As might be expected, which process is optimal will depend jointly upon productivity in the various processes and relative factor costs.

**FIGURE 4-10**
Four production
processes

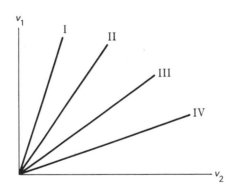

**Some Assumptions about Production Processes**

In this section we introduce two assumptions about the nature of production processes which greatly simplify solution of production problems. To begin, let us agree to call $x^0$ some *unit level* of production. Thus $x^0$ may be one unit of $X$, a hundred units, or a thousand. All we need here is some basic production level as an accounting unit. Now define $(\bar{v}_1^i, \bar{v}_2^i)$ as the *unit level input requirement* in process $i$. We take this to mean that $\bar{v}_1^i$ units of $V_1$ and $\bar{v}_2^i$ units of $V_2$ are needed to produce the unit output $x^0$ in process $i$. If there are only four processes, the unit output levels may be represented as

$$(\bar{v}_1^1, \bar{v}_2^1) \longrightarrow x^0 \quad \text{in process I}$$
$$(\bar{v}_1^2, \bar{v}_2^2) \longrightarrow x^0 \quad \text{in process II}$$
$$(\bar{v}_1^3, \bar{v}_2^3) \longrightarrow x^0 \quad \text{in process III}$$
$$(\bar{v}_1^4, \bar{v}_2^4) \longrightarrow x^0 \quad \text{in process IV}$$

where the $\longrightarrow$ is read "yields." This schema is merely a shorthand way of depicting the input requirements for the unit output in each process. Hence the first line tells us how much $V_1$ and $V_2$ are needed to produce $x^0$ in process I. Keep in mind that $\bar{v}_1^i$ and $\bar{v}_2^i$ are constants in process $i$, since the definition of a *process* is a collection of input combinations in which the proportion of $V_1$ to $V_2$ used is fixed.

We now introduce an important assumption: In each process, proportional changes in factor use lead to equal proportional changes in output. In other words, we now assume that production processes exhibit constant returns to scale. If $k_i$ is any positive number, then in terms of the above representation, this assumption means that

$$(k_1\bar{v}_1^1, k_1\bar{v}_2^1) \longrightarrow k_1 x^0 \quad \text{in process I}$$
$$(k_2\bar{v}_1^2, k_2\bar{v}_2^2) \longrightarrow k_2 x^0 \quad \text{in process II}$$
$$(k_3\bar{v}_1^3, k_3\bar{v}_2^3) \longrightarrow k_3 x^0 \quad \text{in process III}$$
$$(k_4\bar{v}_1^4, k_4\bar{v}_2^4) \longrightarrow k_4 x^0 \quad \text{in process IV}$$

We will say that process $i$ is being utilized at *level* $k_i$ if the output of the process is $k_i$ times the unit level, that is, $k_i x^0$.

*The effect of the constant returns to scale assumption is to turn our above listing of input requirements into the firm's production function*! This follows from the fact that such a listing provides the relationship between inputs and output for any input combination in any process. For example, if process II takes 10 units of $V_1$ and 20 units of $V_2$ to produce 100 units of output, we could display this information as $(10, 20) \longrightarrow 100$ (in process II). Then from constant returns to scale we also know that 30 units of $V_1$ and 60 units of $V_2$ will yield 300 units of output. That is, utilization of process II at level 3 yields three times the unit output. Of course an analogous argument holds for each process and any level of utilization.

The assumption of constant returns to scale is often justified on the basis of the concept of a process. If a certain type of machine can turn out some given number of units per hour, then addition of a second machine with an equally skilled operator will double the hourly output. In many cases this seems to be a reasonable assumption.

The goal of the present discussion is to develop a way of choosing among the various available processes, that process or combination of processes that is most efficient. If we add a second assumption, we not only will be able to accomplish this end but also will have set the production problem up in such a manner that it can virtually always be solved, a consideration that is by no means trivial.

In what follows we will call a given level of utilization of each of the available processes a *production plan*. This is consistent with our prior use of this concept, in that a production plan still amounts to a particular way (input combination) of producing an order. (And as before, our goal is to find a rule for calculating the most efficient plan.) The simplest production plan involves using only one process to produce an order—one process is utilized at a positive level, all other processes are utilized at the zero level.

Our second assumption comes naturally when isoquants are defined for production functions in which there are but a finite number of production processes. To introduce this assumption consider the two processes shown in Figure 4-11, where points $a$ and $b$ indicate the unit production levels in these processes.

**FIGURE 4-11**

Interpreting
line segments
"between"
production
processes

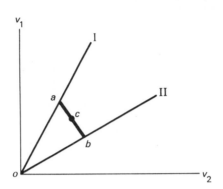

The points $a$ and $b$ have been connected by a straight line. Assumption II arises when we interpret point $c$, which lies between $a$ and $b$. To this end, draw the line $cd$ from $c$ parallel to $ob$ as shown in Figure 4-12. Next choose the point $e$

**FIGURE 4-12**

A production
plan utilizing
two processes

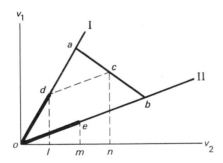

on the line that represents process II so that $dc = oe$. Now consider the production plan that consists of using process I to produce $od$ units of $X$ and process II to produce $oe$ units. At these levels, process I uses $ol$ units of $V_2$ and process II uses $om$ units of $V_2$, and hence the total $V_2$ requirement for this production plan is $ol + om$. But notice that $om = ln$, since lines $dc$ and $oe$ are equal in length and parallel. Therefore *the total $V_2$ requirement at point $c$ is $ol + ln = on$.*

An analogous argument shows that the $V_1$ requirement in this production plan[6] (process I at level $od$, process II at level $oe$) is the $V_1$ requirement at $c$.

---

[6]Students familiar with linear algebra will recognize that the input requirement of a production plan that uses two processes obeys the rules of "vector addition."

We have shown that the coordinates of point $c$ correspond to the total input
requirement of processes I and II being "run" at levels $od$ and $oe$, respectively.
It is for this reason that *point c will be interpreted as the production process formed*
*by combining processes I and II in the given manner.* It should be clear that any
point on the line between points $a$ and $b$ corresponds to some combination of
the two processes. Interpreting points on the line $ab$ as a combination of processes I and II makes sense only if the two processes are *independent* in that if
both processes are used simultaneously one neither hinders nor helps the other.
For example, if machine operators must be pulled off one process to work on
another as the latter is brought into operation, the processes in question are
*not* independent. This is our second assumption: *Production processes are inde-*
*pendent.* Process independence allows us to add inputs and the corresponding
output in one process to inputs and the corresponding outputs in other processes
to obtain total input use and total output when two processes are used simultaneously. If processes are not independent, addition of outputs obtained by
using processes simultaneously at given levels would not in general yield the
output obtained if the same processes were used at the same levels but not
simultaneously.

We have shown that utilizing process I at level $od$ and process II at level $oe$
has exactly the same input requirements as point $c$. Now, if we could also show
that the output associated with this production plan yields the same output as
at points $a$ or $b$, then $c$ lies on an isoquant through $a$ and $b$. And indeed the line
segment between points $a$ and $b$ is a portion of an isoquant. To see this, return
to Figure 4-12 and notice that since output $oa$ equals output $ob$, $\dfrac{\text{output } od}{\text{output } oa} +$
$\dfrac{\text{output } oe}{\text{output } ob}$ is the proportion of output $oa$ produced by using process I at level
$od$ and process II at level $oe$. Since triangles $oab$ and $dac$ are similar, $da/dc =$
$oa/ob$ and hence $da/oa = dc/ob$. But since $dc = oe$ by construction, $da/oa =$
$oe/ob$. Therefore $\dfrac{\text{output } oe}{\text{output } ob} = \dfrac{\text{output } da}{\text{output } oa}$, and since output $oa =$ output $ob$ we
can rewrite the above sum as $\dfrac{\text{output } od}{\text{output } oa} + \dfrac{\text{output } da}{\text{output } oa}$. From Figure 4-12 we see
that this sum is equal to one, that is, the proportion of output $oa$ produced in
this production plan is one. In other words, "all" of output $oa$ is produced by
operating processes I and II at levels $od$ and $oe$, respectively. In still other words,
the output of the production plan given by point $c$ is equal to output $oa$ (or
output $ob$), and hence the points $a$, $c$, and $b$ are points of equal production.
Since $c$ is an arbitrary point on $ab$, the argument could be repeated with any
other point. Therefore line $acb$ is an isoquant.

In Figure 4-13 this process has been completed for four production processes
and a production level $x'$, some multiple of the unit level. As we have seen,
points on the isoquant $x'$ may be interpreted as factor combinations that yield
the output $x'$ by using either a single process or some combination of two
*adjacent* processes. (Why not include input combinations of nonadjacent processes, the broken line in Figure 4-13, as points along an isoquant?) As before,

**FIGURE 4-13**

An isoquant—
piecewise
linear
production
function

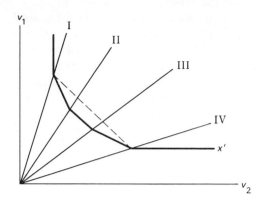

and for the same reasons, these isoquants will have a negative slope in the relevant production region.[7]

### The Isoquant Map—Piecewise Linear Production Functions

We have seen that production functions composed of a finite number of production processes in which processes are independent and exhibit constant returns to scale imply isoquants like those pictured in Figure 4-14. Isoquants of

**FIGURE 4-14**

The isoquant
map—piecewise
linear
production
function

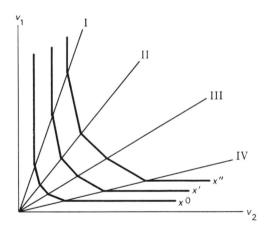

this type are composed of a series of linear segments between processes. Since input requirements are fixed in any given process, a question arises as to exactly what meaning can be given to the rate of technical substitution in the present context. That is, since there is no factor substitution within a given production process, the rate of technical substitution is not even defined in a given process. In the problem now confronting us, however, our interest lies in how substitutable inputs are *between* processes. Therefore we will interpret the rate of technical substitution as a measure of the substitutability of $V_1$ for $V_2$ between processes. Because the slope of an isoquant between processes is constant and

---

[7]Positively sloped segments would imply a negative marginal product for some input.

because constant returns to scale implies isoquants must be parallel, we may conclude that the rate of technical substitution is constant between any two given processes and is always the *same* constant no matter what the production rate happens to be. To illustrate this point, note that the slope of the line segments between processes III and IV in Figure 4-14 is approximately minus two whether $x^0$, $x'$, or $x''$ is being produced. The fact that $RTS_{12} = 2$ between processes III and IV means that a production plan utilizing process IV needs two units less of $V_1$ per unit of $V_2$ used than does a plan using process III. Also, the assumption of constant returns to scale coupled with the fact that the isoquants $x^0$, $x'$, and $x''$ are equidistant from one another and from the origin implies $x' = 2x^0$, $x'' = 3x^0$, and so forth.

### Minimizing The Cost of Producing An Order

Let us return to the problem of efficient use of the firm's inputs. We have solved this problem for firms that have differentiable (smooth) production functions and are now ready to extend those results to firms with piecewise linear production functions in which production processes are independent and exhibit constant returns to scale.

The decision problem of a firm with four available production processes which utilize $V_1$ and $V_2$ in differing intensities is depicted graphically in Figure 4-15. An order is received for $x'$ units and management desires to choose the process or combination of processes that will produce the order at least expense.

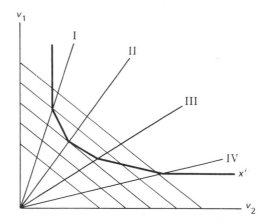

**FIGURE 4-15**
The most
efficient
production
plan: case I

Factor costs are given at $w_1^0$ and $w_2^0$ per unit of $V_1$ and $V_2$, respectively. The graphical solution to this problem is given by proceeding to the lowest isocost function consistent with the order size constraint; $x'$ units must be produced. (The isoquant $x'$ is the feasible region of input space.) Clearly, process II is most efficient, *given* $w_1^0$ and $w_2^0$ are the input costs. Changes in costs lead to changes in the slope of the isocost functions $(-w_2^0/w_1^0)$ and hence *possibly* to a different solution to the cost-minimization problem.

Notice that the problem of choosing the optimal production plan amounts to choosing the values of $k_1, k_2, k_3$, and $k_4$ that minimize the cost of producing

$x'$. In Figure 4-15 $k_1 = k_3 = k_4 = 0$, while $k_2$ is a positive number representing the optimal level of utilization of process II. It is helpful to view the decision problem as one of choosing the optimal level of utilization for each process.

We now want to write a decision rule that could be used to find the optimal process. Recall that the rate of technical substitution of $V_1$ for $V_2$ is defined only between processes, and, in fact, in any particular process there is no substitution between $V_1$ and $V_2$. It is the rate of substitution *between* processes that is needed to write the rule for efficient factor use. Inspection of Figure 4-15 indicates that the rate of technical substitution is *greater than* $w_2^0/w_1^0$ between processes I and II but is *less than* $w_2^0/w_1^0$ between processes II and III and is *still less than* $w_2^0/w_1^0$ between processes III and IV. The *direction* of the inequality between the rate of substitution and relative input prices *changes* as one moves along the isoquant and "passes through" the optimal process. The "further" one is from the optimal process (in this case process II), the more unequal are $RTS_{12}$ and $w_2^0/w_1^0$. Roughly speaking, the "closest" one can get to equality of the rate of substitution and factor prices is in process II, and hence process II is the most efficient way of producing the order.

We may now write the following rule: Process $i$ minimizes the cost of producing a given order if $RTS_{12} > w_2^0/w_1^0$ "between" processes $i - 1$ and $i$, and $RTS_{12} < w_2^0/w_1^0$ "between" processes $i$ and $i + 1$. In Figure 4-15 process II is the optimal process because $RTS_{12} < w_2^0/w_1^0$ between processes I and II and $RTS_{12} > w_2^0/w_1^0$ between processes II and III. Although this rule will hold for most configurations of factor prices and production processes, a special case can occur that requires that the rule be slightly modified. This case is shown in Figure 4-16. It is evident that process II, or process III, or any combination of

**FIGURE 4-16**

The most efficient production plan: a special case

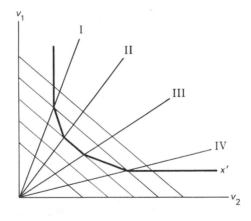

processes II and III that produces $x'$ units is optimal. In the case pictured, $RTS_{12} < w_2^0/w_1^0$ between processes I and II, $RTS_{12} = w_2^0/w_1^0$ between processes II and III, and $RTS_{12} < w_2^0/w_1^0$ between processes III and IV. To modify the above rule, we need only add a third statement. The decision rule in general form is then:

Process $i$ minimizes the cost of producing a given order if

i. $RTS_{12} > w_2^0/w_1^0$ between processes $i - 1$ and $i$ and

ii. $RTS_{12} < w_2^0/w_1^0$ between processes $i$ and $i + 1$. Or, if

iii. $RTS_{12} = w_2^0/w_1^0$ between processes $i$ and $i + 1$, then process $i$, process $i + 1$, or any combination of processes $i$ and $i + 1$ that produces the order is optimal.

Firms whose production functions are composed of a finite number of independent production processes exhibiting constant returns to scale are said to possess a *linear technology.* This definition of a linear technology is not to be confused with the statement that the firm's production function is linear, that is, $f(v_1, v_2) = av_1 + bv_2$ where $a$ and $b$ are parameters. The significance of a linear technology lies in the fact that production problems of firms facing constant factor prices and possessing such technologies are *linear-programming* problems. The advantage of having a production problem that is a linear-programming problem stems from the fact that a set of rules, called the simplex algorithm, has been developed that makes it possible to machine-solve extremely large and complex linear-programming (and hence production) problems very rapidly. In practice, actually solving a cost-minimization or output-maximization problem becomes increasingly difficult as the number of inputs and/or the number of constraints on production processes increases. But under the above conditions, this important decision problem is always solvable.

How does one know whether it is appropriate to use the linear-programming technique to solve a production problem? If the two assumptions underlying a linear technology are "reasonably accurate" for the firm in question, then the problem can probably be viewed as a linear program.[8] So once again we arrive at a familiar theme: Technique alone will not be very helpful (and may actually be harmful) in making firm decisions. But powerful techniques combined with a thorough knowledge of the production process, *and* how to interpret that production knowledge in terms of the techniques available, can be of immense value in reaching correct decisions.

### Cost Minimization With Additional Constraints

The cost-minimization problem we have just analyzed is extremely easy to solve. It is now time to add additional considerations which often constrain real-world optimization problems. Up to this point the minimization problem was only constrained by the requirement that an order of $x'$ units be produced. Now reconsider the same problem, but this time add the additional constraint that some or all factors are available only in limited quantities during the coming production period. As we saw earlier, constraints of this type are present in virtually all production decisions. Machine time for the various classes of machines is rigidly fixed at a maximum of twenty-four hours a day and may be fixed at lesser rates. Union contracts often place maxima and minima on the number of hours union labor will work. Inventories of certain components may be limited, and so forth. If these constraints are not built into the problem, the

---

[8]In more detail, a linear-programming solution to the production problem requires a piecewise linear production function which displays constant returns to scale and a linear isocost function. A linear technology implies the appropriate production function. The linear isocost function means that unit factor costs are constant.

solution may well be impossible to execute. For example, a given set of factor costs may imply that the most efficient way to produce an order is to use a particular machine forty-three hours a day. Of course this is nonsense and merely means that productivity per dollar of expenditure is higher on this machine than on other factors. If the machine hour constraint is not built into the problem, the "solution" will contain "forty-three" as the optimal value of machine hours. Unfortunately the "solution" makes no sense, although the "productivity per dollar" requirement will be met for all factors. In this case we want our solution to tell us to use these machines to capacity and to use all other factors within prescribed bounds and as efficiently as possible.

Figure 4-17 depicts the case where $V_2$ is available at most at level $v_2^0$ while $V_1$, for all practical purposes, is available in whatever amount is needed. The feasible set of input choices is the area on the isoquant $x'$ to the left of, and including, the point $v_2^0$. (The set of feasible production plans is the darkened portion of the isoquant in the figure.) Isocost lines are truncated at the point $v_2^0$,

**FIGURE 4-17**

The most efficient production plan : case II

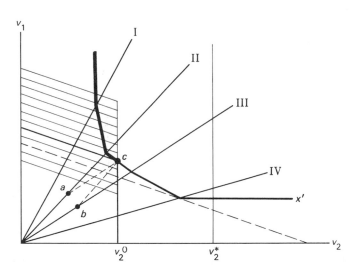

since larger quantities of $V_2$ are not available. Hence, isocost functions are their regular form for $v_2 < v_2^0$ and vertical at $v_2 = v_2^0$. In interpreting the solution to this problem, it is helpful to note that the slope of the isocost function is $-w_2^0/w_1^0$ for $v_2 < v_2^0$ and becomes infinite at $v_2 = v_2^0$. Note that this is precisely the situation we want the problem to incorporate: It is not possible to get more $V_2$ than $v_2^0$ in the present production period, so, for all practical purposes, $w_2^0$ is infinite beyond $v_2^0$.

In Figure 4-17, point $c$ is the most efficient point. Geometrically, this point is obtained by moving along the feasible region until the lowest isocost function is reached. At $c$ the costs of producing $x'$ are as low as they can be and still be consistent with an order of $x'$ units and with the production constraint $v_2 \leq v_2^0$. Notice that if $V_2$ were available in larger quantities, the cost of producing $x'$ would be lower. This point is quite clear in Figure 4-17 where the broken line represents the cost of producing the order if the amount of $V_2$ available is not constrained.

According to the figure, the cost-minimizing strategy is to use a combination of processes II and III to produce the order. In particular, process II would be used at level $a$ and process III at level $b$. If $w_2^0/w_1^0$ is interpreted as being infinite at $v_2^0$, it is easy to see that the same decision rule applies here as in the unconstrained case (Case I, Figure 4-15). Specifically, the rate of technical substitution is greater than $w_2^0/w_1^0$ "left" of the optimal production plan and less than $w_2^0/w_1^0$ "to the right" of the optimal plan. Symbolically

i.   $RTS_{12} > w_2^0/w_1^0$ to the "left" of point $c$, and
ii.  $RTS_{12} < w_2^0/w_1^0$ to the "right" of point $c$.

Intuitively, condition (i) means that a process, or combination of processes, that uses more $V_2$ and less $V_1$ will lower costs. Using more $V_2$ puts us to the right of point $c$ where condition (ii) says that more $V_1$ and less $V_2$ will lower costs. Using more $V_1$ puts us back left of point $c$ where condition (i) is again applicable. All this means is that it is not possible to lower costs any further than by using the plan implied at point $c$. At $c$, costs are minimum.

Notice that the higher is the cost of $V_2$ relative to $V_1$, the less likely it is that the constraint $v_2 \leq v_2^0$ will be binding. This is because the higher is the relative cost of $V_2$, the less intensively will $V_2$ be used. In terms of Figure 4-17, the higher is $w_2^0/w_1^0$, the steeper is the slope of isocost functions, which in turn means that processes using "relatively little" of $V_2$ are most efficient. No matter how short in supply a factor may be, there is always a relative cost ratio high enough that it will not pay to use the available supply.

Of course the constraint on factor availability may not be binding for any given order size and set of input prices. For example, in Figure 4-17 if $V_2$ is available in amounts no greater than $v_2^*$, then the optimal strategy is to produce the order using process IV alone. In fact, this is implicitly the case we analyzed first (Figure 4-15) when input availability constraints were not accounted for.

EXAMPLE. Assume four different processes are available to produce an order. In process I, 40 hours of $V_1$ and 10 hours of $V_2$ yield 100 hours of output; in process II, 20 hours of $V_1$ and 15 hours of $V_2$ are needed; in process III, 10 hours of $V_1$ and 20 hours of $V_2$; and in process IV, 5 hours of $V_1$ and 25 hours of $V_2$.

In terms of the notation we used earlier, the production function for this firm may be represented as

$$
\begin{array}{ll}
(k_1 40, k_1 10) \longrightarrow k_1 100 & \text{in process I} \\
(k_2 20, k_2 15) \longrightarrow k_2 100 & \text{in process II} \\
(k_3 10, k_3 20) \longrightarrow k_3 100 & \text{in process III} \\
(k_4 5, \ k_4 25) \longrightarrow k_4 100 & \text{in process IV}
\end{array}
$$

where $k_1, k_2, k_3$, and $k_4$ are nonnegative numbers.

It is easy to see that rates of technical substitution between processes are given by

$$RTS_{12} = -\left(\frac{40-20}{10-15}\right) = 4 \qquad \text{between processes I and II}$$

$$RTS_{12} = -\left(\frac{20-10}{15-20}\right) = 2 \qquad \text{between processes II and III}$$

$$RTS_{12} = -\left(\frac{10-5}{20-25}\right) = 1 \qquad \text{between processes III and IV}$$

It is now possible to answer several interesting questions: If factor costs are $35.00 and $85.25 per hour and an order for 1,000 units is received, (i) Which process or combination of processes is optimal? (ii) If the amount of $V_2$ available is limited to 110 hours, which process or combination of processes is optimal?

To answer (i) we need only note that $w_2^0/w_1^0 = 2.43$, and hence by the decision rule developed above, process II should be used to produce the order. This situation is depicted graphically in Figure 4-18.

**FIGURE 4-18**

The optimal
production
plan:
an example

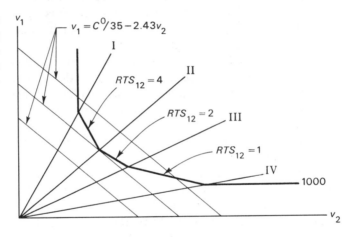

The answer to (ii) may be obtained by graphical methods or by noting that it will not be possible to use process II alone to produce the 1,000-unit order, since the $V_2$ requirement for the order would be 150 hours and only 110 hours are available. (In other than words, any production plan utilizing more than 110 hours of $V_2$ is not in the feasible region.) Therefore, some combination of processes II and I will be optimal, since process I needs only 100 hours of $V_2$ to produce 1,000 units of output. Exactly which combination of processes I and II is most efficient can be found by noting that (a) the optimal combination of processes I and II will use all of the $V_2$ available,[9] and (b) the level of utilization of the two processes combined must be chosen to yield 1,000 units of production. Symbolically, these two conditions are

$$10k_1 + 15k_2 = 110 \tag{a}$$

and

$$k_1 + k_2 = 10 \tag{b}$$

[9] If the order were produced in process I alone, only 100 hours of $V_2$ would be used.

If equations (a) and (b) are solved simultaneously we obtain $k_1$ and $k_2$, the level of utilization of processes I and II that minimizes the cost of producing the order. Equation (a) guarantees that the amount of $V_2$ used in process I plus the amount of $V_2$ used in process II is 110 hours. In this equation, the term $10k_1$ is the amount of $V_2$ needed if process I is used at level $k_1$, while $15k_2$ is the amount of $V_2$ needed if process II is used at level $k_2$. Equation (b) merely ensures that total production in the two processes will be ten times the unit level (100). These two equations may be written as

$$10k_1 + 15k_2 = 110$$
$$10k_1 + 10k_2 = 100$$

Solving yields $k_2 = 2$ and therefore $k_1 = 8$, since $k_1 + k_2 = 10$. Running process I at level 8 (eight times the unit level) and process II at level 2 (twice the unit level) is the most efficient way of producing the order when only 110 hours of $V_2$ are available. That is, produce 200 units in process II and the remaining 800 in process I. The solution to this problem is depicted graphically in Figure 4-19, where we have again used a heavy line to indicate the set of feasible production plans. (Calculate the cost of producing the order with and without the constraint on $V_2$. Notice that the shortage of $V_2$ has increased the cost of the order from \$19,787.50 to \$21,977.50.)

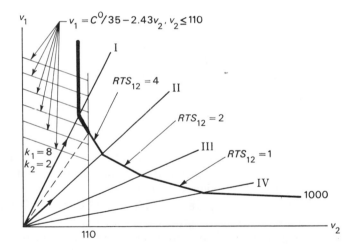

**FIGURE 4-19**

The optimal production plan, given $v_2 \leq 110$: an example

Finally, notice that the cost of factor one would have to decrease *or* the cost of factor two increase by approximately 40 percent before process I alone would be used to produce the order. In such a case the constraint on $V_2$ would no longer be binding—a situation that amplifies our earlier statement that factor "shortages" are relative to a given set of factor costs. Changes in costs of sufficient magnitude will turn what was a "shortage" into a "surplus."

### A Summary of the Problem of Efficient Input Use

Let us begin by summarizing the differences and the similarities between the efficient factor use problem when the production function is "smooth" and when it has "corners." First, it is clear from Figure 4-20 that in *both* cases the rate of technical substitution is greater than the ratio of factor prices for feasible production plans less $V_2$ intensive than the most efficient plan, and that the rate of technical substitution is less than the ratio of input prices for feasible production plans more $V_2$ intensive than the most efficient plan. Firms with linear technologies are merely a special case of the "smooth" production technologies we studied first. As you might expect, in the limit as the number of production processes increases, the former become the latter.[10]

**FIGURE 4-20**

The most efficient production plan: differentiable and piecewise linear production functions

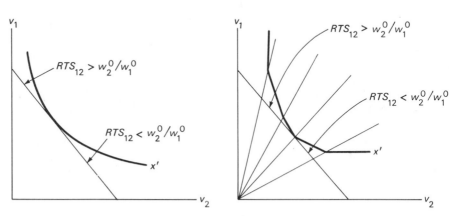

Second, production functions for firms with linear technologies are extremely easy to estimate for two reasons. In the first place, estimation of only one isoquant, say for the unit level of production, yields an estimate of the entire production function. This follows from constant returns to scale which implies that once the input requirements for the unit production level are calculated, the relationship between inputs and *all other* production levels is immediate merely by multiplying unit input requirements and related outputs by a positive constant. In addition, estimating the unit level isoquant amounts only to calculating the factor requirements for the unit output level in each process. Sophisticated statistical techniques are not needed. In terms of the example on page 101, once the input requirements, (40, 10), (20, 15) (10, 20), and (5, 25), for 100 units are established, the production function has been estimated.

The final point is demonstrated in Figures 4-21 and 4-22 in which the effects of a change in relative factor costs are explored. In these figures the solid and broken isocost functions represent relative costs before and after the cost changes. If the firm's production function is differentiable, then before the increase in $w_1$, cost minimization implies $(v_1^0, v_2^0)$ is the optimal production plan. It is clear from Figure 4-21 that any change in the price of a factor will *always* lead the cost-minimizing firm to substitute away from the factor that has become relatively more expensive. (In the figure less $V_1$ and more $V_2$ are utilized.) But, in the world, we see factor prices change and often observe that management keeps on doing things much the same as before the change.

[10]Of course, even in the limit, the linear technology will still exhibit constant returns to scale, which may or may not be the case in general.

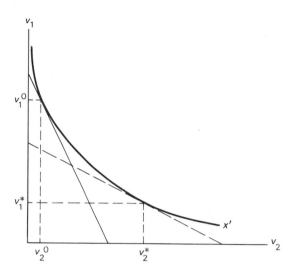

**FIGURE 4-21**

The effects of changes in factor costs: case I

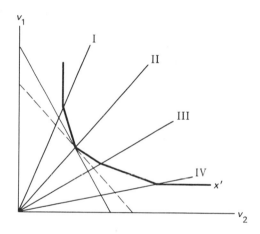

**FIGURE 4-22**

The effects of changes in factor costs: case II

In other words, no factor substitutions are made. In such cases, should management be "called on the carpet"? Figure 4-22 provides a possible explanation for such behavior, behavior that at first may seem to be inconsistent with cost minimization. Again, $w_2/w_1$ is postulated as falling, but this time cost minimization demands sticking with process II (not changing relative factor use). It is evident that there is a large range of input prices for which process II is the cost-minimizing process. The fewer alternative ways of producing the order (the smaller the number of production processes), the more insensitive will be the choice of the optimal process to changes in factor prices; the two limiting cases of finely attuned sensitivity and total insensitivity being given by continuously differentiable production functions and production functions in which there is but one process, respectively. The lack of sensitivity of production decisions to changes in costs are an implication of efficient input use in firms with a "small" number of production processes; an implication that seems to correspond rather closely to observed behavior.

**105**

1. Discuss the role of factor specialization as it pertains to the level of opportunity costs. (Hint: There is an obvious relationship between input specialization and the number of alternative uses to which an input can be put.) Give some examples where the total cost of an input is merely its direct cost, i.e., where opportunity costs are zero.

2. For any given value of $v_1$, the most efficient use of $V_2$ is that level that maximizes the (i) total product of $V_2$; (ii) average product of $V_2$. True or false? Support your answer.

3. Discuss the relationship between the length of time between production decisions and the level of opportunity costs. (Hint: Opportunity costs are defined with respect to a given production period. What happens to alternative uses to which an input can be put as the length of the decision period varies?)

4. The parameters of the production function $x = Av_1^a v_2^b$ are estimated and turn out to be $A = 10$ and $a = b = 1$. Assume the firm in question desires to produce any order it receives at minimum cost and that a large order is received. A decision is reached to produce the order with 1,200 units of $V_1$ and 750 units of $V_2$. At this time factor one costs $0.50 per unit and factor two costs $1.50 per unit.

a. Is this decision consistent with cost minimization? Why or why not?
b. Calculate the response of output to a percentage change in the use of all inputs. Interpret your answer.

5. If you were given a list of every possible input combination in a firm and the corresponding outputs, could you determine the optimal production plan? Explain.

6. You are given the following production function: $x = v_1^{.75} v_2^{.25}$. You know that during the next production period the price of $V_1$ will be $20 and the price of $V_2$ will be $10. Overhead charges are $100,000; and $200,000 has been allocated to production with the dictum "produce as much as possible" with the $200,000.

a. Calculate the rate of technical substitution between $V_1$ and $V_2$.
b. What is the optimal factor combination?
c. Do the same problem if $V_1$ and $V_2$ are limited to 3,000 units and 5,000 units, respectively. What is the feasible region of input space? Compare the optimal production rates in parts b and c. What is the effect of limited factor availability on the level of production?
d. Does the production function exhibit constant, increasing, or decreasing returns to scale?

7. Referring to the production function given in problem 3 at the end of Chapter 3, assume that the company in question is currently producing 180 units of output using 4 units of $V_1$ and 2 units of $V_2$ and that the cost per unit of $V_1$ and $V_2$ is equal. Make a case for changing this production plan based upon cost minimization.

8. Suppose that a product requires two inputs for its production. Then is it correct to say that if the prices of the inputs are equal they will be used in approximately equal amounts?

9.  Given the production function $f(v_1, v_2) = 10v_1\sqrt{v_2}$ answer the following questions:

a.  Are marginal product functions consistent with the implications of the two assumptions we adopted about production functions in Chapter 3?

b.  If $C = 4v_1 + 2v_2$, how much $V_1$ and $V_2$ would be used to produce 80 units at lowest possible cost? What is the minimum cost?

c.  If the amount of $V_2$ available is limited to 3 units, what is the optimal production plan for producing the 80 units? Compare the cost of this plan with that of part b.

d.  Compare feasible production plans in parts b and c.

e.  Show that this production function exhibits increasing returns to scale.

10.  An industrial engineering firm is given a contract to estimate the present production function of Metallux, Inc., and the production function that would be attained if Metallux changed to a different production technology. The two estimates provided are $x = 4LK - L^2 - K^2$ and $x = 24L^{.5}K^{.5}$, respectively, where $L$ and $K$ represent "labor" and "capital." ($L$ and $K$ are indices into which the various types of labor and capital equipment have been aggregated.) The average order size for Metallux is around 1,100 units, wages are $8 per hour, and capital equipment under the present technology costs about $32 per hour to operate. If the new production technology is adopted, wages will remain unchanged but equipment operating costs will fall to $18 per hour. It is now time to make the decision whether to replace the present setup or adopt the new one. (Overhead charges are the same for both.) Which technology would be adopted? Why?

11.  Consider a firm with production function $x = f(L, K)$ where $L$ and $K$ again represent quantities of labor and capital. On the basis of an estimate of the production function it is learned that $1 \leq RTS_{LK} \leq 2$ in the relevant production region. Assuming an effort is made to minimize the cost of producing any given order, what can be said concerning the input decisions of the firm if (i) $w_K/w_L > 2$, (ii) $w_K/w_L < 1$, and (iii) $1 \leq w_K/w_L \leq 2$?

12.  A firm receives an order for 100 units of a certain item in its product line, say $X$. For this item the production function is $x = 20 + 5v_1 + 10v_2$ in the relevant production region. If the firm desires to determine factor use such that the cost of producing the 100 units is minimum, what factor combination would be chosen if $w_1 = \$1$ and $w_2 = \$3$?

13.  Draw an isocost function for a firm using two inputs for the case when price per unit of one input (i) falls with quantity purchased; (ii) rises with quantity purchased.

14.  Consider the production function $x = f(L, K)$ where $L$ and $K$ denote quantities of labor and capital, respectively. Assume that the firm is interested in minimizing the cost of producing an order of $x^0$ units and that for output levels in the neighborhood of $x^0$ the marginal products of capital and labor are constant and equal to 6 and 2, respectively. Given $w_L$ and $w_K$ are the prices of labor and capital, what can be said about the producer's cost-minimization problem (the "best" combination of capital and labor) if

a. Capital is more than three times as expensive as labor?

b. Capital is less than three times as expensive as labor?

c. Capital is exactly three times as expensive as labor?

15. Say there is a choice of three different processes with which to produce an order of $x^0$ units. Process one produces $x^0$ with 30 units of $V_1$ and 10 units of $V_2$, process two produces $x^0$ with 20 units of $V_1$ and 20 units of $V_2$, while process three utilizes 10 units of $V_1$ and 40 units of $V_2$ to produce $x^0$. (i) What range of relative prices of $V_1$ and $V_2$ lead to the adoption of process two (i.e., find the two numbers $a$ and $b$ so that whenever $a < w_2^0/w_1^0 < b$, process two is the most efficient process)? (ii) Will process three ever be utilized? Show why.

16. Earnings on invested capital in a particular firm have hovered around 10 percent for a number of years. As a potential investor in that industry, you must decide whether this return is satisfactory. To help reach a decision, you estimate accounting profits and economic profits. Explain (i) how you calculated these estimates and (ii) their significance in evaluating firm performance.

17. It is possible to produce some commodity $X$ in five alternative ways, i.e., with five different processes. The cost of factor one is $3 per unit, and the cost of factor two is $4 per unit. Assume it is desired to produce a 1,000-unit order at lowest possible costs. Input requirements for 1,000 units are:

Process 1 produces the 1,000 units using 300 units of $V_1$ and 30 units of $V_2$

| // | 2 | // | 250 | // | 50 | // |
| // | 3 | // | 200 | // | 80 | // |
| // | 4 | // | 150 | // | 200 | // |
| // | 5 | // | 100 | // | 400 | // |

a. Which process or processes will be used?

b. What is the minimum cost of producing the 1000 units?

c. Calculate the effect on the firm's production plan of:
  (1) A fall in $w_2$ to $3
  (2) A fall in $w_2$ to $2
  (3) A fall in $w_2$ to $1

18. Do part a and b of problem 17 if only 180 units of $V_1$ are available. What assumption about production processes is implicit in your answer to this problem?

19. Referring to the example that begins on page 101, answer the following questions:

a. Assume that $V_1$ and $V_2$ can be purchased in any amount the firm desires and that the price of $V_2$ has been fixed at $85.25. What range of prices for $V_1$ will lead to the adoption of process 2 as the most efficient process?

b. Assume that it is currently impossible to get additional $V_2$, that the firm receives a 2,000-unit order, and that 350 units of $V_2$ are available in inventory. If $w_1 = $60.00$ and $w_2 = $85.25$, which process or processes should be used to produce the order? At what "level" should these processes be operated?

20. In this chapter we illustrated the firm's cost-minimization problem using the production function $x = 20v_1v_2 - 2v_1^2 - v_2^2$ (see pp. 85–88) and input prices $w_1^0 = \$4$ and $w_2^0 = \$8$. Consider the same problem again, but this time assume the production manager is allocated \$89,600 and told to "produce as much as possible" with this expenditure. What is the most efficient combination of skilled and unskilled labor? Compare your answer with the answer given for the cost-minimization problem in the example.

21. In your own words, explain why isoquants must be parallel for firms with "linear technologies."

22. Referring to problem 17, calculate and graph the isoquant corresponding to 500 units of output. How would you go about graphing the isoquant map?

23. Referring to the example that begins on page 87 (Case II), again assume unskilled and skilled labor are available in amounts not exceeding 5,000 and 15,000 hours, respectively. Find the most efficient production plan if \$89,600 is allocated production. (Assume $b = 0$.) How much is produced? Compare this with the amount produced when there are no constraints on the availability of labor.

# * The Linear Technology: Other Applications

This chapter discusses two additional applications of linear programming to management decision problems. We first examine the problem of optimal product mix and then look at input-output analysis as a means of forecasting industry demand. It is hoped that upon completion of this material the student will have acquired both an appreciation for the scope and complexity of the problems that can be solved via linear programming and a thorough understanding of the conditions that must be satisfied to use this powerful tool. If the solutions to problems are to be meaningful, the assumptions underpinning the required "linear technology" must be fulfilled.

## THE PROBLEM OF OPTIMAL PRODUCT MIX

We first study a multiproduct firm with a linear technology and product line, or potential product line, $X_1, X_2, \ldots, X_n$. ("Potential product" is used to designate products for which the firm has immediate production capabilities and whose production will be undertaken if calculations indicate that such a move is in the interest of the firm.) For the present production period, the prices of $X_1, X_2, \ldots, X_n$ are taken to be $P_1^0, P_2^0, \ldots, P_n^0$. The firm is assumed to utilize $m$ fixed factors $Z_1, Z_2, \ldots, Z_m$ and $r$ variable factors $V_1, V_2, \ldots, V_r$ in the production of $X_1, X_2, \ldots, X_n$.[1] If unit costs of variable factors are constant at, say, $w_1^0, w_2^0, \ldots, w_r^0$, then constant returns to scale in each process plus independence of processes (a linear technology) imply that unit costs of production for each product are constant.[2] If we call these costs $C_1^0, C_2^0, \ldots, C_n^0$, then

---

[1] This model is obviously not a pricing model, since for decision purposes prices are taken as given.

[2] This statement is verified in Chapter 6.

$p_i^0 \equiv P_i^0 - C_i^0$ is the profit contribution per unit of $X_i$ sold, exclusive of the costs of fixed factors (overhead charges).

A number of questions are of vital interest to the firm. Among them, (i) Which of the $n$ products should be produced? (ii) How much of each product should be produced? (iii) Are there bottlenecks or excess capacities in any of the fixed inputs? (iv) What would it be worth to the firm to eliminate existing bottlenecks? (Or, more generally, what return would the firm gain if it were possible to augment the capacities of fixed factors?) Each of these questions refers to a general type of decision problem: How does management optimally utilize existing plant and equipment, given "present" market conditions? In the case we have outlined, the problem is soluble.

### The Optimal Product Mix as a Linear-Programming Problem

To begin, we will need an assumption about the firm's goals, information that is not needed in problems involving efficiency considerations alone. We assume that management desires to choose products and production levels so that firm profits are maximum. Hence the firm's problem is to choose *which* products to produce and *how much* of each to produce subject to the constraints imposed by limited availability of fixed factors. For example, labor time, machine time, and storage capacities will be available only in fixed amounts. Management's problem is to generate as much profit as possible given these fixed resources.

To actually solve this problem, several more definitions are needed. Call $a_{ij}$ the number of units (hours) of fixed input $Z_i$ needed in the production of one unit of $X_j$, and $\bar{z}_i$ the quantity of fixed resource $Z_i$ available in the current production period. The constants $\bar{z}_i$ may be the number and type of machine capacity available, the maximum number of labor hours (by type) available in the given production period, or the fixed availability of any other input.

Given this information, the firm's problem is to[3]

$$\text{maximize } \Pi = p_1^0 x_1 + p_2^0 x_2 + \cdots + p_n^0 x_n$$

subject to the conditions that

$$a_{11}x_1 + a_{12}x_2 + \cdots + a_{1n}x_n \leq \bar{z}_1$$
$$a_{21}x_1 + a_{22}x_2 + \cdots + a_{2n}x_n \leq \bar{z}_2$$
$$\vdots \qquad \vdots \qquad \qquad \vdots \qquad \vdots$$
$$a_{m1}x_1 + a_{m2}x_2 + \cdots + a_{mn}x_n \leq \bar{z}_m$$

and

$$x_1, x_2, \ldots, x_n \geq 0$$

To interpret these conditions notice that since $a_{ij}$ is the amount of $Z_i$ needed to produce one unit of $X_j$, $a_{ij}x_j$ is the amount of $Z_i$ needed to produce $x_j$ units of product $j$. So that for example, $a_{11}x_1 + a_{12}x_2 + \ldots + a_{1n}x_n$ is the total amount

---

[3] Profits as defined here are "gross" profits—profits before overhead charges are deducted. This follows from the fact that $p_i^0 = P_i^0 - C_i^0$, and $C_i^0$ is the unit *variable* cost of producing $X_i$.

of $Z_1$ needed to produce $x_1$ units of $X_1$, $x_2$ units of $X_2$, and so forth. Hence the first inequality condition requires the total $Z_1$ requirement to be no larger than $\bar{z}_1$, the amount of $Z_1$ available. The other conditions place similar requirements on each of the other fixed inputs. Finally, the condition $x_1, x_2, \ldots, x_n \geq 0$ requires that products must be produced either in positive or in zero amounts. Without this condition the solution might instruct management to produce some unprofitable products in negative amounts. This would occur due to the fact that if $p_i^0 < 0$, then a negative value for $x_i$ causes $\Pi$ to increase in value.

The way the problem stands at this point, it cannot be solved. This stems from the fact that little is known about solving sets of inequalities. But a slight modification of the problem transforms the resource constraints into equations and allows solution. The modification in question consists of defining $m$ new nonnegative variables $S_1, S_2, \ldots, S_m$ (one for each fixed input) called *slack variables* and rewriting the original problem as

$$\text{maximize } \Pi = p_1^0 x_1 + p_2^0 x_2 + \ldots + p_n^0 x_n$$

subject to the conditions that

$$a_{11}x_1 + a_{12}x_2 + \cdots + a_{1n}x_n + S_1 = \bar{z}_1$$
$$a_{21}x_1 + a_{22}x_2 + \cdots + a_{2n}x_n + S_2 = \bar{z}_2$$
$$\begin{matrix} . & . & . & . & . \\ . & . & . & . & . \\ . & . & . & . & . \end{matrix}$$
$$a_{m1}x_1 + a_{m2}x_2 + \cdots + a_{mn}x_n + S_m = \bar{z}_m$$

and

$$x_1, x_2, \ldots, x_n \geq 0 \text{ and } S_1, S_2, \ldots, S_m \geq 0$$

Note that slack variables are defined as nonnegative variables which turn the inequality constraints into equalities. As we stated, this procedure is necessary because little is known about solving sets of inequalities, but general procedures exist for solving sets of linear equations. We will see that the variables $S_i$ are more than mathematical conveniences and contain important decision-making information. The problem is now ready for solution.

**Properties of the Solution**

Since we have spent quite a lot of time and effort in setting up this problem, it is worth reemphasizing the reasons for our interest. First, the solution to the problem will tell the firm *which* products in the line to produce and *how much* of each to produce; where *bottlenecks* and *excess capacities* exist in fixed factors; and *the value to the firm of changing the capacity of any of the fixed factors.* Second, the problem we have just posed is a linear-programming problem and hence can be solved even when the number of products, the number of fixed inputs, and the number of variable inputs is very large. And, as we have noted before, this is far from a trivial consideration in real-world decision problems.

Let us agree to call the solution to this linear-programming problem the set of numbers $(x_1^0, x_2^0, \ldots, x_n^0, S_1^0, S_2^0, \ldots, S_m^0)$. These are the profit-maximizing values of all $n + m$ variables in the model (the optimal production levels for the

*n* products and the optimal values for the *m* slack variables). The solution has
the following properties:

1. The optimal values of the $x_i$'s and $S_i$'s are either zero or positive. If $x_j^0 = 0$, then the profit-maximizing strategy is *not* to produce $X_j$. If $x_j^0 > 0$, then product *j* will be produced, the optimal level being the number $x_j^0$. If the $i^{th}$ slack variable is positive, $S_i^0 > 0$, there is "slack" or excess capacity in the $i^{th}$ fixed factor. (The constraint on $Z_i$ is not binding.) When possible, the firm may want to rent out this extra capacity. Finally, if $S_i^0 = 0$, there is no slack in the $i^{th}$ fixed factor—a bottleneck exists in fixed factor $Z_i$.

2. Exactly *m* of the values $(x_1^0, x_2^0, \ldots, x_n^0, S_1^0, S_2^0, \ldots, S_m^0)$ will be positive and *n* will be zero. That is, the solution to the profit-maximization problem will contain *m* positive variables and *n* zero variables.[4] (Keep in mind that both the $x_i$'s and the $S_i$'s are "variables" in this problem.)

3. From property (2), we may conclude that if the number of products or potential products is larger than *m* (if $n > m$), then it will always be most profitable to drop *at least* $n - m$ of them. That is, it will never be profitable to produce more than *m* of the items in the product line. This conclusion results directly from the linearity of the model. If a linear technology combined with constant input and product prices are good assumptions, this conclusion must follow.

As an example of property (3), consider a firm with ten products in a product line which are being produced with a number of variable inputs and four fixed inputs. If the conditions underpinning the linear technology assumption hold, then profit maximization demands that *at least* six of the products in the line be dropped! The solution to the problem tells management which products utilize fixed facilities most profitably given current market and cost conditions (i.e, given $p_i^0$, $i = 1, 2, \ldots, n$). The point here is that specialization in four or fewer products will make most profitable use of fixed resources.

To see why property (3) must hold, imagine a manager who is trying to decide, sequentially, which of *n* products to produce. Since $p_i^0$, the profit per unit of $X_i$, is constant, profit maximization would lead the manager to choose as the first product that product with the highest unit profit. Production of that product would be expanded until capacity was reached in some fixed factor. Then the product with the second highest net revenue would be introduced. Of course this will most likely entail some cutback in the production of the first product. Production of the second product would be expanded until some other fixed factor was being used to capacity. At this point, two products are being produced and *at least* two fixed inputs are being used to capacity. The same reasoning limits the number of products in the line to no more than *m* if there are *m* fixed factors. This reasoning does not prevent all fixed inputs from being used to capacity before *m* products are being produced.

### A Graphical Solution

Up to this point, we have presented a rough overview of the optimal product mix problem. It is now time to take a closer and more concrete look.

[4]To be completely accurate, this statement should read, ". . . the solution will contain *at most m* positive variables . . ." But the case where the number of positive-valued variables is less than *m* is of so little practical importance we shall ignore it.

This is most readily accomplished by choosing a problem small enough to be solved graphically. To this end we rewrite the above problem for the case of two products and three fixed factors ($n = 2$ and $m = 3$). In this case, the problem is to choose $x_1$, $x_2$, $S_1$, $S_2$, and $S_3$ to

$$\text{maximize } \Pi = p_1^0 x_1 + p_2^0 x_2$$

subject to the conditions that

$$a_{11} x_1 + a_{12} x_2 + S_1 = \bar{z}_1$$
$$a_{21} x_1 + a_{22} x_2 + S_2 = \bar{z}_2$$
$$a_{31} x_1 + a_{32} x_2 + S_3 = \bar{z}_3$$

and

$$x_1, x_2, S_1, S_2, S_3 \geq 0$$

In Figure 5-1, the lines $a_{11} x_1 + a_{12} x_2 = \bar{z}_1$, $a_{21} x_1 + a_{22} x_2 = \bar{z}_2$ and $a_{31} x_1 + a_{32} x_2 = \bar{z}_3$ are graphed. Notice that these lines give the *maximum* amount of each of the fixed factors that could be used in producing $X_1$ and $X_2$.

**FIGURE 5-1**

The feasible region

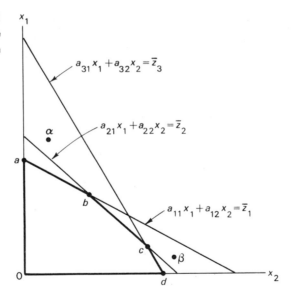

This follows from the fact that slack variables are zero in these equations. The region of $x_1 x_2$ space that satisfies each of the constraints, *the feasible region*, is the area bounded by the dark lines. In this region each of the constraints on fixed factor availability holds as do the constraints requiring production levels and slack variables to be positive or zero. Any point outside the feasible region fails to satisfy at least one of the constraints on the problem. Before proceding make sure you can explain why points like $\alpha$ and $\beta$ in Figure 5-1 are not in the feasible region. Which constraints are not satisfied at these points?

Referring to Figure 5-1 notice that there are five "corners" on the feasible region, the origin and the points labeled $a$, $b$, $c$, and $d$, and that *at each of these*

points exactly three (*the number of fixed factors*) *variables are positive.* For
example, examination of the point *a* indicates that $x_1 > 0$, $x_2 = 0$, $S_1 = 0$,
$S_2 > 0$, and $S_3 > 0$, since at *a* the first constraint holds as an equality ($S_1 = 0$)
and there is slack in the second and third constraint. In other words, point *a*
lies *inside* constraint two and three and *on* constraint one. At point *b*, $x_1 > 0$,
$x_2 > 0$, constraints one and two hold as equalities ($S_1 = 0$, $S_2 = 0$) and there
is slack in constraint three, $S_3 > 0$. At the origin $x_1 = x_2 = 0$, $S_1 > 0$, $S_2 > 0$,
and $S_3 > 0$, since there is slack in each fixed input. Similar findings hold at
points *c* and *d*. Now if the solution to the profit-maximization problem occurs
at a "corner" of the feasible region, then property (2) above has been verified
for the case at hand. Recall that property (2) stated that exactly *m* of the variables
(production levels and slack variables) would be positive in any solution. Here
$m = 3$, and at each corner exactly three variables are positive. We shall see that
profit can be no higher than at a corner of the feasible region.

To carry out our analysis of the profit-maximizing mixture of products, we
need the concept of an isoprofit function. An isoprofit function is a listing of all
combinations of $x_1$ and $x_2$, that is, all product mixes, which yield a constant level
of profit. More precisely, an *isoprofit function* is the set $\{(x_1, x_2) | p_1^0 x_1 + p_2^0 x_2$
$= \Pi^0$, where $\Pi^0$ is a constant level of profit. Four isoprofit functions have been
graphed in Figure 5-2. Obviously, $\Pi^0 < \Pi' < \Pi'' < \Pi^*$.

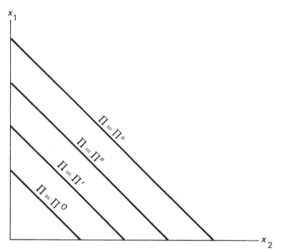

**FIGURE 5-2**
Isoprofit
functions

A graphical solution to the product mix problem may be obtained by combining Figures 5-1 and 5-2, thereby plotting fixed factor availability constraints
and isoprofit functions in one graph, as in Figure 5-3. Figure 5-3 contains all the
information needed to make the optimal product mix decision. In particular, both
relative profitability information and the capacity constraints imposed on the
firm's decision are represented. (Notice that the relative profitability of $X_1$
versus $X_2$ is given by the slope of the isoprofit function.) Geometrically speaking,
profit maximization implies moving to the highest profit level that is consistent
with capacity constraints. Clearly, *profits can be no higher than at a "corner"*

*of the feasible region*—a fact that greatly simplifies the search for a solution, since only "corners" need be considered.[5] In Figure 5-3, profits are maximum at corner $b$ and the optimal product mix is $(x_1^0, x_0^2)$. As we have noted, at this point exactly three ($m$) variables are positive and two ($n$) are zero. Specifically, $x_1^0 > 0$, $x_2^0 > 0$, $S_1^0 = 0$, $S_2^0 = 0$, and $S_3^0 > 0$ are the profit-maximizing levels of the five variables in the model. This result illustrates the principle stated above that the profit-maximizing solution to a problem with $n$ products and $m$ fixed factors would contain $m$ positively valued variables and $n$ zero valued variables.

**FIGURE 5-3**

Solution to the
optimal
product mix
problem with
two products
and three
fixed inputs

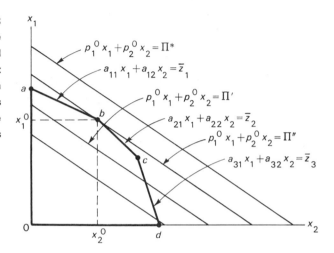

The solution to the problem tells us that both $X_1$ and $X_2$ are to be produced, $X_1$ at level $x_1^0$ and $X_2$ at level $x_2^0$. In addition, $S_1^0 = S_2^0 = 0$ indicates there are bottlenecks in $Z_1$ and $Z_2$. Both of these factors are being used to capacity. $S_3^0 > 0$ indicates excess capacity in $Z_3$.

Notice that increases in the price of the first product, $X_1$, will eventually lead the firm to specialize in the production and sale of $X_1$ (point $a$ in the figure).[6] The production plan at $a$ has a solution in which $x_1^0 > 0$, $x_2^0 = 0$, $S_1^0 = 0$, $S_2^0 > 0$, and $S_3^0 > 0$. Only one product is produced, and only one fixed factor is being utilized to capacity.

Although we have now answered most of the questions of interest to the firm, one problem remains unsolved: Is it worthwhile for the firm to expand (or decrease) capacities of the several fixed factors, if such is possible? Profit maximization implies that if the profit contribution were greater than the cost of expansion, the expansion would be undertaken. We shall see that this is precisely the information contained in the solution to a closely related problem called the *dual* of the profit-maximization programming problem. But first we present a numerical example illustrating the above discussion.

---

[5] If profits are negative at points $a$, $b$, $c$, and $d$, then the optimal "corner" is the origin and neither product is produced.

[6] Increases in $P_1^0$ cause isoprofit functions to be less steep, which will eventually cause point $a$ to be the optimal mix.

EXAMPLE. Consider a firm producing two products, $X_1$ and $X_2$, which sell for \$400 and \$600 each. Unit variable costs of producing these products are \$250 and \$375, respectively. In the present production period, three resources are in fixed supply—labor hours ($z_1$), machine time ($z_2$), and warehouse capacity ($z_3$). The values of these variables are $\bar{z}_1 = 1200$ hours, $\bar{z}_2 = 2100$ hours, and $\bar{z}_3 = 20{,}000$ cubic feet. Input requirements for $X_1$ and $X_2$ are

|  | Requirements for $X_1$ | Requirements for $X_2$ |
|---|---|---|
| Labor (hrs.) | 50 ($a_{11}$) | 20 ($a_{12}$) |
| Machine time (hrs.) | 70 ($a_{21}$) | 70 ($a_{22}$) |
| Warehouse space (cu. ft.) | 400 ($a_{31}$) | 800 ($a_{32}$) |

The profit-maximization problem is then

$$\max \Pi = \$(400 - 250)x_1 + \$(600 - 375)x_2$$

subject to the conditions that

$$50x_1 + 20x_2 \leq 1200$$
$$70x_1 + 70x_2 \leq 2100$$
$$400x_1 + 800x_2 \leq 20{,}000$$

and

$$x_1, x_2 \geq 0$$

As we know, the first constraint requires total hours of labor expended in producing $X_1$ and $X_2$ to be no greater than the amount of labor available in the production period. The second and third constraints are similar statements about machine time and warehouse capacity, respectively. The final constraint requires production of only positive or zero amounts of the two products. Adding slack variables to the problem we have

$$\max \Pi = \$150x_1 + \$225x_2$$

subject to the conditions that

$$50x_1 + 20x_2 + S_1 = 1200$$
$$70x_1 + 70x_2 + S_2 = 2100$$
$$400x_1 + 800x_2 + S_3 = 20{,}000$$

and

$$x_1, x_2, S_1, S_2, S_3 \geq 0$$

The problem as it stands cannot be solved, since a solution requires solving the constraint equations. In general there are an infinite number of solutions to these equations.[7] But recall that the solution to the product mix programming problem always occurs at a corner of the feasible region, and therefore the number of solutions is reduced to the number of corners. Hence one could calculate the solution at each corner and compare the profit levels generated by each solution. The corner yielding the highest profit is the optimal solution.[8]

To assist in our exposition of the solution, the problem has been graphed in Figure 5-4. We will begin at the origin and proceed to calculate the values of $x_1$, $x_2$, $S_1$, $S_2$, and $S_3$ and the level of profits at each corner.

**FIGURE 5-4**

The optimal product mix: an example

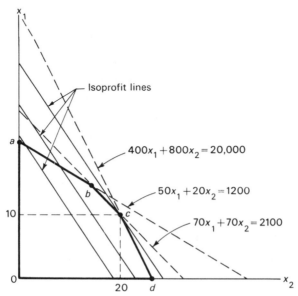

Isoprofit lines

$400x_1 + 800x_2 = 20{,}000$

$50x_1 + 20x_2 = 1200$

$70x_1 + 70x_2 = 2100$

At the origin   $x_1 = x_2 = 0$ and of course

$$\Pi = \$150(0) + \$225(0) = 0$$

Since $x_1 = x_2 = 0$ we have from the constraints

$$S_1 = 1200, \ S_2 = 2100, \ S_3 = 20{,}000$$

This is certainly to be expected, since $X_1$ and $X_2$ are not produced and hence each fixed input is completely slack.

At point $a$   Constraint one is binding, while constraints two and three are not. We therefore need only concern ourselves with the first constraint

$$50x_1 + 20x_2 + S_1 = 1200$$

Notice that at this point $S_1 = 0$ (constraint one is binding) and $x_2 = 0$. Therefore

$$50x_1 + 20(0) + 0 = 1200$$

and                                             $x_1 = 24$

[7]A system of linear equations with more variables than equations generally will have an infinite number of solutions. In our problem there are three equations and five variables.

[8]This method of solving the problem is not used in practice, since much more efficient methods are available.

Since neither constraint two nor constraint three is binding and $x_1 = 24$, $x_2 = 0$, we have

$$70(24) + 70(0) + S_2 = 2100$$

and

$$S_2 = 420$$

Also

$$400(24) + 800(0) + S_3 = 20{,}000$$

and

$$S_3 = 10{,}400$$

At this point both more labor and more warehouse space are available. The amounts are 420 hours and 10,400 cubic feet, respectively.

$$\Pi = \$150(24) + \$225(0) = \$3600$$

**At point b**  Constraints one and two are binding; therefore $S_1 = S_2 = 0$. We may ignore the third constraint, since it is not binding. Then

$$50x_1 + 20x_2 = 1200$$
$$70x_1 + 70x_2 = 2100$$

Multiplying the first equation by 7 and the second by 2 we have

$$350x_1 + 140x_2 = 8400$$
$$140x_1 + 140x_2 = 4200$$
$$\overline{\phantom{350x_1} 210x_1 \phantom{+ 140x_2} = 4200}$$

and

$$x_1 = 20$$

Substituting yields

$$70(20) + 70x_2 = 2100$$

and

$$x_2 = 10$$

To obtain $S_3$ we need merely write constraint three with the solution values of $x_1$ and $x_2$ inserted:

$$400(20) + 800(10) + S_3 = 20{,}000$$

and

$$S_3 = 4000$$

At this point labor and machine time are being used to capacity, but there are 4,000 cubic feet of excess warehouse capacity

$$\Pi = \$150(20) + \$225(10) = \$5250$$

**At point c**  Constraints two and three are binding, while constraint one is slack. Therefore $S_2 = S_3 = 0$ and

$$70x_1 + 70x_2 = 2100$$
$$400x_1 + 800x_2 = 20{,}000$$

The solution to these two equations is

$$x_1 = 10, \quad x_2 = 20$$

Using the first constraint

$$50(10) + 20(20) + S_1 = 1200$$
and
$$S_1 = 300$$

At this point machine time and warehouse space are being utilized to capacity while 300 hours of labor are still available.

$$\Pi = \$150(10) + \$225(20) = \$6000$$

At point $d$   Only the third constraint is binding, and hence $S_3 = 0$. Also $x_1 = 0$. Therefore

$$400(0) + 800x_2 = 20,000$$
and
$$x_2 = 25$$

$S_1$ and $S_2$ are obtained from the first two constraints:

$$50(0) + 20(25) + S_1 = 1200$$
and
$$S_1 = 700$$
Also
$$70(0) + 70(25) + S_2 = 2100$$
and
$$S_2 = 350$$

At this point neither labor nor machine time is fully utilized.

$$\Pi = \$150(0) + \$225(25) = \$5625$$

The results of our calculations are displayed in the following table:

Solution values
at "corners"

| Corner | $x_1$ | $x_2$ | $S_1$ | $S_2$ | $S_3$ | Profit |
|---|---|---|---|---|---|---|
| Origin | 0 | 0 | 1200 | 2100 | 20,000 | 0 |
| $a$ | 24 | 0 | 0 | 420 | 10,400 | $3600 |
| $b$ | 20 | 10 | 0 | 0 | 4,000 | $5250 |
| $c$ | 10 | 20 | 300 | 0 | 0 | $6000 |
| $d$ | 0 | 25 | 700 | 350 | 0 | $5625 |

The profit-maximizing product mix is then at corner $c$, where

$$x_1^0 = 10$$
$$x_2^0 = 20$$

This production plan yields more profit than any other plan, given the availability of labor, machine time, and warehouse space. Both machine time and warehouse space are being utilized to capacity, while more labor time is available (300 hours) than is needed.

Associated with every linear-programming problem is another problem that is the mathematical "negative" of the original problem. It is called the *dual-programming problem*. If the original problem is a maximization problem, then the dual is a minimization problem, symmetrical in all respects to the original problem. The word "dual" arises from the fact that mathematical-programming problems always appear in pairs. Convention has it that one is called the *primal* problem, the other the *dual* problem. Since one problem is implicit in the other, it matters not at all which problem is termed primal. We will, for convenience, call the profit-maximization problem the primal problem, and the related minimization problem the dual problem. Our discussion of the dual will be in terms of the minimization problem associated with the profit-maximization problem we have just analyzed. The best way to begin the discussion is to plunge in and write the dual to the profit-maximization problem.

The dual to the profit-maximization problem contains a new variable, $y_i$, which is the *imputed cost per unit* of fixed input $Z_i$, or the *shadow price of $Z_i$*, and will be discussed in some detail as we proceed. The objective in solving the dual problem is to find these imputed costs, or shadow prices. Keep in mind that imputed costs are associated with *fixed* inputs and it is the desire on the part of management to place a value on these inputs (i.e., to impute costs to them) that leads to this problem. Clearly, historical costs of machines, processes, or fixed inputs in general do not reflect their worth to the firm at a later date. So the whole rationale behind management's interest in the dual is the "costing" of the firm's fixed inputs. The solution to the dual problem imputes values, the $y_i$'s, to each of the fixed inputs, according to what these inputs are worth to a profit-maximizing firm.

For purposes of comparison, the primal is reproduced here and displayed alongside the dual.

| *Primal Problem* | *Dual Problem* |
|---|---|
| max $\Pi = p_1^0 x_1 + p_2^0 x_2$ | min $W = \bar{z}_1 y_1 + \bar{z}_2 y_2 + \bar{z}_3 y_3$ |
| subject to the conditions | subject to the conditions |
| $a_{11}x_1 + a_{12}x_2 \leq \bar{z}_1$ | $a_{11}y_1 + a_{21}y_2 + a_{31}y_3 \geq p_1^0$ |
| $a_{21}x_1 + a_{22}x_2 \leq \bar{z}_2$ | $a_{12}y_1 + a_{22}y_2 + a_{32}y_3 \geq p_2^0$ |
| $a_{31}x_1 + a_{32}x_2 \leq \bar{z}_3$ | $y_1 \geq 0, \ y_2 \geq 0, \ y_3 \geq 0$ |
| $x_1 \geq 0, \ x_2 \geq 0$ | |

Comparison of these two problems shows that the primal and the dual are related by the following operations: (i) interchange rows and columns of coefficients in the constraints—$a_{ij}$ in the primal is replaced by $a_{ji}$ in the dual; (ii) reverse the direction of the inequalities in the constraints—$\leq$ in the primal becomes $\geq$ in the dual; (iii) interchange the constants on the right in the constraints and the constants in the expressions to be maximized or minimized—the $\bar{z}_i$ from the primal go into the function $W$ in the dual, while the $p_i^0$ from the primal go to the right-hand side of the inequality constraints in the dual; and

(iv) reverse the direction of optimization—the primal is a maximization problem so the dual is a minimization problem.

Since the variable $y_i$ is defined as the imputed cost per unit or shadow price of fixed input $Z_i$, $\bar{z}_i y_i$ is the imputed cost associated with using $\bar{z}_i$ units of $Z_i$, that is, $\bar{z}_i y_i$ is the imputed cost of using input $Z_i$ to capacity. The objective in the dual problem is to choose the values of $y_1$, $y_2$, and $y_3$ such that *total imputed costs*, $\bar{z}_1 y_1 + \bar{z}_2 y_2 + \bar{z}_3 y_3$, $W$, are minimum. Of course this problem by itself is trivial, since choosing the $y_i$'s to be zero minimizes cost. But there are constraints on how the $y_i$'s may be chosen. To interpret these constraints, note that $a_{ij} y_i$ is the imputed cost of $Z_i$ per unit of $X_j$ produced. Therefore, $a_{1j} y_1 + a_{2j} y_2 + a_{3j} y_3$ is the imputed *unit* cost of $X_j$ in terms of the amount of $Z_1$ needed, plus the imputed unit cost of $X_j$ in terms of the $Z_2$ requirement, plus the imputed unit cost of $X_j$ in terms of the $Z_3$ requirement. The sum $a_{1j} y_1 + a_{2j} y_2 + a_{3j} y_3$ is then the *total* imputed cost of fixed factors *per unit* of $X_j$ produced.

The first constraint requires that the cost imputed to fixed factors, *per unit* of $X_1$ produced, be at least as large as the profit per unit of $X_1$ sold. The second constraint requires that the imputed cost of fixed factors used in the production of a unit of $X_2$ be at least as large as the profit per unit of $X_2$ sold. The final requirement is that imputed costs be nonnegative. Again, these costs are not known, and the objective of the dual problem is to determine the $y_i$ such that each of these conditions is met.

A legitimate question at this point is why the constraints in the dual problem require total imputed costs per unit, for each product, to be greater than or equal to the product's profit contribution per unit. To answer this question, note first that for any product that ends up being produced, profit maximization requires production to be pushed to the point where imputed costs per unit *equal* the profit contribution (if costs per unit of producing $X_i$ were less than $p_i^0$, then profits could be increased by increasing production of $X_i$). Second, for products that are not produced, it must be true that imputed costs per unit are *larger than* the unit profit contribution. So the equality in $a_{1j} y_1 + a_{2j} y_2 + a_{3j} y_3 \geq p_j^0$ must hold for products that are produced, and the strict inequality for those that are not produced.

Although interpretation of the dual is by no means as straightforward as that of the primal, some headway can be made. As has been stated repeatedly, the dual of the linear-programming problem we have been studying is concerned with determining the worth or value to the firm of each of its fixed resources. The criterion for valuation that is implicit in the dual of the profit-maximization problem is the contribution these fixed factors make to firm profits at the margin. More specifically, in the dual problem values are imputed to fixed factors $Z_1$, $Z_2$, and $Z_3$ ($y_1$, $y_2$, and $y_3$) according to what *the reduction in profit would be if less of these factors were available*. Alternatively, the solution to the dual tells the firm *the profit contribution that would be brought about by increasing the capacity of $Z_i$ beyond $\bar{z}_i$* and hence is the value[9] to the firm of increased availability of $Z_i$.

Imputed costs calculated in this manner represent the marginal value of

[9] Mathematically, the imputed value of, say, $Z_1$ is $\partial\Pi/\partial\bar{z}_1$, and in general $y_j = \partial\Pi/\partial\bar{z}_j$. Of course this is precisely what is stated in nonmathematical terms in the text.

$Z_i$ to the firm and are the appropriate "price" or basis for "costing" $Z_i$. After all, a profit-maximizing firm would like to "cost" fixed factors by their profit contributions, which *is* their value to the firm.

In summary, the solution to the dual program assigns values to each of the firm's fixed factors. For example, the value to the firm of $Z_1$ is given by the solution value of $y_1$ and is the profit contribution the firm would realize if the availability of fixed factor one were expanded by one unit (say, one hour). Clearly, this number is the correct "internal cost" for $Z_1$, since this is what $Z_i$ is worth to the firm at the margin. Likewise, it is evident that historical costs of these factors are of no use whatsoever in this context. The crucial consideration to a manager making the decision whether or not to expand the capacity of a fixed input is the profit generated by doing so.

### The Relationship Between Dual and Primal Solutions

As with the primal problem, solution of the dual requires that the inequality constraints be written as equalities. To do this, introduce the two nonnegative *surplus variables* $L_1$ and $L_2$ which, when subtracted from the constraints, convert them into equalities. Again, both the primal and the dual are presented to facilitate exposition.

| *Primal Problem* | *Dual Problem* |
|---|---|
| $\max \Pi = p_1^0 x_1 + p_2^0 x_2$ <br> subject to the conditions <br> $a_{11}x_1 + a_{12}x_2 + S_1 = \bar{z}_1$ <br> $a_{21}x_1 + a_{22}x_2 + S_2 = \bar{z}_2$ <br> $a_{31}x_1 + a_{32}x_2 + S_3 = \bar{z}_3$ <br> $x_1, x_2, S_1, S_2, S_3 \geq 0$ | $\min W = \bar{z}_1 y_1 + \bar{z}_2 y_2 + \bar{z}_3 y_3$ <br> subject to the conditions <br> $a_{11}y_1 + a_{21}y_2 + a_{31}y_3 - L_1 = p_1^0$ <br> $a_{12}y_1 + a_{22}y_2 + a_{32}y_3 - L_2 = p_2^0$ <br> $y_1, y_2, y_3, L_1, L_2 \geq 0$ |

We have emphasized that the primal and dual are symmetric problems, the "positive" and "negative" of the same print so to speak. To bring out this symmetry, call the solution to the dual the numbers $(y_1^0, y_2^0, y_3^0, L_1^0, L_2^0)$. The number $y_i^0$ is the imputed cost of the fixed input $Z_i$, and $L_i^0$ is the cost-minimizing value of surplus variable $L_i$. There is an intimate relationship between the solution of the primal $(x_1^0, x_2^0, S_1^0, S_2^0, S_3^0)$ and the solution of the dual $(y_1^0, y_2^0, y_3^0, L_1^0, L_2^0)$. To see this, one need only examine the dual and primal constraints to observe that

✓ 1. If $a_{1i}y_1^0 + a_{2i}y_2^0 + a_{3i}y_3^0 > p_i^0$, then $L_i^0 > 0$ and imputed unit costs of producing $X_i$ are greater than unit profits and $X_i$ will not be produced. Hence $L_i^0$ is the subsidy (per unit) that would be needed for $X_i$ to break even. In other words, $L_i^0 > 0$ implies $x_i^0 = 0$ ($X_i$ will not be produced). It also follows that $x_i^0 = 0$ implies $L_i^0 > 0$. (If $X_i$ is not produced, it is because $X_i$ does not make a positive contribution to profits.)

2. If $a_{1i}y_1^0 + a_{2i}y_2^0 + a_{3i}y_3^0 = p_i^0$, then $L_i^0 = 0$, no subsidy is needed, and $X_i$ is produced. That is, $L_i^0 = 0$ implies $x_i^0 > 0$. Also $x_i^0 > 0$ implies $L_i^0 = 0$. (Why?)

3. We interpreted $S_j^0 > 0$ as meaning that there was excess capacity (slack) in the fixed factor $Z_j$. But, if there is excess capacity in $Z_j$, the value to the firm (the imputed cost) of additional $Z_j$ is zero, since additional units of $Z_j$ would add nothing to profits. That is, $S_j^0 > 0$ implies $y_j^0 = 0$. Also, if $y_j^0 = 0$, then $Z_j$ must be in excess supply ($S_j^0 > 0$).

4. If a bottleneck exists in factor $Z_j$, we saw that $S_j^0 = 0$. But existence of a bottleneck means the factor is in short supply and therefore has *some* value to the firm. In other words, relieving the bottleneck will add *something* to profits. (Whether or not it will pay to eliminate the bottleneck depends on the cost of $Z_j$ relative to the magnitude of $y_j^0$.) In summary, $S_j^0 = 0$ implies $y_j^0 > 0$. Also, $y_j^0 > 0$ implies $S_j^0 = 0$.

5. Finally, we note one further property of the primal and dual of the linear-programming problem: The cost-minimizing value of $W$, say $W^0$, is equal to the profit-maximizing value of $\Pi$, $\Pi^0$. To interpret this condition, note that $\Pi$ is profit before allocations are made to cover fixed factors (overhead) and is that portion of revenue that is generated by the firm's fixed inputs. (Recall that the cost of variable inputs has been netted out.) Therefore, the condition $W^0 = \Pi^0$ tells us that the value of output generated by the firm's fixed inputs, $\Pi^0$, has been totally allocated to these inputs. In other words, the services of the fixed inputs have been costed so as to exhaust the value they have generated.

We have seen that the slack variables in the primal problem are intimately related to the imputed costs calculated in the dual, and that the surplus variables in the dual are intimately related to the profit-maximizing product mix determined in the primal. These relations may be shown schematically as follows:

Solution to primal:  $(x_1^0, x_2^0, S_1^0, S_2^0, S_3^0)$
$$\updownarrow \quad \updownarrow \quad \updownarrow \quad \updownarrow \quad \updownarrow$$
Solution to dual:  $(L_1^0, L_2^0, y_1^0, y_2^0, y_3^0)$

In the problem we solved graphically (Figure 5-3), $x_1^0 > 0$, $x_2^0 > 0$, $S_1^0 = 0$, $S_2^0 = 0$, and $S_3^0 > 0$. Therefore, if we solved the dual to this problem, we would find $L_1^0 = 0$, $L_2^0 = 0$, $y_1^0 > 0$, $y_2^0 > 0$, and $y_3^0 = 0$. From these calculations we know that the firm produces both $X_1$ and $X_2$, uses two fixed inputs $Z_1$ and $Z_2$ to capacity, and would be willing to pay up to $y_1^0$ and $y_2^0$ for each unit of expansion of these inputs. Fixed input $Z_3$ is not used to capacity, and the value to the firm of additional units of $Z_3$ is then $y_3^0 = 0$.

The relationship between the primal and the dual of a linear-programming problem is even closer than the discussion of the preceding paragraph indicates. In fact, the solution of the primal *contains* the solution of the dual, and vice versa. In particular, knowledge of the relationship between primal and dual variables permits use of the solution of the primal to directly calculate imputed costs (the value of dual variables). Or alternatively, the same knowledge permits use of the solution of the dual to directly calculate the optimal product mix (the value of primal variables). We now illustrate this important fact using the example presented in Figure 5-3.

The solution of the primal problem and its implications for the dual variables are

$$x_1^0 > 0 \Longrightarrow L_1^0 = 0$$
$$x_2^0 > 0 \Longrightarrow L_2^0 = 0$$
$$S_1^0 = 0 \Longrightarrow y_1^0 > 0$$
$$S_2^0 = 0 \Longrightarrow y_2^0 > 0$$
$$S_3^0 > 0 \Longrightarrow y_3^0 = 0$$

where the symbol $\Longrightarrow$ is read "implies."

we may write the dual constraints as

$$a_{11}y_1 + a_{21}y_2 = p_1^0$$
$$a_{12}y_1 + a_{22}y_2 = p_2^0$$
$$y_1 > 0 \text{ and } y_2 > 0$$

*The solution to these two equations is $y_1^0$ and $y_2^0$, the imputed costs of fixed inputs $Z_1$ and $Z_2$!* All that was needed to solve for these values is the solution to the primal and a knowledge of the relationship between primal and dual variables.

In a similar manner, if one knows the solution to the dual problem, the optimal product mix is readily determined. Let us use the dual of the same problem to illustrate. The relationship between the solution to the dual and the solution of the primal is

$$y_1^0 > 0 \Longrightarrow S_1^0 = 0$$
$$y_2^0 > 0 \Longrightarrow S_2^0 = 0$$
$$y_3^0 = 0 \Longrightarrow S_3^0 > 0$$
$$L_1^0 = 0 \Longrightarrow x_1^0 > 0$$
$$L_2^0 = 0 \Longrightarrow x_2^0 > 0$$

Since $y_3^0 = 0$ implies $S_3^0 > 0$, the third constraint in the primal problem is not binding and may be ignored. This follows from the fact that $y_3^0 = 0$ means that in the solution to the primal problem $Z_3$ is in excess capacity. Therefore we know that the constraint on availability of $Z_3$ is satisfied and hence may be ignored in our calculations. Also, $y_1^0 > 0$, $y_2^0 > 0$ means $S_1^0 = S_2^0 = 0$ and implies the constraints on the primal problem are

$$a_{11}x_1 + a_{12}x_2 = \bar{z}_1$$
$$a_{21}x_1 + a_{22}x_2 = \bar{z}_2$$
$$x_1 > 0 \text{ and } x_2 > 0$$

*The solution to these two equations is $x_1^0$ and $x_2^0$, the optimal product mix* shown in Figure 5-3!

In summary, the primal and dual of a linear-programming problem are merely different ways of viewing the same problem. The solution of the primal problem implies the solution of the dual, and similarly the solution of the dual problem implies the primal solution.

EXAMPLE.   To help clarify the relation between dual and primal solutions, we return to the numerical example used above (p. 117) to illustrate solution of the primal problem. Recall that the solution was $x_1^0 = 10$, $x_2^0 = 20$, $S_1^0 = 300$, $S_2^0 = S_3^0 = 0$, and $\Pi = \$6000$. From this information we may readily compute the solution to the dual problem. To actually calculate the value to the firm of increasing the capacity of fixed inputs, it is necessary to write the dual to this problem. Let us include the surplus variables and write the constraints as equalities.

$$\min W = 1200y_1 + 2100y_2 + 20{,}000y_3$$

subject to the conditions that

$$50y_1 + 70y_2 + 400y_3 - L_1 = 150$$
$$20y_1 + 70y_2 + 800y_3 - L_2 = 225$$

and

$$y_1, y_2, y_3, L_1, L_2 \geq 0$$

As we have noted, the solution to the primal problem is

$$x_1^0 = 10, \ x_2^0 = 20, \ S_1^0 = 300, \ S_2^0 = S_3^0 = 0$$

We have seen that

$$x_i^0 > 0 \Longrightarrow L_i^0 = 0$$
$$S_i^0 > 0 \Longrightarrow y_i^0 = 0$$
$$S_i^0 = 0 \Longrightarrow y_i^0 > 0$$

and therefore we know that $L_1^0 = L_2^0 = y_1^0 = 0$.

Using this information in the dual we may solve for $y_2^0$ and $y_3^0$. Evaluating the dual constraints yields

$$50(0) + 70y_2 + 400y_3 - 0 = 150$$
$$20(0) + 70y_2 + 800y_3 - 0 = 225$$

The solution to these two equations is

$$y_2^0 = \$1.07$$
$$y_3^0 = \$0.187$$

Of course $y_1^0 = 0$, since labor is in excess capacity and additional labor would add nothing to firm profitability. But the shadow price (imputed cost) of machine time is $1.07, which says that firm profits would increase $1.07 if one more hour of machine time were available. Analogously, an additional cubic foot of warehouse space is worth about $0.19. These calculations indicate that it is worthwhile to expand the available machine capacity if it can be done for $1.07 per hour or less, and warehouse space should be expanded if the cost of doing so is less than $0.19 per cubic foot. Just how much capacities should be increased requires further analysis and depends upon the labor time constraint. Finally, since $L_1^0 = L_2^0 = 0$, we know neither product requires a subsidy to break even.

### Postscript

Although one encounters no particular difficulties in solving small linear programs such as the one we have used as an example, problems encountered in practice are usually quite large. Solving a problem with $n$ products in the product line entails solving a set of $n$ equations in $n$ variables at each corner of the feasible region. And in a realistic problem there are often millions of corners. Obviously such problems are much too complex to be solved in the manner used above. However, a very efficient rule for searching for the optimal solution, called the *simplex algorithm*, has been designed. When this algorithm is incorporated into a computer program it is usually possible to solve both primal and dual problems in a matter of seconds.

## INPUT-OUTPUT ANALYSIS

In 1970 an article in the *Wall Street Journal* noted that fifty major U.S. corporations were using input-output analysis to generate industry sales forecasts, up from "... just a handful three or four years ago. In a couple of years, companies using I-O (input-output) could easily number 500."[10] Due to the growing importance of input-output analysis as a method of forecasting industry demand, we now examine the input-output model with the purpose of delineating underlying assumptions and assessing forecasting capabilities.

To begin, let us consider an economy with a linear technology and a given set of input and output prices. In this context, we take "linear technology" to mean that each industry in the economy experiences constant returns to scale and that productivity in any one industry does not materially influence productivity in any other industry. (This is analogous to the assumption of process independence.) More precisely, this latter requirement stipulates that the *production level* of any one industry does not enter the *production function* of any other industry. Under these conditions, it is possible to answer the following very interesting question: Given the factor requirements per unit of output in each industry and an estimate of *final* demand for each product, what should the production level of each industry be if *all* demands are to be met?

To understand the significance of this capability, keep in mind that total demand for an industry's output is derived from two distinct sources: The first consists of other industries that buy the output for use in some production process, the output of one industry being a factor of production in other industries. The second group of buyers consists of those that buy an output for "final" use or consumption, that is, not for use in a production process. Demands of this type are termed *final* (consumer) demands, while the former are termed *intermediate* (industry) demands. Now, given the technology of each industry in the economy and an estimate of *final* demand for each industry's output, the input-output model provides a means of calculating the production levels in each industry in the economy needed to meet all intermediate and final demands. For any single industry the calculated production rate is an estimate of total industry demand at the going price—an estimate that fully accounts for the interrelatedness of industries in a modern economy.

Before proceeding, it is well to point out that demand estimates generated using I-O analysis differ significantly from such estimates obtained by estimating demand functions. In the first place, demand estimates generated using I-O are estimates of *industry* demands and hence are not firm specific. Second, I-O demand estimates are not estimates of industry demand *functions* but rather are estimates of *one point* on each industry demand function—that point associated with current prices. (Remember, one of the assumptions of the I-O model is

[10] *Wall Street Journal*, February 17, 1970.

that prices are taken as given.) Nonetheless, used either in conjunction with traditional demand estimation procedures as a means of cross-checking predictions, or alone as a technique for forecasting industry demand, I-O analysis provides a fairly simple way of generating industry demand forecasts under different assumptions about market conditions.

Since the input-output model of the economy was developed by Professor Leontief over thirty years ago, one might wonder why it took so long for the business community to pick up such a potentially useful tool. The answer is simple. Determining the production levels of every industry in the economy so that all demands (household demands plus business demands) are met is an extraordinarily difficult task. Although the theoretical model was worked out over thirty years ago, it is only recently that machine-computing capabilities have been sufficient to actually solve large realistic problems. The reason this problem is so difficult is that industries in a modern economy are inextricably interdependent. The output of one industry is an input in another, while the output of the second industry is the input in still other industries. For example, the output of the steel industry is an input in the automobile, aircraft, construction, computer, and numerous other industries. At the same time, the output of most of these latter industries are inputs in the former. In the words of the *Wall Street Journal*, when discussing Union Carbide's input-output model:

> When a Carbide economist asks the effect of a drop in auto production on steel [demand], the I-O system does much more than merely calculate the reduced steel requirements of the auto industry. It assumes also that less textiles will be used in auto upholstery, that less chemicals will be used to process textiles, and that less glass will be used in auto windows and headlights. And, it then calculates the reduced steel requirements of the textile, chemical and glass industries into the steel production forecast, accomplishing all this within seconds.[11]

The result is an estimate of the change in steel demand due to a change in the steel needs of the automobile industry which is brought about by a decrease in the demand for automobiles. This estimate takes into account the decreased steel needs of all other industries in the economy which is brought about by the fall in automobile demand.

**The Input-Output Model**

In this section we define the various components of the I-O model. This formalization is necessary to get the model into a form that is machine solvable. To this end consider an $n$ industry economy and define

$a_{ij} \equiv$ the number of dollars' worth of commodity $X_i$ needed to produce one dollar's worth of commodity $X_j$, $i, j = 1, 2, 3, \ldots, n$

$x_i \equiv$ the number of dollars' worth of commodity $X_i$ produced

$d_i \equiv$ household demand (in dollars) for $X_i$

$a_{0j} \equiv$ the number of dollars' worth of labor needed to produce one dollar's worth of commodity $X_j$

[11]Ibid.

The production function for industry $s$ is then $(a_{0s}, a_{1s}, a_{2s}, \ldots, a_{ns})$, a point in $n + 1$ dimensional space, just as $(a_{1s}, a_{2s})$ is a point in two-dimensional space. This point is the production function for industry $s$ because it represents the input requirement for producing one dollar's worth of $X_s$, and due to constant returns to scale, the input requirement for any other output level can be calculated from this basic input requirement. In other words, the input combination $(ka_{0s}, ka_{1s}, \ldots, ka_{ns})$ will yield $k$ dollars' worth of $X_s$ for any $k > 0$, and hence given $(a_{0s}, a_{1s}, \ldots, a_{ns})$, we know the relationship between inputs and all possible outputs in industry $s$. That is, we know the production function for industry $s$.

Arranging the *nonlabor* input requirements of all industries into columns and grouping, we get the *technology matrix* of the economy:

$$A = \begin{bmatrix} a_{11}a_{12} & \cdots & a_{1n} \\ a_{21}a_{22} & \cdots & a_{2n} \\ \cdot & \cdot & \cdot \\ \cdot & \cdot & \cdot \\ \cdot & \cdot & \cdot \\ a_{n1}a_{n2} & \cdots & a_{nn} \end{bmatrix}$$

Each *column* of matrix $A$ is a production function for a particular industry exclusive of the industry's labor requirement. Of course in practice a number of the $a_{ij}$'s will be zero, since few industries use the output of all other industries as inputs.

The problem of interest in this model is the calculation of industry production levels that would be sufficient to meet all business and household demands. To see how this is done, note that $a_{ij}x_j$ is the *total input requirement of industry j for commodity $X_i$* and is the number of dollars' worth of $X_i$ needed to produce $x_j$ units of $X_j$. Therefore, if production of $X_i$ is to meet both intermediate and final demands, the following equation must hold for industry $i$:

$$x_i = a_{i1}x_1 + a_{i2}x_2 + a_{i3}x_3 + \cdots + a_{in}x_n + d_i, \qquad i = 1, 2, \ldots, n \qquad (5\text{-}1)$$

This equation says that the production of $X_i$ must equal the sum of the amounts of $X_i$ demanded by each of the $n$ industries *plus* final demands, $d_i$. Equations (5-1) are $n$ equations in $n$ unknowns whose solution, $x_1^0, x_2^0, \ldots, x_n^0$, is the production level in each industry that is necessary to meet all demands.

### Setting Up the Problem for Solution

As we have noted, equations (5-1) are a system of $n$ equations in $n$ unknowns —the production levels needed to meet all demands. To solve these equations, notice that the first equation in (5-1) has $x_1$ on the left-hand side and $a_{11}x_1$ on the right-hand side, while the second equation has $x_2$ on the left-hand side and the term $a_{22}x_2$ on the right-hand side. A similar statement holds for each of the other equations. Now if we bring all terms containing $x_i$ to the left-hand side of equation $i$ and collect similar terms, we have

$$
\begin{aligned}
(1 - a_{11})x_1 - \quad\; & a_{12}x_2 - \cdots && -a_{1n}x_n = d_1 \\
-a_{21}x_1 + (1 - a_{22})x_2 - \;\; & \cdots && -a_{2n}x_n = d_2 \\
-a_{31}x_1 - \quad\; & a_{32}x_2 - \cdots && -a_{3n}x_n = d_3 \\
\phantom{.} & \phantom{.} && \phantom{.} \\
-a_{n1}x_1 - \quad\; & a_{n2}x_2 - \cdots && +(1 - a_{nn})x_n = d_n
\end{aligned}
\tag{5-2}
$$

These equations are the mathematical equivalent of the requirement that production levels in each industry be sufficient to meet intermediate plus final demands.

In general, it is possible to solve very large sets of linear equations, like equations (5-2), with the aid of modern electronic computers.[12] But any old solution to (5-2) will not do. To see what additional requirements must be imposed upon industry production levels, recall that we denoted the production levels that satisfy (5-2) as $x_1^0, x_2^0, \ldots, x_n^0$. Obviously, each of these production levels must be nonnegative. In addition, the labor requirement for all industries combined must be no greater than the amount of labor available. Calling $\bar{x}_0$ the total amount of labor (in dollars) available in the economy, these two conditions may be written as[13]

$$
x_i^0 \geq 0,\ i = 1,2,\ldots, n,\ \text{and}\ \sum_{i=1}^{n} a_{0i}x_i^0 \leq \bar{x}_0
\tag{5-2'}
$$

Equations (5-2) and (5-2') completely specify the input-output problem.

As the problem now stands, the major obstacle confronting a firm preparing to use I-O for forecasting is how to calculate the elements of the technology matrix $\mathbf{A}$, the $a_{ij}$'s. In an $n$ industry economy there will be $n^2$ of these coefficients to calculate. So even in a "small" model of a one-hundred-industry economy, there are ten thousand of these input-output coefficients to calculate. Fortunately for prospective users of this technique, in 1970 the Department of Commerce finished a $1.25 million data-gathering effort and produced a set of estimated I-O coefficients which are available to business in either printed or magnetic-tape form. The coefficients have been estimated for 370 industrial sectors. In other words, the technology matrix contains 136,900 entries ($370^2$), and equations (5-2) are 370 equations in 370 unknown industry production levels.

**Solving for Industry Production Levels**

To investigate the general solution to equations (5-2) and (5-3) in any detail, the student must be familiar with the techniques of matrix algebra. A second-best approach, which we will follow here, is to examine rather carefully

[12]Although the matter will not be pursued here, the input-output model may be viewed as a linear-programming problem.

[13]In practice, it is often desirable to be more specific about the labor variable. This can be accomplished by disaggregating $\bar{x}_0$ into the various types of labor used in an economy.

a small I-O model and use it to indicate the properties of the general model. We will use the case of a two-industry economy for this purpose ($n = 2$). Clearly, such a model is hopelessly unrealistic, but the properties we will be discussing hold for a model of any size. The model is then

$$(1 - a_{11})x_1 - \qquad a_{12}x_2 = d_1$$
$$-a_{21}x_1 + (1 - a_{22})x_2 = d_2$$

(5-3)

subject to the conditions that

$$x_1^0, x_2^0 \geq 0 \quad \text{and} \quad \sum_{i=1}^{2} a_{0i}x_i^0 \leq \bar{x}_0$$

(5-3')

We now solve equations (5-3) keeping in mind that in any given application the constants $a_{ij}$ are given, although typically one does not specify the value of final demand, the $d_i$'s. Not specifying the elements $d_i$ makes the solution of the I-O problem a function of the final demands and hence allows one to generate the required production levels associated with different assumptions about final demands.

The solution to equations (5-3) is then [14]

$$x_1^0 = \frac{(1 - a_{22})d_1 + a_{12}d_2}{(1 - a_{11})(1 - a_{22}) - a_{12}a_{21}}$$

$$x_2^0 = \frac{a_{21}d_1 + (1 - a_{11})d_2}{(1 - a_{11})(1 - a_{22}) - a_{12}a_{21}}$$

(5-4)

Equations (5-4) give the production levels required in each industry to meet intermediate plus final demands for each output. As we noted above, in any given application the technological coefficients are given and production levels are a function of the unspecified levels of final demand for the various commodities, the $d_i$'s. A solution of this type is quite flexible, as it permits the required production levels to be calculated using a number of different assumptions about the level and composition of final demands.

To illustrate our discussion, consider the estimation problem confronting firms in the domestic steel industry when a decrease in tariffs on foreign-produced automobiles is proposed. A tariff reduction would lead to decreased sales of domestically produced automobiles, which in turn would have direct and indirect effects on the steel industry (and of course on numerous other industries in the economy). Firms in the steel industry would be most interested in estimating the effect on steel sales of the proposed tariff reduction. One possible way of attacking this estimation problem is to solve the I-O model for steel production requirements, using the two most extreme assumptions about the effect of the tariff change on automobile sales. That is, if we call $x_s$ the production level in the steel industry needed to meet total demand and let $d_a$ represent the final demand for domestically produced automobiles, then the problem posed

---

[14]Equations (5-3) may be solved by multiplying the first equation by $a_{21}$ and the second by $(1 - a_{11})$. Adding yields $x_2^0$ as given in (5-4). Substitution of $x_2^0$ into either the first or the second equation of (5-3) yields $x_1^0$.

consists of calculating $x_s$ once for the lowest reasonable value of $d_a$ and once for the highest reasonable value of $d_a$. This procedure generates two values of $x_s^0$, an upper and a lower bound on the level of steel demand.

It is worth emphasizing once more that calculations of the type described in the preceding paragraph are formidable without the I-O technique. Modern economies are highly interdependent, and demand changes in any one industry induce long chains of direct and indirect effects in other industries, which eventually further change the level of demand in the first industry. Any attempt to account for such a high degree of interdependence is doomed to failure without the I-O model or its equivalent.

### The Responsiveness of Production Requirements to Changes in Final Demands

One other calculation is of considerable interest to managers using input-output analysis for prediction purposes. This calculation concerns the response of production levels in one industry due to a shift in final demand in some other industry. This situation arises, for example, if management of firms in the steel industry decide to assess the effect on steel production of a decline in the final demand for automobiles. If an input-output model is available, such a calculation is straightforward.

To see this, note that the solutions to the general I-O model, equations (5-2) above, are linear functions of the values of final demands in each of the industries in the economy, just as $x_1^0$ and $x_2^0$ in our two-industry example are linear functions of $d_1$ and $d_2$. Mathematically, the calculation we have been discussing amounts to nothing more than calculating the partial derivative of the solution for industry, say, $s$, with respect to a change in, say, $d_a$, that is, $\partial x_s^0/\partial d_a$. Again, referring to our two-industry example (equations (5-4)), we see that

$$\partial x_1^0/\partial d_2 = \frac{a_{12}}{(1 - a_{11})(1 - a_{22}) - a_{12}a_{21}} \tag{5-5}$$

and

$$\partial x_2^0/\partial d_1 = \frac{a_{21}}{(1 - a_{11})(1 - a_{22}) - a_{12}a_{21}} \tag{5-5'}$$

These equations illustrate an important principle: *The response of production in any one industry due to a change in demand in any other industry depends upon the magnitude of each of the coefficients in the technology matrix.* In a general model with $n$ industries the same principle obtains. Also note that these derivatives are a function only of the technological coefficients, the $a_{ij}$'s. So if a firm had the "Commerce" estimates, the derivatives would require no additional information.

### Limitations of Input-Output Analysis

Our discussion up to this point should have given the reader some feeling for the power of I-O analysis in solving an immensely complex problem. In fact, a good deal of this "power" derives from the assumption that the economy

in question is characterized by a linear technology. Some of the implications of
this assumption are rather strong and are made explicit in this section.

Two of the assumptions implicit in the required *linear economy* are most troublesome. First, as we know, it is necessary to assume that all industries in the economy are subject to constant returns to scale. There is no doubt that this assumption is violated in practice, the question is whether deviations from constant returns to scale are significant enough to preclude use of the model. Current evidence would seem to indicate that at the industry level of aggregation, the assumption probably is not too damaging.

The second restriction implicit in the linear technology assumption is that all inputs are employed in rigidly fixed proportions. In other words, industry production functions allow only one way of producing industry output (since production coefficients are a set of fixed constants for all production levels). If one method of production is used at some output rate, the same method must be used at all other output rates. Whether this assumption is relatively harmless or does significant violence to the results obtained from the model is still being debated. One thing is certain, the assumption is probably never completely true.

Finally, we note one further assumption: Each industry is assumed to produce but one, homogeneous product (our $X_i$'s)—there are no joint products. This restriction usually is not too bothersome, since it can be relaxed to some extent by interpreting each industry's output as a composite commodity composed of numerous items produced in fixed proportions.

Our discussion of input-output analysis has necessarily been quite sketchy due to the somewhat more advanced level of mathematics needed to present a thorough analysis. Hopefully, we have provided enough detail to indicate the potential of this model in the area of demand forecasting. To provide a bit more concreteness to our discussion, we next present a rather detailed example.

EXAMPLE. About the largest model we can handle without more specialized tools is a model of a three-industry (sector) economy. So, for purposes of illustration, consider the following technology matrix:

$$\mathbf{A} = \begin{bmatrix} 0 & .5 & .4 \\ .2 & .1 & .4 \\ .3 & .2 & 0 \end{bmatrix}$$

Let us calculate the production levels in industries one, two, and three that will be required to meet \$20, \$30, and \$60 million final demands, respectively, for the outputs of these industries. Using equations (5-2) and the technology matrix, we may write the conditions that industry production levels must satisfy:

$$\begin{aligned} x_1 - .5x_2 - .4x_3 &= d_1 \\ -.2x_1 + .9x_2 - .4x_3 &= d_2 \\ -.3x_1 - .2x_2 + x_3 &= d_3 \end{aligned} \qquad (5\text{-}6)$$

Notice that although $d_1$, $d_2$, and $d_3$ are given, we will not use specific values until we have calculated $x_1^0$, $x_2^0$, and $x_3^0$. At that point it is a simple matter to plug in 20, 30, and 60 for these parameters.

It is a trifle laborious to solve even three linear equations without the appropriate tools, but let's get started. We may begin by solving the first equation in (5-6) for $x_1$, which gives

$$x_1 = d_1 + .5x_2 + .4x_3 \qquad (5\text{-}7)$$

Next, eliminate $x_1$ from equations two and three by substituting for $x_1$ using (5-7). This yields

$$\begin{aligned} .8x_2 - .48x_3 &= d_2 + .2d_1 \\ -.35x_2 + .88x_3 &= d_3 + .3d_1 \end{aligned} \qquad (5\text{-}8)$$

Now, solve the first equation of (5-8) for $x_2$, which yields

$$x_2 = .6x_3 + .25d_1 + 1.25d_2 \qquad (5\text{-}9)$$

Here $x_2$ is a function of only one unknown, $x_3$. We may now use this equation to eliminate the variable $x_2$ from the second equation in (5-8). This is done by substituting (5-9) into the second equation of (5-8), which results in

$$x_3^0 = .58d_1 + .65d_2 + 1.49d_3 \qquad (5\text{-}10)$$

This is the value of $x_3$ required to meet all demands. To calculate $x_2^0$, substitute $x_3^0$ into (5-9), which gives

$$\begin{aligned} x_2^0 &= .6x_3^0 + .25d_1 + 1.25d_2 \\ &= .60d_1 + 1.64d_2 + .89d_3 \end{aligned} \qquad (5\text{-}11)$$

Finally, substitute $x_2^0$ and $x_3^0$ into (5-7) to get

$$\begin{aligned} x_1^0 &= d_1 + .5x_2^0 + .4x_3^0 \\ &= 1.53d_1 + 1.08d_2 + 1.04d_3 \end{aligned} \qquad (5\text{-}12)$$

If projected levels of final demand are \$20, \$30, and \$60 million respectively, industry production rates needed to meet these demands *plus* intermediate demands may be calculated from equations (5-10), (5-11), and (5-12):

$$\begin{aligned} x_3^0 &= \$120.5 \text{ million} && (5\text{-}10') \\ x_2^0 &= \$114.6 \text{ million} && (5\text{-}11') \\ x_1^0 &= \$125.4 \text{ million} && (5\text{-}12') \end{aligned}$$

Comparing final demands ($d_1$, $d_2$, and $d_3$) with industry production rates (equations (5-10'), (5-11'), and (5-12')), we see that about 50 percent of the production of industry three is purchased by other industries, about 74 percent of the production of industry two, and about 84 percent of the output of industry one is used by other industries.

One interesting question remains: How do industry production quotas respond to changes in the level of final demands? As we have seen, the answer to this question is obtained by differentiating the general solutions, equations (5-10), (5-11), and (5-12), with respect to the final demands of interest. If we postulate a change in final demand for the output of industry three, we have

$$\partial x_1^o / \partial d_3 = 1.04$$
$$\partial x_2^o / \partial d_3 = .89$$
$$\partial x_3^o / \partial d_3 = 1.49$$

as the changes in the production rates of industries one, two, and three that will be required if all demands are to be met. These are the required production responses *per $1 million change in $d_3$*. We see, for example, that the demand for $X_1$ will increase $1.04 million for every million dollar increase in final demand for $X_3$. Interpret the other two derivatives.

1. Because of the ease with which very large cost-minimization problems can be solved, it is often tempting to assume that the firm's production problem can be adequately represented by a linear program. Under what conditions can the linear-programming production model be used?

**PROBLEMS AND QUESTIONS**

2. Referring to the optimal product mix example (pp. 117–20) in the text, answer the following questions:

a. If the profit contribution of $X_2$ should rise to $325, what is the optimal product mix? What is additional warehouse capacity worth to the firm? Additional labor? Machine capacity? What is the optimal value of the surplus variable $L_1$? Interpret.

b. If the variable cost of producing $X_2$ should fall to $300 per unit, what is the optimal product mix?

3. The Jurard Machine Shop produces two items which, for convenience, we will call $X_1$ and $X_2$. Production of a single unit of $X_1$ requires 1.5 hours of lathe time, 2 hours of milling, 3.5 hours of assembly time, and 5 cubic feet of storage space. Each unit of $X_2$ requires 1 hour of milling, 3 hours of assembly time, and 9 cubic feet of storage space. ($X_2$ requires no lathe time.) Jurard has 30,000 hours of lathe capacity, 50,000 hours of milling machine capacity, 120,000 hours of assembly time capacity, and 300,000 cubic feet of usable storage space in the current production period. At current market prices and under current cost conditions the profit contributions of both $X_1$ and $X_2$ are $350 per unit.

a. What are the profit-maximizing levels of production?

b. Calculate and interpret the marginal profit contribution of *additional* lathe capacity, milling capacity, assembly capacity, and storage capacity.

c. How much excess capacity exists in lathe and milling machine capabilities?

d. Assume that management is reasonably confident that the price of $X_1$ is "firm" into the foreseeable future but that the price of $X_2$ is "soft." Also assume that Jurard has the opportunity to buy additional lathes at a very good price but does not want to unless there is a strong possibility of a shortage of lathe capacity. To help reach a decision on whether or not to purchase the lathes, the operations research department is asked to calculate how low the profit contribution of $X_2$ will have to fall before current lathe capacity would be inadequate. Based upon this calculation, management will decide how likely a shortage of lathe capacity is and will then use this judgment to reach a decision concerning the lathes. How far will the profit contribution of $X_2$ have to fall before current lathe capacity is exhausted?

e.  Given the present production technology and capacity constraints, would it be possible for Jurard to specialize in the production and sale of $X_1$? Under what conditions would specialization in the production of $X_2$ be called for?

f.  At the original profit contributions of $350 for both $X_1$ and $X_2$, what realignment of the product mix is called for if the profit contribution of $X_1$ should rise to $425? Explain.

g.  Jurard's production capabilities depend upon one fixed production facility other than the lathing, milling, assembly, and storage facilities we listed above. This facility is a small foundry where certain metal components are cast. The maximum amount of foundry time available in a production period is 30,000 hours. If it takes one-half hour of foundry time per unit of $X_1$ produced and one-half hour per unit of $X_2$, can you find a legitimate reason why the constraint imposed by this fixed facility was not included in the problem you have solved?

4.  Consider a firm that produces two products, $X_1$ and $X_2$, with three fixed resources, $Z_1, Z_2,$ and $Z_3$. The profit contribution is $20 per unit of $X_1$ sold and $25 per unit of $X_2$ sold. Production of $X_1$ requires 10 units of $Z_1$, 15 units of $Z_2$, and no $Z_3$ per unit, while $X_2$ requires no $Z_1$, 10 units of $Z_2$, and 30 units of $Z_3$ per unit produced. $Z_1, Z_2,$ and $Z_3$ are available in amounts of 5,000, 9,000, and 12,000, respectively.

a.  Find the profit-maximizing product mix.

b.  Are there any bottlenecks in the production process?

c.  What is it worth to the firm to increase the capacity of each of the fixed resources?

d.  How much would the price of $X_1$ have to rise before the product mix would be changed?

5.  Imagine that you are an economist in a centrally planned economy. The industries in the economy have been aggregated into three large industrial sectors, and the technology matrix has been estimated to be

$$A = \begin{bmatrix} 0 & .2 & 0 \\ .5 & .7 & .2 \\ 0 & 0 & .5 \end{bmatrix}$$

All production coefficients are in dollars' worth of commodity $i$ needed to produce one dollar's worth of commodity $j$. In addition, combined government and household demands have been estimated to be $2, $1, and $5 billion for outputs one, two, and three, respectively. Your problem is twofold:

a.  Determine the number of dollars' worth of outputs one, two, and three that should be produced if intermediate and final demands are to be met.

b.  Calculate expressions for the response in production rates which will be needed to meet a change in final demand for commodity three. How much of an increase in output will be required in sector one if government demand for the output of sector three increases by $2.5 billion?

# The Costs
# of Production

In this chapter we will investigate portions of the theory of cost that are especially useful for managerial decision making. We begin by deriving cost functions from their theoretical underpinnings, an approach that displays in the clearest possible manner the assumptions upon which this important constituent of optimal managerial decision making rests. After cost functions are derived, several topics concerned with estimation of these functions are discussed. Generally cost functions may be estimated in one of two ways: either by directly estimating the relationship between cost and the production rate or by estimating the firm's production function and then deriving the implied cost function. Both methods are discussed.

### Efficient Input Use: The Expansion Path of the Firm

Up to this point, one particular type of problem has been investigated: The firm was assumed to have chosen an output rate (for example, an order for $x^0$ units was received) which it desired to produce at minimum cost.[1] The solution to this problem was demonstrated under different assumptions about the firm's production technology and the availability of resources. But the manager's decision problem is often more complicated than this, since, in general, the production rate of the firm is not given and a decision must be made as to the "best" production and sales rates. The "best" rate will depend jointly upon (i) the goals of the firm, (ii) the costs of production, and (iii) the demand conditions in the market for the firm's product or products. The problem of determining the "best" sales and production rates is most conveniently analyzed when cost is expressed as a function of the production rate.

[1] The one exception to this statement is the optimal product mix problem we investigated in the preceding chapter.

The first step in deriving the relation between cost and the production rate is to define the locus of efficient production plans, which is called the expansion path of the firm:

> **The Expansion Path of the Firm**—the locus of efficient production plans corresponding to all possible production rates. Symbolically, the firm's expansion path is given by the set $\{(v_1, v_2) \mid RTS_{12} = w_2^0/w_1^0$, for all possible $x\}$.

The expansion path for a firm with a "smooth" production function is shown in Figure 6-1.

**FIGURE 6-1**

The expansion
path:
differentiable
production
function

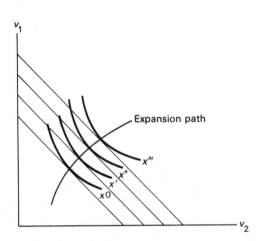

Expansion path

### Calculation of the Expansion Path—An Example

To illustrate calculation of the firm's expansion path, recall the example used above of a shop employing skilled labor, $V_2$, and unskilled labor, $V_1$, in the production of some product $X$. The production function was $x = 20v_1v_2 - 2v_1^2 - v_2^2$, and $v_1$ and $v_2$ were measured in hours. The wages of skilled and unskilled labor were given as \$8 and \$4 per hour, respectively. By definition, the expansion path is the collection of efficient production plans associated with all feasible production rates. Efficient production plans are those input combinations that satisfy $RTS_{12} = w_2^0/w_1^0$. Therefore the expansion path for the shop is given by

$$\frac{20v_1 - 2v_2}{20v_2 - 4v_1} = \$8/\$4, \text{ or}$$

$$v_1 = 1.5v_2 \tag{6-1}$$

The relation $v_1 = 1.5v_2$ is the optimal input proportion and holds for an arbitrary output. To calculate the amount of $V_1$ and $V_2$ needed to produce $x$ units most efficiently, substitute the equation of the expansion path into the production function, which yields

$$x = 20(1.5v_2)v_2 - 2(1.5v_2)^2 - v_2^2$$
$$= 24.5v_2^2$$

Notice that the calculations we have done here are precisely what we did above when we first solved the firm's cost-minimization problem for an order size of 1,000 units, except that here we have solved the problem for an arbitrary production rate, $x$. The expressions $x = 24.5v_2^2$ and $v_1 = 1.5v_2$ yield the amount of $V_1$ and $V_2$ needed to produce $x$ units most efficiently, *given* wages are \$4 and \$8 an hour and *given* the particular production technology implied by the production function $x = 20v_1v_2 - 2v_1^2 - v_2^2$. Several points on the firm's expansion path are tabulated in Table 6-1. We will return to this example later

| Production Rate, $x$ (output/unit time) | Most Efficient Input Combination | |
|---|---|---|
| | $v_1$ (thousands of hrs. of unskilled labor) | $v_2$ (thousands of hrs. of skilled labor) |
| 612.5 | 7.5 | 5.0 |
| 1000.0 | 9.6 | 6.4 |
| 2450.0 | 15.0 | 10.0 |
| 3528.0 | 18.0 | 12.0 |
| 5512.5 | 22.5 | 15.0 |
| 9800.0 | 30.0 | 20.0 |

in the chapter and calculate cost as a function of the production rate for this shop.

### Deriving Production Cost Functions

Once the firm's expansion path has been obtained, production cost functions follow immediately. In Figure 6-2 the cost of producing several different

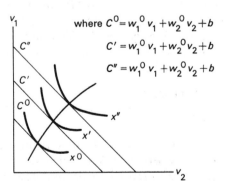

**FIGURE 6-2**

Deriving the production cost function

outputs as efficiently as possible are listed. The cost of producing $x^0$ is $C^0$, the cost of $x'$ is $C'$, and the cost of $x''$ is $C''$. These points are the minimum costs of producing these outputs. The collection of all pairs of cost and output points so obtained constitute the firm's production cost function. The points $(x^0, C^0)$, $(x', C')$, and $(x'', C'')$ are plotted in Figure 6-3. As we mentioned previously,

**FIGURE 6-3**

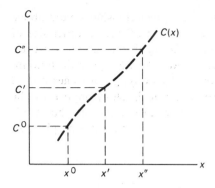

the set of all such points would yield $C(x)$, the positively sloped curve shown in Figure 6-3.

A number of comments are in order: First, our derivation of the cost function makes it clear that production cost functions depend jointly upon (i) input costs (as given in $C^0$, $C'$, and $C''$), (ii) the firm's production function (as given by the isoquant map), and (iii) the efficient behavior of decision makers. (Only input combinations along the expansion path enter the calculations.) Second, since only one set of factor prices and one production function (one set of isoquants) are used in the derivation of $C(x)$, both input costs and the firm's production technology are parameters in the cost function, $C = C(x)$. To make this explicit, let $\tau$ represent the technology of the firm as given by its production function and $\tau^0$ denote a *given* production technology. Then, the production cost function we have derived is $C = C(x, w_1^0, w_2^0, \tau^0)$, where $w_1^0$, $w_2^0$, and $\tau^0$ are the conditions under which the cost function was derived. That is, $w_1^0$, $w_2^0$, and $\tau^0$ are parameters in the firm's cost function. Third, since $C(x)$ is based upon efficient input decisions, if input decisions are not efficient, then the function relating cost to output will be everywhere above $C(x)$. Finally, the "shape" given to the cost function in Figure 6-3 was arbitrary. The only requirement at this point is that $C(x)$ be positively sloped. (Do you see why this must be so?) Shortly, we will determine the conditions under which $C(x)$ will rise at a decreasing, a constant, or an increasing rate.

## SHORT-RUN COST FUNCTIONS (OPERATING COST FUNCTIONS)

Operating cost functions express the relation between costs and output in decision periods within which at least one factor is fixed and hence are often called *short-run cost functions*. The extent to which factors are fixed depends upon two things, the length of the decision period and the degree of specialization of the factors under the firm's control. Highly specialized factors have few alternative uses and are therefore difficult, if not impossible, to liquidate. As far as firm decisions are concerned, factors of this type are fixed factors for their productive lifetimes. Nonspecialized factors (which are by definition factors used by many firms) are often easy to liquidate through resale markets

**140**

and hence may be classified as variable factors even in relatively short decision periods.

In a discussion of firm decision making, it is useful to establish the categories of *variable costs*, *fixed costs*, and *marginal* or *incremental costs*. We will use $D(x)$ to represent costs that vary with the production rate, *variable costs*. Costs that are fixed with respect to the production rate will be denoted by the letter $b$, *fixed costs*. *Total costs*, $C(x)$, are then the sum of variable and fixed cost components:

$$C(x) = D(x) + b$$

If $b \neq 0$, then at least one factor is fixed and $C(x)$ is *short-run total cost*.

*Marginal* (*incremental*) *cost* is the change in total cost brought about by a change in the production rate. If $C(x)$ is differentiable, marginal cost is either $dC(x)/dx$ or $dD(x)/dx$, since fixed costs do not vary with the output rate. Marginal cost is the slope of either the total or the variable cost function. Geometrically, $C(x)$ and $D(x)$ are parallel at every value of $x$. If $C(x)$ is not differentiable, marginal costs are $\Delta C/\Delta x$ or $\Delta D/\Delta x$.

One other cost category will be used—average or unit costs. *Average total costs* are by definition

$$\frac{C(x)}{x} = \frac{D(x)}{x} + b/x$$

Average total cost is equal to *average variable cost* plus *average fixed costs*.

Figure 6-4 shows the relationship between the various cost functions when the total cost function is a cubic equation. Average total costs at output $x$ may be read off the total cost function as the slope of a ray to $C(x)$ at the point $x$. Average total cost is minimum where this slope is minimum (point $x^0$ in the figure). An analogous statement holds for the average variable cost function except that the ray must originate at $b$, thereby excluding fixed costs. (Average variable costs are minimum at $x'$). Marginal cost is minimum at the inflection point in $C(x)$ (point $x^*$ in the figure), since total costs increase at a decreasing rate before the inflection point and increase at an increasing rate after the inflection point. In addition, marginal cost must cut average variable and average total costs at their minimum points, since, if marginal cost is below an average cost function, average costs must be falling; if marginal cost equals average cost, then average cost must be constant; and if marginal is above average, average must be rising. The average fixed cost function declines continuously in the production rate and, mathematically, is a rectangular hyperbola.

### The "Shape" of Short-Run Cost Functions

We saw above that one of the determinants of the firm's cost function was its production function. We now examine this relation more closely. We are interested in the relationship between cost functions and productivity functions and especially in whether we can draw any conclusions about the "shape" of cost functions from our knowledge of productivity functions. To begin, consider a firm that uses but two factors of production and whose decision period is

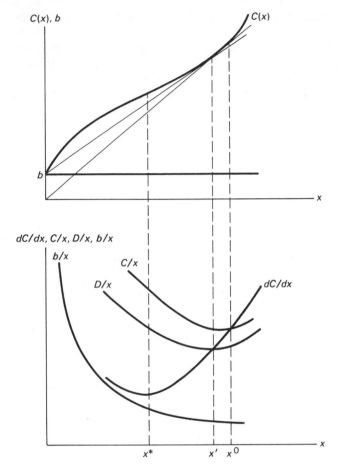

FIGURE 6-4
Relationships
between cost
functions

$C(x), b$

$C(x)$

$b$

$x$

$dC/dx, C/x, D/x, b/x$

$b/x$

$C/x$

$D/x$

$dC/dx$

$x$

$x^*$  $x'$  $x^0$

short enough that one of the factors is fixed. Under these circumstances, the firm's production function in the short run is $f(v_1, v_2^0)$, with $v_2^0$ being the fixed amount of $V_2$ available in the period. Total costs written as a function of input prices are $C = w_1^0 v_1 + w_2^0 v_2^0$ or $C = w_1^0 v_1 + b$, where $b \equiv w_2^0 v_2^0$. Using this relationship we now calculate marginal, average variable and average total costs as a function of $x$, the production rate. Differentiating $C$ yields

$$\frac{dC}{dx} = w_1^0 \frac{dv_1}{dx} = w_1^0 \left(\frac{1}{MP_1}\right)$$

where $dv_1/dx$ is the reciprocal of the marginal product function for $V_1$. Since $D = w_1^0 v_1$, average variable costs are

$$\frac{D}{x} = \frac{w_1^0 v_1}{x} = w_1^0 \left(\frac{1}{AP_1}\right)$$

where $v_1/x$ is the reciprocal of the average product function for $V_1$. Finally,

$$\frac{C}{x} = \frac{w_1^0 v_1 + b}{x} = w_1^0 \left(\frac{1}{AP_1}\right) + b/x$$

These three expressions clearly indicate the relationship between productivity and costs: *Productivity functions and production cost functions are inversely related.* Let us first take a look at the marginal cost function. We see that marginal production cost is the mirror image of the marginal productivity of the variable factor. If marginal product is rising, marginal cost is falling. If marginal product is maximum, then marginal cost is minimum, and if marginal productivity is falling, marginal cost must be rising. By the "law of diminishing returns" we know that marginal productivity must eventually decline in any production function in which there is at least one fixed factor. We may then conclude that *in the short run, marginal production costs must rise*, a situation implicit in the notion of capacity. Although this principle is both simple and intuitive, it has been responsible on numerous occasions for drastic differences between expected profits and actual profits.

Since average variable costs and average productivity of the variable factor are also inversely related, falling average productivity would imply increasing unit variable costs. But falling marginal productivity, as implied by "diminishing returns," must eventually mean falling average productivity. Hence the "law of diminishing returns" implies that *short-run average variable costs must rise*. Finally, we would expect average total costs to fall, level off, and then rise in the presence of fixed factors. This expectation is based on the fact that average fixed costs are "large" at low production rates and will dominate average variable costs, but as the production rate is increased, $b/x$ falls, and as we have seen, unit variable costs must rise eventually dominating "overhead charges" which are being spread over an increasing number of units. A combination of falling unit overhead charges and "diminishing returns" is then seen to be responsible for the customary $U$-shape given to short-run average total cost functions.

### Cost Functions For Firms With Linear Technologies

The expansion path of a firm with linear technology is shown in Figure 6-5 as the heavy line. This line is the ray that represents the cost-minimizing process (process II) for the given set of input prices, $w_1^0$, $w_2^0$. Not only is the expansion path linear, but a linear technology also means there are constant

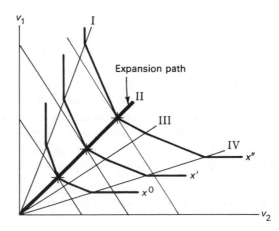

**FIGURE 6-5**
The expansion
path of a firm
with a linear
technology

returns to scale in each process. To see the cost implications of a linear technology, let $(v_1^0, v_2^0)$ be the input requirement for producing $x^0$ in process II when input prices are $w_1^0$ and $w_2^0$. The variable cost of producing $x^0$ is then $D^0 = w_1^0 v_1^0 + w_2^0 v_2^0$. Constant returns to scale implies that "running" the process at level $k$, $(kv_1^0, kv_2^0)$, produces $kx^0$ units of output, for any $k > 0$. Therefore, the variable costs associated with operating process II at level $k$ are $w_1^0(kv_1^0) + w_2^0(kv_2^0) = kD^0$. A $k$-fold increase in output is accompanied by $k$-fold increases in variable costs, that is, *variable costs are proportional to the production level in linear technologies.* If variable costs are proportional to output, $D(x) = \bar{a}x$ (where $\bar{a}$ is the factor of proportionality), and average variable costs and marginal costs are each constant and equal to $\bar{a}$. Since total cost is variable cost plus fixed cost, $C(x) = \bar{a}x + b$ and total cost is linear in the production rate. Average total cost must then be everywhere falling and approaching average variable cost, $\bar{a}$, in the limit. Each of these cost functions is shown in Figure 6-6.

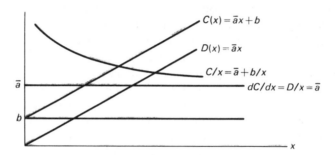

**FIGURE 6-6**

Production cost functions for a firm with a linear technology

If the factor of proportionality $\bar{a}$ were known, all of the firm's cost functions could be written immediately. And, of course, $\bar{a}$ is known. If $D^0$ is the total variable cost of operating the optimal process at the unit level $(x^0)$, then $D^0/x^0$ is equal to $\bar{a}$. So, for firms with linear technologies, once the cost of operating the optimal process at the unit level is calculated, *all* of the firm's production cost functions are known. No sophisticated estimation techniques are needed.[2]

Implicit in the derivation of these cost functions is the assumption that it is possible to continually increase the level of process utilization. In other words, there are no limitational factors in any process. In the short run, this is of course not possible, and diminishing returns must eventually set in against fixed factors. The result of diminishing factor returns, as we have seen, is rising average and marginal cost functions. Therefore, the cost functions pictured in Figure 6-6 must be thought of as being applicable only at production rates where plant capacity is not being pressed. In the following example we investigate the effects of capacity limitations on a firm's cost functions.

EXAMPLE.   Consider a firm that utilizes two factors, $V_1$ and $V_2$, to produce some product $X$. Assume that these factors cost \$7 and \$12 per hour, respectively, and that the conditions underpinning the "linear technology" production

---

[2]Keep in mind that the parameter $\bar{a}$ depends upon a given set of input prices and a given production technology and way of "doing things."

model are valid. The input requirements and corresponding outputs in each

of the four available processes are given by

| Process | $v_1$ | $v_2$ | $x$ |
|---------|-------|-------|-----|
| I       | 160   | 40    | 500 |
| II      | 135   | 45    | 500 |
| III     | 95    | 65    | 500 |
| IV      | 55    | 105   | 500 |

It is easy to see that rates of technical substitution between processes I and II, II and III, and III and IV are 5, 2, and 1, respectively. Since $w_2^0/w_1^0 = \$12/\$7 = 1.71$, the decision rule developed in Chapter 4 implies that process III is the most efficient process. It follows that the ray from the origin of $v_1v_2$ space with slope 95/65 is the expansion path for the given input costs. Of course this line is the ray that graphically defines process III.

Since a linear technology has been postulated, we know that variable costs are proportional to $x$ and that only the factor of proportionality $\bar{a}$ is needed to determine all of the firm's cost functions. But $\bar{a}$ is merely average variable cost, so the only calculation needed is $D/x$ for the efficient process. $D(500) = \$7(95) + \$12(65) = \$1445$ is the variable cost of producing 500 units, and $D(500)/500 = 2.89 = \bar{a}$. The firm's cost functions are then

$$D(x) = 2.89x$$
$$C(x) = 2.89x + b$$
$$dC/dx = 2.89, \text{ etc.}$$

Now, let us ask a further question. How would cost functions "behave" if only 130 hours of $V_2$ were available in the current production period? To answer this question we must first calculate the firm's expansion path and then the cost of production at various production rates along the expansion path.

The firm's expansion path is shown as a dark line in Figure 6-7. Up to a

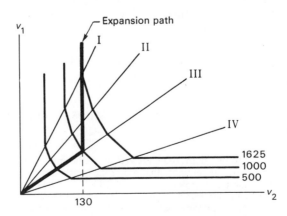

FIGURE 6-7

The expansion path for a firm with a linear technology and a capacity constraint on factor two

production rate of 1,000 units the expansion path, as before, is merely the ray representing process III, the optimal process. At $x = 1000$ the constraint on $V_2$ availability becomes binding, and the expansion path proceeds along the line $v_2 = 130$ as shown. For production rates greater than 1,000 units, the firm can do no better than use all of the $V_2$ available in combination with less efficient processes (processes which are less $V_2$ intensive). The higher is the production rate, the more will the firm be forced to use more costly combinations of processes. This can be easily seen in Figure 6-7 from the fact that as the production rate increases the firm is forced to use combinations of processes ever further from "pure" process III, which is the most efficient process *if* more hours of $V_2$ were available.

Let us now derive the variable cost function, $D(x)$. First of all we know that

$$D(x) = 2.89x \qquad x \leq 1000 \qquad \text{(a)}$$

since the constraint on $V_2$ is not binding until 1,000 units are being produced. Do you see why? Probably the easiest method of calculating the remaining portions of $D(x)$ is to compute costs at a number of different points along the expansion path and then deduce the behavior of $D(x)$ from these points.

Let us start by calculating the cost of producing 1,100 units. A glance at Figure 6-7 shows that the most efficient manner of producing an order of this size is to use some combination of processes II and III.[3] Exactly which combination can be found by noting that (1) on the firm's expansion path all of the available $V_2$ will be used, and (2) the total production forthcoming from both processes must be 1,100 units (2.2 times the unit level of 500 units). Actually what we must find here is $k_2$ and $k_3$, the level of utilization of processes II and III such that the two conditions we just stated hold. These conditions may be written

$$45k_2 + 65k_3 = 130$$
$$k_2 + k_3 = 2.2$$

and merely say that $k_2$ and $k_3$ must be chosen so that the total amount of $V_2$ used is 130 units (the production plan must be on the expansion path) and that the combined utilization level of processes II and III is 2.2 (i.e., 1,100 units are produced). Solving these equations yields $k_2 = .65$ and $k_3 = 1.55$. The total amount of $V_2$ used is 130 units, and the total amount of $V_1$ used is given by $.65(135) + 1.55(95) = 235$ units. This is the amount of $V_1$ used when process II is utilized at level .65 and process III is utilized at level 1.55. Variable costs are then

$$\begin{aligned} D(1100) &= \$7(235) + \$12(130), \quad k_2 = .65 \\ &= \$3205 \qquad\qquad\qquad\quad k_3 = 1.55 \end{aligned} \qquad \text{(b)}$$

---

[3]To see that 1,100 units are most efficiently produced in some combination of processes II and III, merely note that along the expansion path, a production plan using pure process II would utilize process II at level $130/45 = 2.889$ (the availability of $V_2$ divided by the unit level $V_2$ requirement in process II). Therefore, $2.889 \times 500 = 1,444$ would be produced in this plan—implying that 1,100 units would be produced using a combination of processes II and III.

Similar calculations show

$$D(1200) = \$7(280) + \$12(130), \quad k_2 = 1.3 \qquad \text{(c)}$$
$$= \$3520 \qquad\qquad\qquad k_3 = 1.1$$

$$D(1300) = \$7(325) + \$12(130), \quad k_2 = 1.95 \qquad \text{(d)}$$
$$= \$3835 \qquad\qquad\qquad k_3 = .65$$

$$D(1400) = \$7(370) + \$12(130), \quad k_2 = 2.6 \qquad \text{(e)}$$
$$= \$4150 \qquad\qquad\qquad k_3 = .2$$

As you have probably noticed, the efficient production plan requires increasingly heavy utilization of process II and diminishing use of process III as the production rate increases. For production rates greater than 1,444 units (approximately), combinations of processes *I and II* must be used. To see this, divide the $V_2$ requirement of process II into the available $V_2$, $130/45 = 2.889$. This tells us that if process II were used alone at level 2.889 ($k_2 = 2.889$, $k_3 = 0$), all available $V_2$ would be depleted. At level 2.889, process II turns out $2.889(500) = 1444$ units of output. In terms of cost, what we have just stated is

$$D(1444) = \$7(390) + \$12(130), \quad k_2 = 2.889 \qquad \text{(f)}$$
$$= \$4290 \qquad\qquad\qquad k_3 = 0$$

Higher production rates require combining processes II and I. To find the most efficient manner of producing, say, 1,500 units, we must ensure that between processes I and II all 130 units of $V_2$ are used and that the combined level of use is 3(1,500 units). These requirements may be written as

$$40k_1 + 45k_2 = 130$$
$$k_1 + k_2 = 3$$

The solution to these equations is $k_1 = 1$, $k_2 = 2$. This plan uses 130 units of $V_2$ and $1(160) + 2(135) = 430$ units of $V_1$. Variable costs are then

$$D(1500) = \$7(430) + \$12(130), \quad k_1 = 1 \qquad \text{(g)}$$
$$= \$4570 \qquad\qquad\qquad k_2 = 2$$

The cost of a production rate of 1,600 units is

$$D(1600) = \$7(502) + \$12(130), \quad k_1 = 2.8 \qquad \text{(h)}$$
$$= \$5074 \qquad\qquad\qquad k_2 = .4$$

It is impossible to produce more than 1,625 units with the given availability of $V_2$. (Before reading on be sure you understand why this is so.)

By looking over cases (a)–(h) we see that marginal costs are constant until the production rate reaches 1,000. To get a clear idea of the behavior of firm cost functions after $x = 1,000$, we need only calculate marginal costs, $\Delta D(x)/\Delta x$, for $x > 1,000$. For production rates between 1,000 and 1,100 units marginal costs are

$$\frac{D(1100) - D(1000)}{1100 - 1000} = \$3.15$$

and remain $3.15 for each of the following increments:

$$\frac{D(1200) - D(1100)}{1200 - 1100} = \frac{\$3520 - \$3205}{100} = \$3.15$$

$$\frac{D(1300) - D(1200)}{1300 - 1200} = \frac{\$3835 - \$3520}{100} = \$3.15$$

$$\frac{D(1400) - D(1300)}{1400 - 1300} = \frac{\$4150 - \$3835}{100} = \$3.15$$

Now recall that at a production rate of 1,444 units process III could no longer be used, higher output rates must be produced by utilizing processes I and II. For this reason we calculate marginal costs between 1,400 and 1,444 units and then between 1,444 and 1,500 units. The idea here is to check to see if marginal costs change as the firm is forced to change from production plans utilizing combinations of processes II and III to plans utilizing combinations of processes I and II.

$$\frac{D(1444) - D(1400)}{1444 - 1400} = \frac{\$4290 - \$4150}{44} = \$3.15[4]$$

$$\frac{D(1500) - D(1444)}{1500 - 1444} = \frac{\$4570 - \$4290}{56} = \$5.04[5]$$

Marginal costs increase 60 percent as it becomes necessary to use combinations of processes I and II instead of II and III! The next calculation will allow us to infer the behavior of the entire marginal cost function.

$$\frac{D(1600) - D(1500)}{1600 - 1500} = \frac{\$5074 - \$4570}{100} = \$5.04$$

Marginal costs are constant at $5.04. We now see a familiar pattern emerging which may be stated as the following general principle:

> Marginal costs are *constant* for all production plans that are a combination of any two given processes. Production plans that utilize combinations of any other pair of processes are associated with different levels of marginal costs.

In our example, marginal costs are constant at all production rates utilizing combinations of processes II and III ($3.15) and at all production rates that utilize combinations of processes I and II ($5.04). Since marginal costs are constant between adjacent processes, we may conclude $D(x)$ is linear in these regions with slope equal to marginal costs.

Total variable and marginal cost functions for the cases where there is no capacity constraint on $V_2$ and where only 130 hours of $V_2$ are available are graphed as Figures 6-8 and 6-9 for purposes of comparison.

If there are no capacity constraints, $D(x)$ is a ray from the origin with slope 2.89, and marginal and average variable costs are constant and equal to $2.89.

---

[4]Due to rounding error this calculation is not exactly $3.15. But if decimal places are carried incremental costs are $3.15.

[5]If decimal places are carried, incremental costs are $5.04 as we show.

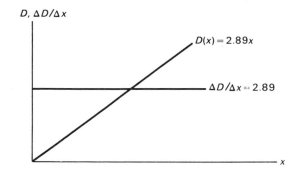

D, ΔD/Δx

$D(x) = 2.89x$

$ΔD/Δx = 2.89$

x

**FIGURE 6-8**
Total variable
and marginal
cost functions:
no capacity
constraints

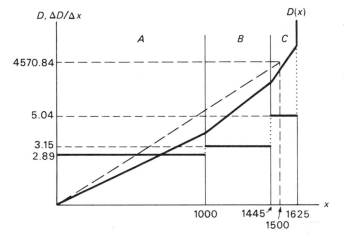

D, ΔD/Δx

A

B

C

D(x)

4570.84

5.04

3.15
2.89

1000   1445   1625
       1500

x

**FIGURE 6-9**
Total variable
and marginal
cost functions:
$v_2 \leq 130$

But as soon as a bottleneck is experienced in any factor, marginal costs must rise. Since increasing marginal costs are due to falling marginal productivity (see p. 142), we see that capacity limitations on any resource imply the law of diminishing returns is operative. In Figure 6-9 the total variable cost function is piecewise linear with increasing slope, since the marginal cost function is an increasing step function.[6]

From our discussion it is a simple matter to write an expression for the firm's marginal cost function. Specifically,

$$\frac{\Delta D(x)}{\Delta x} = \begin{cases} \$2.89, x \leq 1,000 \\ \$3.15, 1,000 < x \leq 1,444 \\ \$5.04, 1,444 < x \leq 1,625 \end{cases}$$

Can the same be done for the total variable cost function $D(x)$? The answer is yes, if we are careful. To this end note first that $D(x) = 2.89x$ for $x \leq 1,000$. Second, note that $D(x)$ is $3.15x$ for production rates *between* 1,000 units and 1,444 units *plus* the costs of producing 1,000 units ($2.89 \times 1,000 = \$2,890$). Therefore, $D(x) = 2,890 + 3.15(x - 1,000)$ for $1,000 < x \leq 1,444$.[7] Finally,

[6]Of course, Figure 6-8 is a special case of Figure 6-9 for production rates of less than 1,000 units.

[7]1,000 must be subtracted from x so that the cost of $3.15 per unit is charged only to the number of units produced in excess of 1,000 since the $2,890 charge accounts for $x \leq 1,000$.

an analogous argument, using the fact that $D(1,444) = \$4,288.60$, allows us to write $D(x) = 4,288.60 + 5.04(x - 1,444)$ for $1,444 < x \le 1,625$. In summary

$$D(x) = \begin{cases} 2.89x, \ x \le 1,000 \\ 2,890 + 3.15(x - 1,000), \ 1,000 < x \le 1,444 \\ 4,288.60 + 5.04(x - 1,444), \ 1,444 < x \le 1,625 \end{cases}$$

In Figure 6-9 average variable costs are given by the slope of a ray through the origin to a point on $D(x)$. For example, the slope of the ray at $x = 1500$ (the broken line) is $D(1500)/1500 = \$3.05$ and is the variable cost per unit of producing 1,500 units. Notice that unlike marginal costs, after a production rate of 1,000 units is reached average variable costs will increase continuously between processes, since the slope of the ray continuously increases. Also we see that beginning at a production rate of 1,000 units, the slope of the ray to any point on $D(x)$ is less than the slope of $D(x)$ at that point. Therefore average variable costs are equal to marginal costs until $x = 1000$, after which average variable costs lie beneath marginal costs—the increasing marginal costs pulling up average variable costs. The regions labeled $A$, $B$, and $C$ represent respectively, production regions in which process III alone is used, processes III and II are used in varying combinations, and finally a region where processes I and II are used in varying combinations.

## LONG-RUN COST FUNCTIONS

Managerial decisions are constrained in the short run to choices that are available with the given production technology. And short-run cost functions are used for making day-to-day operating decisions within this given technological framework. But there is some decision period long enough that the firm will have no fixed commitments and will be free to choose many aspects of future production processes under which it will operate. The cost functions associated with this decision period are called long-run cost functions. Since all inputs are variable inputs in the long run, there is no distinction between variable costs and total costs. Hence we need consider only one cost function, the long-run average cost function—all others are derivable from it. In addition, we should emphasize at this point that for decision purposes, the collection of resources and production processes we commonly call "plant" are completely characterized by the set of cost curves associated with the plant. Because all short-run cost functions are derivable from the short-run average total cost function, we will represent a given plant by the associated average total cost function.

### Long-Run Average Cost

Short-run cost curves are derived under the assumption that management consciously and successfully utilizes *existing* plant and equipment in a cost-minimizing manner. So, short-run, say, average cost functions give the *minimum* unit costs of all outputs that are possible in a *given* plant. As we saw above, if inputs are not used as efficiently as possible, the firm's actual cost functions will lie everywhere above those we have derived. Analogously, long-run cost curves are the set of minimum unit cost points when "plant" is also a variable factor. That is, if one plotted the minimum unit costs of production over the entire range of output that is technically possible given the state of technology within an industry, the result would be the firm's long-run average cost function. In other words, a long-run average cost curve is a "list" of minimum unit production costs when all technical possibilities (plants) open to the firm are considered.

The long-run average cost function for a firm that has only three plant possibilities is shown as the heavy scalloped line in Figure 6-10. The curves

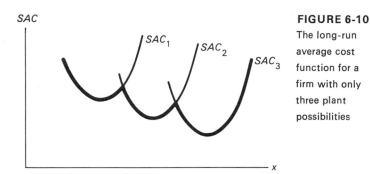

labeled $SAC_1$, $SAC_2$, and $SAC_3$ are the short-run average total cost functions associated with the three plants. One point should be emphasized. The plant represented by the cost function $SAC_3$ may not be the "best" of the three plants from the firm's point of view. Which plant is optimal will depend upon the goals of the firm and the nature of the demand for $X$. Even if the firm's goal is profit maximization, this plant may not be optimal. We will return to this point later.

### ★ Cost Curves and Uncertain Production Rates: A Digression

A related question that emphasizes a different aspect of the dictum that "plants with lowest unit costs are not necessarily optimal" is depicted in Figure 6-11. Plant 1 utilizes highly specialized equipment and achieves very low unit

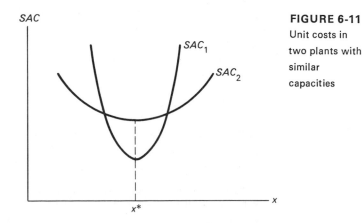

**FIGURE 6-11**

Unit costs in two plants with similar capacities

costs within a limited range. Outside of this range, unit costs rise rapidly. On the other hand, plant 2 is less specialized, and consequently costs are less sensitive to changes in the production rate. Is it better to specialize with a chance of experiencing very low production costs, or is it better to "play it safe" and pay the higher unit costs? The answer is the same as before: Both the goals of the firm and the nature of product demand are needed to answer this question.[8]

In somewhat more detail, the answer will depend first upon the decision maker's preference for risk and the strength of these preferences. Roughly, if two investments yield the same expected (average) returns but the variability of returns is significantly greater in investment one than in investment two, then a *risk averse* decision maker will tend to choose investment two, while a *risk preferring* decision maker will tend to choose investment one. The fact that the investment with the more variable returns could lead to significantly higher returns (and consequently significantly higher losses) is appealing to a decision maker who prefers risk and unappealing to a risk averse decision maker. If expected returns and not the riskiness of returns is all that matters, then the decision maker is said to be *risk neutral*. A risk neutral manager will choose that plant that yields highest *average* returns. The fact that there is "a lot of variability" in returns has no effect on a risk neutral decision maker's choice of plant. All that matters is that returns on the average are higher in one plant than in another.

Risk averse managers *tend* to "insure" expected returns by taking less risky actions, while managers who have a preference for risk *tend* to gamble with expected returns in the hope of higher returns. Notice that the word "tend" was emphasized both times it was used in the preceding sentence. This was done to indicate that the behavior noted is only a tendency and that there are unit costs low enough with high enough probability to make a risk averse manager gamble on plant 1, and there are losses high enough with a high enough probability that a manager with a preference for risk would choose plant 2.

This brings us to the second determinant of the optimal plant, the characteristics of product demand. What determines the probability of those "low enough" unit costs and "high enough" losses we spoke of above? The dispersion or variability of demand—the more variance, the more likely is a period of high or low demand. Industries whose products have high-income elasticities of demand, for example, find their sales strongly influenced by the business cycle and hence rather volatile. On the other hand, industries producing products with low-income elasticities of demand, often experience more stable patterns of demand.

### The Envelope Curve

Figure 6-10 showed the long-run average cost function for a firm with three possible plants. Generally, a firm will have a choice of many production technologies, and in the limit there will be an infinite number of alternative plants.

[8]The word *capacity* (see Figure 6-11) is used by different authors to mean different things. We use *capacity* to mean the point of minimum costs.

The long-run average cost function for this situation is shown in Figure 6-12 and is called the *envelope* of the short-run curves. Notice that the most efficient plant for any output level will usually not be a plant in which short-run average costs are at a minimum. For example, the lowest cost of producing $x^*$ is attained in the plant labeled with two asterisks in the figure, while "unit costs are being minimized" in the plant labeled with the single asterisk. The point here is that the words "minimum cost" may be interpreted in several ways, and hence care should be exercised in their use.

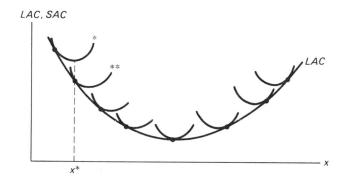

Notice that the long-run average cost function does not exist apart from the short-run curves and is defined as being that portion of each short-run curve that is most efficient relative to all other plant possibilities. This means that every point on the long-run curve corresponds to a point on *some* short-run curve—each of which is a possible choice for the firm's optimal plant. The eight plants shown in Figure 6-12 generate eight points on the long-run average cost function. The long-run unit cost function is often called the firm's *planning curve*, since the unit costs of all plant possibilities are represented along it.

### Returns to Scale

At the time the idea of returns to scale was first introduced, we stated that there existed a close relationship between the measure of returns to scale, $\varepsilon$, and the firm's cost functions. It is now time to investigate this relationship.

Recall that $\varepsilon$ measures the response of output to an equal percentage change in the use of *all* inputs and that in Chapter 3 we showed that

$$\varepsilon = \varepsilon_1 + \varepsilon_2$$

where $\varepsilon_i$ is the output elasticity for input $V_i$. We also saw that the output elasticity of input $i$ was equal to the ratio of the marginal product to the average product for input $V_i$. Our measure of returns to scale may then be written as

$$\varepsilon = MP_1\left(\frac{v_1}{x}\right) + MP_2\left(\frac{v_2}{x}\right)$$

or

$$= \frac{MP_1}{w_1^0}\left(\frac{w_1^0 v_1}{x}\right) + \frac{MP_2}{w_2^0}\left(\frac{w_2^0 v_2}{x}\right)$$

For efficient firms, $MP_1/w_1^0 = MP_2/w_2^0$, and hence

$$\varepsilon = \frac{MP_1}{w_1^0}\left[\frac{w_1^0 v_1 + w_2^0 v_2}{x}\right]$$

The term in brackets is average variable cost. In addition, we showed above[9] that $dC/dx = w_1^0/MP_1$. Therefore, $\varepsilon$ is the ratio of average variable to marginal costs:

$$\varepsilon = \frac{AVC}{MC} \tag{6-2}$$

The responsiveness of output to equiproportional changes in the use of all inputs depends upon the relative sizes of average variable and marginal costs. If marginal costs are higher than unit variable costs, then output will increase less than 1 percent in response to a 1 percent increase in inputs; and the response of output is smaller, the higher is marginal cost relative to unit variable costs. The three possibilities are

$$MC > AVC \text{ which implies } \varepsilon < 1$$
$$MC = AVC \text{ which implies } \varepsilon = 1$$
$$MC < AVC \text{ which implies } \varepsilon > 1$$

The result given as equation (6-2) is especially interesting because it shows that returns to scale—a purely technical relationship given by the firm's production function—is expressible in terms of costs. In other words, the firm's production function determines the "shape" of its cost curves. The relationship between costs and returns to scale is shown graphically in Figure 6-13.

**FIGURE 6-13**

Regions of increasing, constant, and decreasing returns to scale

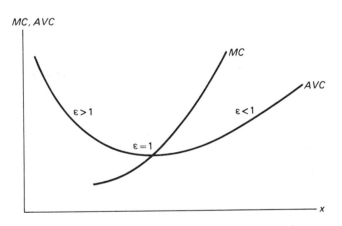

**Factors Responsible for Increasing and Decreasing Returns to Scale**

The definition of returns to scale requires variation in the use of all inputs. Two interpretations of the definition are possible: All *variable* inputs are

---

[9]See page 142. Strictly speaking, we showed that marginal cost equals $w_1^0/MP_1$ only for the case where factor one alone was variable. But if more than one factor is variable, the same result holds. For example, if two factors are variable, say $V_1$ and $V_2$, then $dC/dx = w_1^0/MP_1 = w_2^0/MP_2$ for any firm in which inputs are utilized efficiently.

varied, fixed inputs remaining constant, or *all* inputs are varied. The latter of course means that there are no fixed inputs and that returns to scale is a long-run concept. In practice, the interpretation adopted depends upon the use to which the measure is to be put. In this section we will interpret $\varepsilon$ as a long-run concept, that is, $\varepsilon = LAC/LMC$.

We have seen that capacity restrictions on fixed factors were responsible for increasing costs in the short run. In the long run, all factors are variable and increasing costs are no longer inevitable. Consequently, the cost functions shown in Figure 6-13 exhibit but one of several types of behavior possible for long-run cost functions. For example, in some industries we might expect to find increasing returns to scale over a great range of output. Specialization and division of labor and/or technological factors could be responsible. In small organizations, laborers are likely to perform a number of different tasks and may never be as efficient at any one task as would individuals hired for specialized jobs. If this is the case, the productivity of labor will be higher in large plants, and hence costs will be lower in large plants. On the technological side, we often find that highly specialized mass-production equipment significantly lowers costs. These savings may be the result purely of specialization or of the fact that productivity increases faster than costs as size increases. For example, building a warehouse with four hundred thousand square feet of floor space will usually not cost twice that of a warehouse with two hundred thousand square feet of floor space. That is, a proportional increase in the use of all inputs needed to produce warehouse capacity leads to a more than proportional increase in warehouse capacity.

It has often been argued that economies of scale cannot persist indefinitely due to the fact that the ability of management to coordinate activities within the firm decreases as firm size increases. Basically, this argument says that as the size of the firm increases, there will come a point where the organization is so large that communication along an increasingly long chain of command becomes inefficient and thwarts attempts to coordinate activities within the organization. Whether decreasing returns to scale is inevitable is open to debate. It is certainly possible that technological economies will outstrip managerial inefficiencies in all relevant plant sizes, in which case the long-run average cost function behaves as shown in Figure 6-14. Notice that the interpretation of Figure 6-14 is *not* that "overhead is being spread" over an increasing number of units, since there is no overhead in the long run. Instead, long-run unit cost

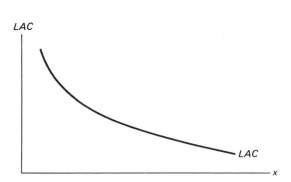

**FIGURE 6-14**

Increasing returns to scale

functions such as the one depicted in Figure 6-14 indicate that *large plants are more efficient than small plants*, which in turn means that economies generated by specialization of labor, plant, and equipment dominate any diseconomies of large size that may exist.

From a public policy point of view, the shape of long-run average cost functions is quite important. Here we will mention but one area of interest—the area of antitrust policy. Briefly, antitrust statutes in the United States speak of the *intent* to monopolize. To convict a firm of violating these laws, the Justice Department must prove intent. And this is where long-run unit cost functions come in. Typically, firms will attempt to justify large market shares by claiming that unit costs fall as plant capacity is expanded and therefore the dominant market position of the firm is the result of "natural market forces," rather than any *intention* to monopolize. Whether unit costs fall continuously as plant capacity is expanded is an empirical question which must be answered on a case-by-case basis. But, in industries where this occurs, it is difficult to show intention to monopolize.

# DIRECT ESTIMATION OF
# PRODUCTION COST FUNCTIONS

We have written the firm's cost function as $C = C(x, w_1^0, w_2^0, \tau^0)$. Cost is a function of the production rate, the costs of factors used in the production process and the production technology of the firm. The function $C$ may be estimated either directly or, alternatively, indirectly by estimating the firm's production function. We first discuss direct estimation of $C$, then indirect estimation. In either case, one must account for all systematic influences on cost if a satisfactory estimate is to be obtained. In particular, if input costs or production technology varies over the estimation period, it is imperative that such variations be properly "accounted for."

To directly estimate the firm's production cost function, data are needed on cost and *all other variables* that actively affect cost. We have written the production cost function as $C(x, w_1^0, w_2^0, \tau^0)$. This expression is a relation between costs and the production rate *given* the input costs $w_1^0$ and $w_2^0$, and *given* some particular "way of doing things," denoted by $\tau^0$. If input costs or production methods change over the estimation period, then $w_1$, $w_2$, and $\tau$ are variables and not parameters in $C$ and must be accounted for explicitly in the estimation process.

### Accounting for Changes in Production Methods

If input costs change over the period in which data have been gathered, then input costs must be included as variables, along with the production rate, in the function to be estimated. We return to this topic below. Changing methods of production are often more difficult to handle, since one does not have data representing the different production methods. What is needed is an estimation process that can differentiate between the costs associated with the various production methods used. In practice, this is usually accomplished by using what is known as *dummy variables*. Examples of situations in which several production processes are regularly utilized are widespread. For example, power-generating utilities generally have "normal," "standby," and "emergency" generating capacities. The cost of generating power increases rapidly as the utility moves from "normal" to "standby" capacity and from "standby" to "emergency" capacity. To estimate this cost function the estimation technique must be able to "separate out" the costs arising from the different power-generating technologies. Dummy variables are designed to do just this type of job.

To get an idea of how dummy variables are used, assume that input prices have been constant over the period on which we have data, that three different methods of production were utilized over this period (i.e., $\tau$ is *not* a parameter), and finally that the relation between cost and the production rate is approximately linear over the range covered by the data.[10] Under these conditions, an appropriate model of costs is

$$C_t = b_0 + b_1 x_t + b_2 D_{1t} + b_3 D_{2t} \qquad (6\text{-}3)$$

The $b_i$ are parameters to be estimated, and $D_{1t}$ and $D_{2t}$ are the values of two dummy variables in period $t$, which have been introduced to account for the three production methods. The variable, $D_1$, takes on the value one in each period production method one was used and is zero whenever production methods two or three were used. The variable $D_2$ takes on the value one in each period production method two was used and is zero whenever production method one or three was used. Note that it is not necessary to introduce a third dummy variable, since equation (6-3) is, in fact, the three equations

$$
\begin{aligned}
C_t &= b_0 + b_1 x_t + b_2, \text{ when } D_1 = 1, D_2 = 0\\
C_t &= b_0 + b_1 x_t + b_3, \text{ when } D_2 = 1, D_1 = 0 \qquad (6\text{-}3')\\
C_t &= b_0 + b_1 x_t, \text{ when } D_1 = D_2 = 0
\end{aligned}
$$

The first of these equations is the cost function when production method one is used, the second equation is the cost function associated with production method two, and the third equation represents the cost function when neither method one nor method two was used; that is, when production method three was used. The two dummy variables turn the estimate of equation (6-3) into an estimate of three "different" cost equations, one for each production method. Notice that these equations differ only in the "level" of costs. They do not differ in slope. That is, the assumption in this model is that different methods of production affect only the level of cost and not incremental costs. The "level" of the first equation is $b_0 + b_2$, the "level" of the second equation is $b_0 + b_3$, and $b_0$ is the "level" of the third equation. In each equation, marginal cost is the same and equal to $b_1$.

What if it is known that the different production methods also affect incremental costs? This situation is easily handled by writing our model of costs as

$$C_t = b_0 + b_1 x_t + b_2 D_{1t} + b_3 D_{2t} + b_4 x_t D_{1t} + b_5 x_t D_{2t} \qquad (6\text{-}4)$$

[10]Linearity is not needed here, but is introduced merely to focus attention on the role of dummy variables. Other more general functional forms for the cost function are introduced later in this chapter.

In equation (6-4) the dummy variables $D_1$ and $D_2$ take on the same values as before. But now, during the time production method one is being used, the cost function is

$$
\begin{aligned}
C_t &= b_0 + b_1 x_t + b_2 + b_4 x_t \\
&= (b_0 + b_2) + (b_1 + b_4)x_t
\end{aligned}
\tag{6-4'}
$$

Again, the level of the function $C_t$ is $b_0 + b_2$ during this period, but introduction of $x_t D_{1t}$ implies that marginal production costs are $b_1 + b_4$ during this period. Similar calculations show that marginal costs are $b_1 + b_5$ when production method two is used, and $b_1$ when method three is used.

Cost models (6-3) and (6-4) both have the same data requirements. Data are needed on costs, on production rates, and on $D_1$ and $D_2$. Of course the "observations" on $D_1$ and $D_2$ are obtained merely by writing columns of ones and zeros according to the above criterion.

### Data Requirements

As we have noted, statistical estimation of a production cost function will require data on costs and the production rate and any other variable that affects costs. In addition, accurate estimation will require the adoption of accounting methods that maximize the information content of the firm's accounting records. If the data used are taken from ordinary cost-accounting records, there is but a small chance that the estimated cost function will be useful to the firm. Several of the more important data requirements and the implied accounting procedures are now briefly discussed.

First, the length of the recording period must be chosen with estimation in mind. Should observations on the relevant variables be taken daily, weekly, monthly, or at some other interval? A primary requirement is that time periods be long enough to allow production in a period to be paired with the costs generated *by that production*. Lags between production and the recording of costs associated with *that* production must be eliminated or adjusted for. On the other hand, the recording period must be short enough so that there are not large variations in the production rate over the period. If there are, cost variations that occur will be averaged out, and the true relationship between costs and output will be obscured.

Second, it is desirable to have observations on cost and output over as wide a range as possible. The narrower the range of observations, the smaller the segment of the cost function that ends up being estimated. In the limit, if there is no variation in cost and the output rate, it is impossible to estimate the cost function.

Third, if a firm produced a number of products, some costs will be common, that is, jointly incurred in the production of the several products. In economic theory, costs are "joint" if they cannot be traced to a single product. Overhead charges are joint costs in this sense. But for most decision-making purposes, only joint costs that *vary* with output need be accounted for. The electric power that runs machines is an example of a joint cost that varies with output.

If joint costs are allocated to products in an arbitrary manner that is un-related to the production of the products, estimates of the coefficients of the cost function will be biased. (For example, allocating utility charges according to a floor space rule makes no sense at all. Virtually any intelligent guess yields a better allocation.) An effort must be made to allocate joint costs, in some rational manner.[11] If this is not done, it would be better to estimate a cost function *sans* joint costs and adjust for joint costs later. At least with this approach the estimated relation will not contain deliberate bias.

### The Functional Form of Cost Functions

Once basic data requirements are met, a general *class* of functions must be chosen of which the firm's cost function is assumed to be a member. To expand on this remark, consider the case when the production rate is the only variable affecting cost. That is, input prices, technology, production methods and processes, and so forth, are unchanged in the period in which the data were collected. In this case, the statistician must decide upon the functional form of $C(x)$. A good first step is to plot the values of $C$ and $x$ one is going to use for estimating $C(x)$ and see if any conclusions can be drawn. Is the plot approximate-ly linear, quadratic, or cubic? Another way of stating this question is, Are incremental costs constant? Do they increase or decrease with the production rate, but at a fairly constant rate? Or do they change at a nonconstant rate? If the answer to the first question is affirmative, then a *linear* function should be used for $C(x)$. If the answer to the second (third) question is affirmative, then a *quadratic* (*cubic*) function should be used for $C(x)$. If the production manager believes that *percentage* changes in the production rate lead to the same *per-centage* changes in cost over the relevant range of production, then a *power* function is an appropriate choice. These four functions are listed as equations (6-5)–(6-8).

$$C_t = b_0 + b_1 x_t, \qquad b_0 > 0, b_1 > 0 \tag{6-5}$$

In equation (6-5) costs are linear in the production rate, and hence marginal costs are constant.

$$C_t = b_0 + b_1 x_t + b_2 x_t^2 \tag{6-6}$$

In equation (6-6) costs are a quadratic function of the production rate. This implies that marginal cost increases or decreases at a constant rate, depending upon whether $b_2 > 0$ or $b_2 < 0$.

$$C_t = b_0 + b_1 x_t + b_2 x_t^2 + b_3 x_t^3 \tag{6-7}$$

In equation (6-7) costs are a cubic function of the production rate, implying

---

[11]Much work has been done on this problem in recent years. For those with some mathe-matical background, R. L. Weil, Jr.'s, "Allocating Joint Costs," *American Economic Review*, December 1968, is a brief and excellent account of the problem. Weil shows that allocation of joint costs can be done in a rational manner by solving a specific mathematical programming problem. This is of particular interest to decision makers, since many types of these problems can be solved.

that marginal costs can fall and rise at different rates depending upon the output rate and the values of $b_2$ and $b_3$.

$$D_t = b_0 x_t^{b_1}, \qquad b_0, b_1 > 0 \qquad (6\text{-}8)$$

In (6-8) variable costs are related to the production rate as a power function. Marginal cost is $b_0 b_1 x_t^{b_1-1}$ and is increasing if $b_1 > 1$, constant if $b_1 = 1$, and falling if $0 < b_1 < 1$. (Why must $b_0, b_1 > 0$?) Also note that $(dD/dx)(x/D) = b_1$ —the elasticity of costs with respect to output (the percentage response of costs to a percentage change in the output rate)—is constant for all production rates. If percentage changes in output lead to approximately the same percentage change in costs over the relevant production region, then this particular function may be a good choice for the *variable* cost function. Why can't a power function be used to represent the total cost function?

The cost functions given in equations (6-5)–(6-8) are pictured in Figure 6-15 along with the associated average and marginal cost functions. Each of these equations may be estimated using regression analysis. As we have noted, the accuracy of the estimated equation depends heavily upon the manner in which cost and production information are recorded.

**FIGURE 6-15**
Total, average, and marginal cost functions: several functional forms

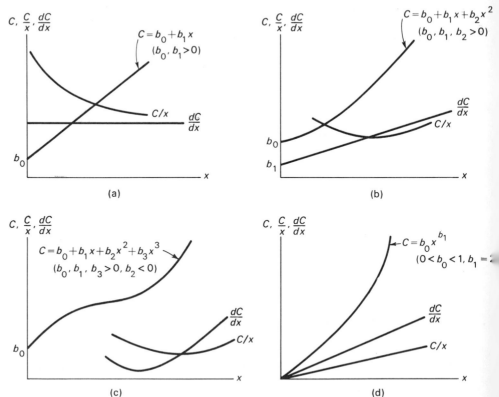

(a)

(b)

(c)

(d)

The cost functions expressed in equations (6-5)–(6-8) have one common underlying assumption: all influences on cost except the production rate are constant in the period for which costs are to be estimated. But if there are differences in production methods or production technologies in the period, these differences must be accounted for if the estimated function is to be meaningful. We have seen above that dummy variables may be used to accomplish this. If input costs change over the period, then input costs must be incorporated as variables in the cost function to be estimated. If changes in input costs merely raise the "level" of costs but do not affect marginal costs, they have a linear influence on costs. In such a case, adding $c_0 w_1 + c_1 w_2$ to cost equations (6-5), (6-6), or (6-7) ($c_0$ and $c_1$ are parameters to be estimated) will probably adequately account for changing input prices.

If changes in input costs affect marginal costs, many alternatives are possible. A widely used option is to rewrite equation (6-8) as

$$D_t = b_0 x_t^{b_1} w_{1t}^{b_2} w_{2t}^{b_3}$$   (6-8′)

Marginal cost in period $t$ is then

$$\partial D_t / \partial x_t = b_0 b_1 x_t^{b_1 - 1} w_{1t}^{b_2} w_{2t}^{b_3}$$   (6-9)

and, unlike equation (6-8), depends not only upon the production rate in period $t$ but also upon the costs of $V_1$ and $V_2$ in period $t$.

The decision as to the appropriate functional representation of the relationship between input prices and costs must be reached in precisely the same manner as the decision about the appropriate functional form of the relation between costs and the output rate: Each functional form has particular implications for the various components of costs; the form is chosen that best fits observed cost behavior. Implicit in this choice is cooperation between production managers and accountants in an attempt to glean as much information about costs as is possible from those with long experience in the everyday operation of the plant.

## INDIRECT ESTIMATION OF THE PRODUCTION COST FUNCTION

Indirect estimation of $C(x)$ is accomplished by estimating the firm's production function and then deducing the cost function. Specifically, one estimates the parameters of the firm's production function; then, using the estimated production function, one derives the associated production cost function as follows: (i) Calculate the least cost combination of inputs given existing factor prices. The least cost combination of inputs is obviously a function of the production rate. (ii) Multiply the least cost quantities of $V_1$ and $V_2$ by their respective prices and sum. This yields the cost of production as a function of the production rate, given factor prices and a given production technology, that is, $C = C(x, w_1^0, w_2^0, \tau^0)$. As with direct estimation, a change in either input price or production methods would yield a different cost function. Cost functions estimated in this manner are usually termed *engineering estimates* of cost because they are based upon estimating the technical or "engineering" relation between inputs and output, the production function. We now present an example to illustrate the calculations involved.

### Estimating Production Cost Functions by Estimating Production Functions—An Example

At the beginning of this chapter we calculated the expansion path for a shop with production function $x = 20v_1v_2 - 2v_1^2 - v_2^2$, where $v_1$ and $v_2$ represented hours of unskilled and skilled labor, respectively. Skilled labor earned $8 per hour, unskilled labor $4 per hour. The locus of efficient input combinations (the expansion path) was given by $v_1 = 1.5v_2$.

To transform this information into the firm's variable cost function, merely substitute $v_1 = 1.5v_2$ into $D = 4v_1 + 8v_2$. Then

$$D = 4(1.5v_2) + 8v_2$$
$$= 14v_2$$

But we want variable costs as a function $x$, not $v_2$. This is obtained from the production function by substituting $v_1 = 1.5v_2$ for $v_1$ (since we are only interested in efficient input combinations). We then have $x = 24.5v_2^2$. This is the relationship between output and $v_2$ when inputs are utilized efficiently, and is needed to turn $D = 14v_2$ into a function of $x$. Solving $x = 24.5v_2^2$ for $v_2$ we have $v_2 = \sqrt{x/24.5}$, and hence

$$D = 14\sqrt{x/24.5}$$
$$= 2.83\sqrt{x} = 2.83x^{.5}$$

Notice that this is the *variable* cost function of the shop and is a power function with parameters $b_0 = 2.83$ and $b_1 = .5$ [see equation (6-8)]. So for the technology given by the existing production function and for existing wage rates, a 1 percent increase in the production rate leads to a 0.5 percent increase in costs. Production in this shop is characterized by increasing returns to scale.

We could have added overhead charges to $D = 4v_1 + 8v_2$ if we had been interested in obtaining the total cost function, $C$. But, in practice, calculation of overhead charges leaves much to be desired, and since most short-run decisions are invariant to the level of fixed charges, estimation of the variable cost function is usually sufficient for decision purposes.

This brings up a second point about the above cost function: It is an *estimate* based upon the parameters estimated for the production function. Recall that the general form of the production function that was estimated for the shop is $x = av_1v_2 + bv_1^2 + cv_2^2$. The estimates of $a$, $b$, and $c$ were 20, $-2$, and $-1$, respectively. If, for example, new equipment is introduced or new "ways of doing things" are tried, these parameters will undoubtedly change. Hence the production function must be reestimated and a new cost function derived from this estimate.

In Figure 6-16 the estimated cost function is graphed along with the associated average and marginal cost function (solid lines). As has already been mentioned, it is imperative to remember that the estimated cost function has as parameters the wages of skilled and unskilled labor and the given production technology and "way of doing things." A change in either *shifts* each cost function. The broken curve in Figure 6-16 is the variable cost function that results from a new union contract that increases the wages of skilled labor to $12 per hour. Calculation of the associated average and marginal cost functions would show that both have shifted upward from their original positions. If input costs change often, $w_1$ and $w_2$ must be treated as variables in the derivation of the cost function. Although the algebra is messier, the same procedure we have used here would be followed to calculate the firm's cost function. The resulting production cost equation would be a function of three variables, the production rate and input prices, that is, $C = C(x, w_1, w_2)$.

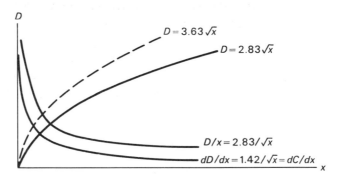

**FIGURE 6-16**

Cost functions associated with the production function

$$X = 20v_1v_2 - 2v_1^2 - v_2^2$$

**PROBLEMS AND QUESTIONS**

1. Using the example in the text of the shop with production function $20v_1v_2 - 2v_1^2 - v_2^2$ with $w_1 =$ $4/hr. and $w_2 =$ $8/hr., answer the following questions. (Recall that this production function is a special case of $x = av_1v_2 + bv_1^2 + cv_2^2$ where $a = 20$, $b = -2$, and $c = -1$.)

a. It is asserted that the productivity of unskilled labor has increased. The production function is reestimated and it is found that $a = 20$, $b = -1.5$, and $c = -1$. Graph the marginal product function of unskilled labor for several values of $V_2$. If "productivity" is interpreted to mean "marginal productivity," is the above assertion justified? Explain.

b. Derive the variable, marginal, and average variable cost functions. Compare these cost functions with the ones derived in the text. Can any conclusions be drawn about the effect on costs of changes in productivity?

c. Derive the same cost functions if the wages of unskilled labor increase 25 percent.

d. Derive the same cost functions if the wages of skilled and unskilled labor both increase 25 percent.

2. Derive the variable cost function associated with the production function $x = 10v_1v_2^5$ if $w_1^0 = w_2^0 =$ $4. Graph the total variable, average variable, and marginal cost functions.

3. Derive the variable cost function if $x = 10v_1^5 v_2^5$ and $w_1^0 = \$10$, $w_2^0 = \$2$. Again, graph the variable, average variable, and marginal cost functions and compare with the preceding problem. Notice the influence on cost of the different production functions.

4. Referring to problem 17, Chapter 4, in which a commodity $X$ may be produced in five alternative ways, assume that the cost of factor one is \$3 per unit and the cost of factor two is \$4 per unit:

a. Calculate the variable cost function $D(x)$, assuming a "linear technology."

b. Graph the average total, average variable, and marginal cost functions associated with $D(x)$.

c. Find the expansion path if the amount of $V_1$ is limited to 180 units.

d. Find the variable cost function when $V_1$ availability is limited to 180 units. (Hint: First find $D(x)$ for output rates where $v_1 < 180$. Then, beginning where the constraint on $V_1$ is binding, calculate $D(x)$ at 50-unit intervals in $x$ following the procedure we used in the example on pp. 144–50.)

e. Graph the average variable and marginal cost functions associated with part d.

5. Assume that the variable cost function of some firm is $D(x) = 5.4x^{-.5}w_1^5 w_2$, where $D$ is in thousands of dollars, $w_1$ and $w_2$ are measured in dollars, and $x$ is in thousands of units. In the past four quarters, a period of rapidly increasing production, the following data were recorded:

| Quarter | D | x | $w_1$ | $w_2$ |
|---|---|---|---|---|
| 1 | 16.2 | 1.00 | 9 | 1 |
| 2 | 21.6 | 2.25 | 9 | 2 |
| 3 | 25.9 | 6.25 | 9 | 4 |
| 4 | 37.8 | 9.00 | 9 | 7 |

Now, suppose that the firm does not know what its variable cost function is and decides to have it estimated. Those responsible for estimation calculate the function $D(x) = b_0 x^{b_1}$, i.e., they neglect to include one of the active influences on cost over the time period in question, $w_2$. Using the above data, plot the relationship between $D$ and $x$ alone. If the function $D(x) = b_0 x^{b_1}$ is estimated, what sign will $b_1$ have? Contrast this to the "true" sign of $b_1(-.5)$ given above. What does this mean as far as the "true" and estimated cost functions are concerned? Plot the "true" cost function in a two-dimensional diagram with $D$ and $x$ as axes. Notice the difference in interpretation of the sentence "Costs have risen over the four quarters" when applied to the estimated cost function and the "true" cost function.

6. Some time ago the *Wall Street Journal* carried an article about the cost calculations of a bankrupt company. The company had bid a job and landed a contract to produce 100,000 units at a given contract price. Company accountants estimated, on the basis of considerable past experience, that profit per unit would be \$11.50. Just as production was beginning, the contracted order

was increased to 150,000 units. Accounting predicted a $575,000 increment to profits (11.50 × 50,000), but instead the company *lost* $6.00 per unit, and because of similar previous mistakes declared bankruptcy. What implicit assumption did "accounting" make in its prediction? Under what conditions can such an assumption be made?

7. Suppose a product $X$ may be produced in three alternative ways and that factor one costs $10 an hour and factor two costs $6 an hour. Input requirements for 500 units of production are:

300 hours of $V_1$ and  30 hours of $V_2$ in Process I
200  //        //   //  80   //      // in Process II
100  //        //   // 400   //      // in Process III

a. Derive the firm's variable cost function, assuming a linear technology.
b. Derive $D(x)$ if the cost of $V_1$ falls to $6 per hour.
c. Derive $D(x)$ if the cost of $V_1$ falls to $2 per hour.

# Optimal Pricing and
# Volume Policies:
# Preliminary Concepts

Our discussion in the remaining chapters is concerned with pricing and sales volume decisions. In general, these decisions are constrained by what economists call the structure of the market. *Market structure* is used to denote the characteristics of demand and cost functions that are common to firms within an industry and which determine the extent to which firms in an industry are able to control price. Traditionally, economists have classified markets as being *purely competitive, monopolistic, monopolistically competitive,* or *oligopolistic.* As for pricing, the major difference between these markets arises from the degree of control managers have over price. In purely competitive industries, managers have no control over price and hence no pricing decision—although a sales volume decision must be made. In monopolistic markets, managers have more control over price than in any other market structure; and for this reason, the pricing decision is often regulated in monopoly markets. In the other two traditional market structures, monopolistic competition and oligopoly, the number of firms in the industry constrain the pricing decision of individual firms. In monopolistic competition it is the large number of firms in the industry that is responsible for the limited pricing options open to the firm, while in oligopoly it is the fewness of competitors that limits pricing options. We now take a brief look at the primary characteristics of these market structures and then return to each in some detail in Chapters 8, 9, and 10.

### Market Structures

• *Pure Competition.* The distinguishing feature of a purely competitive product market is that the individual firm has no control whatever over market prices. Two conditions are fundamental to such a situation: (1) the firm is very small relative to the market in which it sells its product, and (2) the product of each producer in the industry is identical. These conditions ensure that the firm will have no perceptible influence on price. Condition one implies that any one seller withholding all of its production from the market will not affect market price, while condition two rules out *product differentiation*. If products are not identical, then firms will in some sense have "unique" products, in which case differences in buyers' tastes and preferences will lead to differences in product prices between firms.

**167**
Optimal Pricing
and Volume
Policies:
Preliminary
Concepts

One additional condition is necessary to ensure that pure competition persists in an industry. That condition requires "entry" and "exit" of firms into and from the industry to be relatively easy. There can be no restrictions that would prevent new firms from entering industries with relatively high returns. The existence of patents on needed production technology or labor unions that would prevent new firms without union labor from entering an industry are commonplace examples of entry restrictions that are not consistent with pure competition.[1]

The inability of any single firm to influence market price is illustrated in Figure 7-1. The firm, say firm $i$, is able to sell whatever quantity of $X$ it chooses,

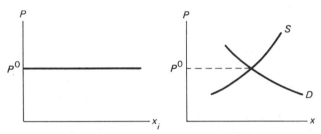

**FIGURE 7-1**
Pure
competition in
the market for
$X$: the firm and
the industry

$x_i$, at the existing market price, $P^0$. The line $P^0$ is the demand function for $X$ *as far as the firm is concerned* and is determined by the intersection of industry demand and supply functions as shown. Markets where demand conditions roughly approximate those depicted in Figure 7-1 include stock and commodity markets and many agricultural markets. For example, when you sell stock from your portfolio only one decision must be made: How much should be sold at the existing market price? If you sell none or all of your holdings the price of the stock will be unaffected, that is, your transaction has absolutely no effect on the price of the stock. Before proceeding, check to see if the conditions for pure competition are met in markets for common stocks.

• *Monopoly.* Monopoly exists whenever there is only one seller in a well-defined market. An alternative definition could be phrased in terms of cross demand elasticities: The producer of $X$ is a monopolist in the marketing of $X$ if the cross-elasticity of demand between $X$ and all other commodities is non-positive. That is, commodity $X$ has no substitutes.

In pure competition, the firm's demand function is market price. This price is independent of the quantity the firm chooses to sell and is determined by the

[1] A requirement that is implicit in each of the above conditions is that all buyers and sellers have full knowledge of market conditions. In other words, cost and price information is available to all buyers and sellers in the market. If market prices are not known to buyers, sellers will necessarily have some control over price. But if buyers know market prices, it will be impossible for sellers to ask any price other than the market price.

intersection of industry demand and supply functions. In monopoly there is only one seller, so the firm is the industry and the industry (market) demand function is the demand function facing the firm.

• *Monopolistic Competition.* If the "identical product" condition underlying pure competition is removed and the other conditions retained, we have the market structure known as monopolistic competition. Monopolistically competitive industries are characterized by a large number of firms producing highly substitutable (not perfectly substitutable, i.e., identical) products. As with pure competition, (1) entry into monopolistically competitive industries is relatively easy, and (2) the "large number of sellers" condition ensures that each firm is very small relative to the total market and hence individual firm decisions have no effect on any other firm in the industry.

The name "monopolistic competition" comes from the fact that these markets contain, in a sense, an element of both monopoly and competition. The competitive element derives from the "large number of sellers" condition. The element of monopoly derives from each firm's being the only seller of its particular product, but unlike monopoly, the products of other firms in the industry are close substitutes. That is, firms have been able to slightly differentiate their products. Product differentiation means that some buyers will be willing to pay more for one product than for another because of real or imagined differences. This implies the firm will have some control over price, but since differentiation is only slight, pricing options will be quite limited.

Monopolistic competition is a common market structure in the United States and includes most small retailers. Retail clothing stores, taverns, restaurants, dry cleaners, and so forth, come close to meeting the requirements we have listed. Typically, factors such as location and personalities of owners provide whatever product differentiation exists.

• *Oligopoly.* Oligopoly is defined as the type of market organization in which there are but a small number of firms in a market selling substitutable products. The salient feature of oligopolistic markets derives from the small number of sellers. Fewness of sellers implies that market decisions of individual sellers affect other sellers in the market. That is, marketing decisions of firms are mutually interdependent—a situation that greatly complicates firm decision making.

Instances of oligopoly are easy to find in the United States and in most of the world. Lead, copper, zinc, and aluminum refining and steel, cigarette, automobile, computer, and rubber manufacturing are but a few of many examples in the U.S. economy. In each case the production of a few firms is sufficient to satisfy much or all domestic demands, and in some cases, even most of world demand.

The market structures we have discussed and their influence on firm pricing and volume decisions will be studied in some depth in succeeding chapters.

### Market Structure: Another Perspective

Because the focus of our discussion in coming chapters is primarily on the pricing decision and because pricing rules in general depend upon the structure of the market in which the firm operates, it is often instructive to view market structure from a pricing perspective. To this end, we categorize firms as either *price-takers* or *price-makers*, depending upon whether or not a price decision is made by the firm. The price-taker category includes all markets in which price is taken as given by sellers and contains as a special case purely competitive firms. The price-maker category includes all remaining types of markets in which pricing decisions are made and is further divided into two subcategories: (1) price-makers who for decision purposes need not consider the pricing policies of other firms—the case of *pricing autonomy*; and (2) price-makers who must account for the "reactions of competitors" when planning their own pricing policies—the case of *pricing interdependence*. In terms of our discussion above, pricing autonomy occurs in monopolistic and monopolistically competitive markets, while pricing interdependence arises in oligopolistic markets. But whatever the structure of the market, the optimal price and volume decision will be a function of the goals of the firm. We next make an assumption about firm motivation.

**169**
Optimal Pricing
and Volume
Policies:
Preliminary
Concepts

### The Goals of the Firm

The traditional but by no means the only assumption about firm motivation is that firm decisions are taken so as to maximize profits. We adopt this assumption in our study of pricing. Simply put, profit maximization means that managers, when choosing between alternative courses of action, give highest priority to those actions that increase profits. If one wanted a single goal that would be most descriptive of observed business behavior in the United States, profit maximization would undoubtedly be chosen. This does not necessarily mean that all firms maximize profits—instead it means that "on the average" profit maximization adequately describes firm behavior. The goals of sales maximization, growth maximization, and numerous other hypotheses are plausible alternatives in some market structures. But even in such cases, profit maximization is often quite descriptive. For this reason, we will assume that firm decisions are taken with the goal of increasing profits. But so as to not give the impression that other goals are not plausible, and in some instances preferable to profit maximization, we now briefly discuss several alternative hypotheses about firm motivation.

• *Sales Maximization.* According to the sales-maximization hypothesis, firms are more interested in sales volume than they are in the level of profits. This does not mean that firms maximize sales revenues without any reference to profits. Instead the hypothesis means that firms maximize sales revenue subject to a minimum profit constraint. The difference between maximum profits and the minimum profit constraint is often termed "sacrificeable profits," since these profits will be voluntarily given up in order to increase sales revenue (for example, by opening or maintaining an unprofitable sales outlet).

Few proponents of sales maximization contend that it is a universally acceptable explanation of firm behavior, nor do they contend that sales maximization is always inconsistent with profit maximization. But at this time the empirical evidence is almost totally at odds with the sales-maximization hypo-thesis.[2] We will return to this topic in more detail in the next chapter.

• *Growth Maximization.*   Another plausible objective for a firm is to maximize the rate of growth of a certain aspect of its activities—for example, its sales revenues, its profits, its assets, or some other variable that describes firm activities. The problem with this hypothesis is that to finance most types of growth the firm must either generate considerable profits or borrow in capital markets. And since the firm's ability to borrow is usually closely tied to its profitability, the decision to maximize growth will normally constrain the firm to behave in a manner very similar to that of a profit maximizer. So unless firms maximize growth subject to well-defined constraints, it will not be possible to distinguish between growth and profit maximization. Even if constraints are well specified, serious difficulties surround testing the growth-maximization hypothesis because of its predictive similarity to profit maximization. To my knowledge no empirical tests exist that successfully distinguish between the two hypotheses.

• *Managerial Theories.*   The type of theory we will discuss in this section focuses attention on the behavior of the managers who operate the firm. These theories are built upon the fact that the individuals who run the typical modern corporation are usually not the primary owners of the corporation. This separation of ownership and management is alleged to have important implications for the behavior of managerial personnel and for the performance of the firm.

The argument goes as follows: Stockholders are primarily interested in high dividends and therefore favor profit-maximizing actions on the part of the firm. Managers, however, have different motives and goals. Managers, it is said, are more interested in the size of their offices, the number of employees reporting to them, the absolute size of the firm, and the perquisites that accompany their jobs. These interests are usually not consistent with profit maximization. Crucial to this argument is a strong independence of managerial actions from owner control—a topic upon which there is considerable disagreement.

In general, managerial theories contend that managers will not be interested in the profit-maximizing behavior that stockholders desire. But it seems that this position would often be difficult to defend, since frequently a great deal of an executive's compensation takes the form of stock options and profit sharing. And since the share price of a firm's stock is closely tied to the profitability of the firm, the separation of financial interests between owners and managers often does not exist. Most actions taken by management will affect the share price of a firm's stock and therefore management's own welfare.

There are many managerial models of the firm, some more carefully formulated than others. There is still no definitive empirical evidence on one side or the other.

• *Satisficing Models of Firm Behavior.*   The satisficing firm does not attempt to maximize or minimize anything but rather attempts to meet reasonable goals in various areas. The standards of achievement that the firm adopts are often

[2]See, for example, M. Hall, "Sales Revenue Maximization: An Empirical Investigation," *Journal of Industrial Economics*, April 1967, pp. 143–56.

"minimum standards" designed to "guarantee the firm's existence," and seldom

**171**

Optimal Pricing
and Volume
Policies:
Preliminary
Concepts

to achieve any single goal such as profit maximization.[3]

Since a satisficing firm does not have a well-defined objective function that dictates its behavior, its actions cannot be predicted except by a detailed examination of its decision process. For this reason, the properties of satisficing models are usually discovered by computer simulation. The predictive ability of these computer simulation models is limited primarily by how realistically the decision process of the firm is represented. In certain cases these models have predicted quite accurately.

### Revenue Functions

As we have already mentioned, the topic of investigation in the remaining chapters is the pricing and volume decision of the firm. Heretofore this problem has not been considered.[4] Our primary interest lies in determining rules for choosing the optimal price and volume. In general, production costs, the characteristics of demand, and the firm's goals jointly determine optimal pricing rules and optimal volume rules. The origin of costs has been studied in some detail, and the goal of the firm has been assumed to be the maximization of profits. The other determinant of the optimal price and volume, the characteristics of product demand, enters the firm's decision problem by way of firm revenue functions. These functions are now introduced.

Let $x = \tilde{f}(P)$ represent the quantity of product $X$ demanded as a function of the price of $X$, for given values of the other determinants of demand. We will find it convenient to express firm revenues as a function of the quantity of $X$ sold. To do this, the demand function must be rewritten as $P = g(x)$. That is, solve $x = \tilde{f}(P)$ for $P$, which yields price as a function of quantity, $P = g(x)$. *Total revenue*, $R(x)$, is then

$$R(x) = P \cdot x = g(x) \cdot x \qquad (7\text{-}1)$$

The response of revenue to a change in sales volume is called *marginal revenue* and is merely the change in $R(x)$ as the sales rate changes. If the demand function is differentiable, then marginal revenue is

$$
\begin{aligned}
dR/dx &= P + x(dP/dx) \\
&= P/P[P + x(dP/dx)] \\
&= P[1 + (x/P)(dP/dx)] \\
&= P(1 + 1/\eta)
\end{aligned}
\qquad (7\text{-}2)
$$

where $\eta$ is the price elasticity of demand.[5] We will find this latter representation of the marginal revenue function particularly useful in pricing problems, since

[3] If the markets in which the firm sells its products are competitive, policies that "guarantee the firm's existence" *are* profit-maximizing policies.

[4] The one exception to this statement is the optimal product mix problem studied in Chapter 5, in which profit-maximizing sales volumes were determined.

[5] When the sales rates and prices of competing products enter management's decision problem, we will revert to the usual subscripts on $\eta$ to denote the various demand elasticities. But for the case of price-takers and price-makers possessing pricing autonomy, only the price elasticity enters management's calculations and hence omission of subscripts causes no confusion.

marginal revenue is expressed as a simple function of product price and the price elasticity of demand.

It is informative to examine (7-2) a little more closely. Notice that $1/\eta = (dP/dx)(x/P)$ measures the sensitivity of price to changes in sales volume. Usually price will have to be lowered to increase sales (i.e., $dP/dx < 0$), in which case marginal revenue must be less than price (see equation (7-2)). A special case occurs when $1/\eta = 0$ and demand is said to be infinitely elastic. The interpretation here is that the firm has no control over price (the firm is a *price-taker*) and can therefore sell whatever volume it chooses at the current market price. Note that an "infinitely elastic" demand function implies marginal revenue is equal to price (by equation (7-2)), and price, as far as the firm is concerned, is a given constant (i.e., $dP/dx = 0$). The decision problem in these circumstances concerns choosing the optimal sales volume.

Revenue per unit of $X$ sold is *average revenue*,

$$R/x = P. \tag{7-3}$$

Average revenue is price, and since $P = g(x)$ is the firm's demand function, *the firm's average revenue function is its demand function*. Total, marginal, and average revenue functions are displayed in Figure 7-2 for the case where the demand function possesses a finite price elasticity. The same functions for the case of an infinitely elastic demand function are shown in Figure 7-3.

**FIGURE 7-2**
Total,
marginal, and
average revenue
functions:
the case of
a finite price
elasticity

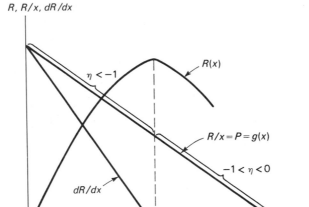

**FIGURE 7-3**
Total, average,
and marginal
revenue
functions:
the case of an
infinitely elastic
demand function

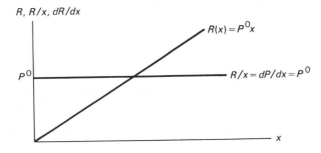

**173**

Optimal Pricing
and Volume
Policies:
Preliminary
Concepts

• *Firm Revenues and the Price Elasticity of Demand.* Since marginal revenue is the rate of change of total revenue, one can easily obtain several elementary relationships between the price elasticity of demand and firm revenues. To examine these relationships it is helpful to write firm revenues as a function of the price of $X$ instead of the sales volume. We will denote this revenue function as $r(P)$ so it will not be confused with the revenue function $R(x)$ introduced above. (Hereafter when we speak of revenue functions we will *always* be referring to $R(x)$ unless we specifically indicate otherwise.) Since revenue is price times sales,

$$r(P) = P \cdot x = P \cdot \bar{f}(P) \qquad (7\text{-}4)$$

where $x = \bar{f}(P)$ is the firm's demand function with quantity written as a function of price. The question of interest here is how firm revenues respond to percentage variations in price. The variation in revenue due to a variation in price is given by

$$\begin{aligned}
\frac{dr}{dP} &= P\frac{dx}{dP} + x \\
&= x/x\left[x + P\frac{dx}{dP}\right] \qquad (7\text{-}5) \\
&= x(1 + \eta)
\end{aligned}$$

which is precisely analogous to (7-2) above. To turn (7-5) into a statement about percentage changes in revenues due to percentage changes in price, merely multiply (7-5) by $P/r = 1/x$. Then

$$\frac{dr}{dP}\left(\frac{P}{r}\right) = 1 + \eta \qquad (7\text{-}6)$$

As is clear from (7-6), the behavior of revenue as price changes depends upon whether $\eta < -1$, $\eta = -1$, or $-1 < \eta < 0$.

    Case 1—If $\eta < -1$, (7-6) is negative, and price changes cause revenues to respond in the opposite direction. Price decreases increase revenue and price increases decrease revenue. Therefore we may conclude that marginal revenue is positive ($dR/dx > 0$), since revenue moves in the same direction as *volume*, $x$ (remember $P$ and $x$ move in opposite directions). In other words, $dr/dP < 0$ implies $dR/dx > 0$.

    Case 2—If $\eta = -1$, (7-6) is equal to zero, and changes in price in either direction cause no change in revenues. Therefore, we may conclude that if demand has unitary elasticity, marginal revenue is zero ($dR/dx = 0$).

    Case 3—If $-1 < \eta < 0$, (7-6) is positive, and revenues move in the same direction as price. This is another way of saying that *volume* and revenues are inversely related, i.e., $dR/dx < 0$. If demand is inelastic, then marginal revenue must be negative.

The regions of elastic and inelastic demand and their relationship to revenue functions are shown in Figure 7-2 for the case of a linear demand function.

    EXAMPLES.  Assume the following transactions are recorded in the market for $X$.

| x (1000s) | 30 | 35 | 40 | 45 | 50 | 55 |
|---|---|---|---|---|---|---|
| P ($/unit) | 280 | 260 | 240 | 220 | 200 | 180 |

*If* all influences on demand except the price of $X$ were constant over the period in which these transactions were recorded, then the following are the firm's total and marginal revenue functions:

| x (1000s) | R(x) (millions of $) | ΔR (millions of $) | ΔR/Δx ($) |
|---|---|---|---|
| 30 | 8.4 | | |
| | | .7 | 140 |
| 35 | 9.1 | | |
| | | .5 | 100 |
| 40 | 9.6 | | |
| | | .3 | 60 |
| 45 | 9.9 | | |
| | | .1 | 20 |
| 50 | 10.0 | | |
| | | −.1 | −20 |
| 55 | 9.9 | | |

The observations on sales and prices, under the conditions stated, yield six points on the revenue function between volumes of 30,000 and 55,000 units and five points on the marginal revenue function.

In the third column of the table changes in revenues are recorded for 5,000-unit increments in sales. We have converted $\Delta R$ to marginal revenues in the last column of the table. The effect of calculating a marginal revenue function from a series of points on the total revenue function as we have done is to get an "average of marginal revenues" between the points, which turns the marginal revenue function into a step function. Total, marginal, and average revenue functions are graphed in Figures 7-4 and 7-5.

As a second example, suppose the demand function for $X$ has been estimated to be $x = 10,000 - 5P$. Average, total, and marginal revenue functions

**FIGURE 7-4**
Total and marginal revenue functions: an example

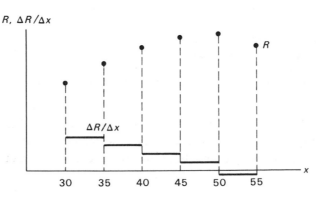

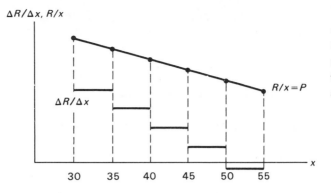

FIGURE 7-5

Average and
marginal
revenue
functions:
an example

are then

$$R/x = P = 2000 - .2x$$
$$R(x) = 2000x - .2x^2$$
$$dR/dx = 2000 - .4x$$

and are graphed as Figure 7-6. (The average revenue function is obtained by solving the demand function for $P$ as a function of $x$.)

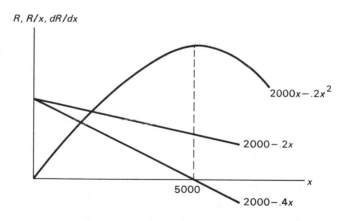

FIGURE 7-6

Total, average,
and marginal
revenue
functions
associated with
the demand
function
$x = 10,000 - 5P$

## Profit Maximization

If revenue and cost functions are differentiable, one can derive the equation that must be satisfied if profits are to be maximum merely by differentiating the profit function and equating the result to zero (see the appendix to Chapter 1). Since by definition profits are total revenues minus total costs, the profit function is

$$\Pi(x) \equiv R(x) - C(x) \qquad (7\text{-}7)$$

Differentiating equation (7-7) and equating the result to zero yields

$$d\Pi/dx = dR/dx - dC/dx = 0 \qquad (7\text{-}8)$$

Equation (7-8) is the familiar rule that volume should be chosen to equate

**175**

marginal revenues and marginal costs. If revenue and cost functions are not differentiable or if estimates of demand and cost functions are not available, the rule becomes

If $\Delta R/\Delta x > \Delta C/\Delta x$, then increase volume
If $\Delta R/\Delta x < \Delta C/\Delta x$, then decrease volume

In words, if increases in volume add more to revenues than to costs ($\Delta R/\Delta x > \Delta C/\Delta x$), further increases in volume are warranted; but if increased volume increases costs more than revenues ($\Delta R/\Delta x < \Delta C/\Delta x$), volume is too high and should be cut back. In still other words, additional batches should be sold if and only if they add more to firm revenues than to firm costs. Since the revenue accruing to the last batch sold is marginal revenue and the costs associated with producing that batch are marginal costs, profit maximization tells the manager to increase sales volume (lower price) whenever marginal revenue is greater than marginal cost and to decrease volume (raise price) whenever marginal revenue is less than marginal cost. If demand and cost functions were known, it would be possible to find an output rate where marginal revenues and costs are equal, and hence profits are maximum.

The rule for profit maximization is perfectly general and may be used to evaluate the desirability of many managerial decisions. In general, if revenues associated with taking an action (say a project) are larger than the costs associated with the action, profit maximization implies the action should be undertaken (since *marginal* costs are less than *marginal* revenues). The costs associated with an action include *only* those costs that originate because the action is taken. They are variable with the action (project). It should be noted that fixed (fully allocated) costs are missing from this decision criterion, since such costs do not originate with a project. All that matters is the level of *marginal* revenues and *marginal* costs. Projects must be evaluated by comparing the costs *generated by the project* with the revenues the project is expected to generate. If these costs are less than expected revenues, the project should be undertaken. If not, the project should be dropped. *In no case should a project be dropped because it does not cover a portion of general overhead charges.* These charges go on whether or not the project is undertaken, and hence any project that generates revenues in excess of direct costs makes a contribution to overhead charges. So for project evaluation, the only cost considerations that are relevant are those costs that vary with the project.

In this section we have been discussing two different types of decision problem. One of these was concerned with a "two-state" world. That is, the decision maker had but two choices, either take an action or do not take the action. The rule was simple: If the revenue generated by the action (marginal revenue) is greater than the costs generated by the action (marginal cost), the action is taken. If not, the action is not taken. In the other type of problem, the decision maker is faced with choosing among many alternatives: Which sales volume of all possible volumes generates the most profits? Here there are numerous alternatives, and profit maximization requires that price be lowered (volume increased) until, at the margin, revenue and costs are equal. In both cases, the problem required comparison of *marginal* revenues and *marginal* costs, which implies that the same decision will be reached regardless of the level of fixed costs, since fixed costs do not affect marginal costs.

**177**

Optimal Pricing
and Volume
Policies:
Preliminary
Concepts

### The Role of Fixed Costs in Profit Maximization

One must be suspicious of a decision rule that allegedly picks the profit-maximizing output but makes no mention of the level of fixed charges. Surely there are levels of fixed costs that will cause a profit-maximizing firm to close down. To investigate this question, write the firm's profit function

$$\Pi(x) = R(x) - C(x)$$

and assume that maximum profits are attained when $n$ units are produced and sold. Now let us deduce the conclusions implicit in this statement. First, $\Pi(n) \geq \Pi(m)$ where $m$ is any other output. In particular, $\Pi(n) \geq \Pi(0)$. That is, if $n$ units maximize profits, then the profits attained at this output must be greater than the profits associated with producing zero units (shutting down). Writing out this inequality in detail provides the information we desire:

$$\Pi(n) \geq \Pi(0),$$

or

$$R(n) - D(n) - b \geq R(0) - D(0) - b,$$

where $D(x)$ represents the variable costs associated with producing $x$ units and $b$ is fixed costs. Since $R(0) = D(0) = 0$,

$$R(n) - D(n) \geq 0$$

Dividing by $n$,

$$P \geq D(n)/n$$

If $n$ is the profit-maximizing output and $n$ is not zero, then price must at least cover average variable costs at this output. Otherwise the firm will find it more profitable to shut down. Notice that profit-maximizing behavior may mean operating at a loss, since a price at least as large as average *variable* cost does not guarantee that all costs are covered. In conclusion, *if* it pays to operate, then the marginal revenue–marginal cost rule yields the optimal output. But if price is less than average variable costs, the optimal policy is not to operate, and marginal revenues and costs are irrelevant. This is the role of fixed costs.

1.  Show that if $-1 < \eta < 0$, it will *always* pay a profit-maximizing firm to increase price.

2.  If profits *per unit* of production are maximum, are total profits maximum? Discuss.

3.  Suppose you are instructed to determine the production volume that would "optimize costs" where this is taken to mean the volume that would minimize costs per unit. Is this the volume that yields the highest profit for the firm? Substantiate your answer.

4. "To be sure, the whole business cannot make a profit unless average total costs are met; but covering average total costs should not determine whether a particular activity should be undertaken." True or false? Why?

5. Would a change in the level of business activity affect the marginal revenue function of a firm? How about a change in the price of a competitor's product? Substantiate your answer.

6. A marketing executive with considerable experience is asked to estimate sales volumes for a particular product at several different prices. His estimates are as follows:

| Prices (dollars) | 40.5 | 40 | 39 | 37 | 34 | 30 | 25 | 19 |
|---|---|---|---|---|---|---|---|---|
| Estimated sales (1000s of units) | 18 | 20 | 22 | 24 | 26 | 28 | 30 | 32 |

a. Calculate the marginal revenue function implied by these estimates.
b. Calculate the price elasticity of demand at several prices. What happens to $\eta$ as price is lowered?
c. Would the firm ever set a price as low as $34? Justify your answer.

7. Explain in your own words why a profit-maximizing firm will stay in business if price is greater than average variable costs but less than average total costs. After all, the firm is experiencing a loss on every unit produced.

8. In deciding whether to accept an additional order, which would entail near capacity operation for the next quarter, the production manager is asked to estimate any additional costs that would be generated by the order. Her calculations show that raw material costs would increase by $54,000 and labor costs would increase by $63,000, and that the contribution to profits and overhead of an order of this size should be about $21,000. She does not expect any other costs to change. The order is for 1,200 units. What is the minimum price that a profit-maximizing firm could charge and accept the order? Why?

9. It is in the interest of the firm to have any *given* output produced in such a way that the cost of producing that *given* output is minimum. But it is not in the firm's interest to choose among *all possible* outputs that output whose average cost is least. Explain.

10. The demand function $x = 500P^{-2}Y^{1/3}$ has been estimated, where $Y$ represents an index of disposable income:
a. Calculate total, average, and marginal revenue functions.
b. If the "index" currently stands at 125, graph these functions.
c. Does marginal revenue ever become negative? Explain.

11. Show that a profit maximizing firm will never choose a sales volume so large that demand is inelastic at the chosen volume.

# The Price-Taker

CHAPTER

8

In this chapter we study a class of decision problems that arise when management takes the current price of the firm's product or products as given, that is, as a parameter in firm decisions. This may come about for a number of reasons, the most important of which are the following: First, the firm may be selling in a *purely competitive* market, in which case it is unable to affect price. Although we have seen that existence of a purely competitive market requires a large number of small firms producing a homogeneous product, a large firm may find itself in an essentially purely competitive situation in one or more of its markets. If this occurs, it implies that the firm has been unable to differentiate its product in the markets in question and that there are numerous sellers in these markets. Second, the firm may be subject to price controls of some sort. Controls may be in the form of *price ceilings* of the type governments are fond of imposing during inflationary periods, or they may be *price floors* which are minimum price levels, below which no firm may sell. "Fair trade" laws are price floors. Third, there are a number of markets in which sellers have so little pricing power, due to the highly substitutable nature of products and the large number of sellers, that for all practical purposes, the firm makes a volume decision at the existing market price. Finally, management may not want to "rock the boat," and therefore existing prices are left unchanged even though the firm has the ability to alter prices. In each of these cases, the decision problem facing management is to choose the sales volume that maximizes profits *given* an admissible set of market prices. (The admissible set of prices may contain but one price—the existing market price.)

### The Pure-Competitor's Revenue Functions

As we have seen, the total, average, and marginal revenue functions of a pure competitor are given by

**179**

$$R(x) = P^0 x \tag{8-1}$$
$$dR/dx = P^0 \tag{8-2}$$
$$R/x = P^0 \tag{8-3}$$

where $P^0$ is the established market price which management takes as given in the sales volume decision. These functions are graphed in Figure 8-1.

**FIGURE 8-1**

Total, average,
and marginal
revenue:
the pure
competitor

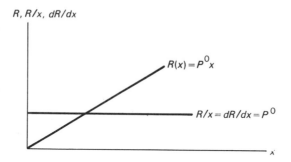

$R, R/x, dR/dx$

$R(x) = P^0 x$

$R/x = dR/dx = P^0$

It is important to realize exactly what the horizontal demand function of Figure 8-1 implies for firm decisions. Quite simply it means that the firm may sell whatever quantity it likes at the existing market price of $P^0$. And no matter what the firm's volume decision turns out to be, it will have absolutely no effect on the current price. In mathematical terms this means $dP/dx = 0$, and hence the price elasticity of demand is infinitely large in absolute value. The interpretation of an "infinitely elastic" demand function is simple; sales are "extremely sensitive" to changes in price, and in fact if the firm (say a Kansas wheat farmer) were to ask 1 percent more than the existing market price for its output, it would sell none. In other words, the individual producer has no control over price.

The conditions underlying purely competitive markets are quite restrictive and are seldom completely fulfilled in the real world. Nonetheless, there are a number of industries and circumstances where individual firms have little control over price, and in these cases the purely competitive model affords a close enough approximation to reality to be helpful in decision making.

### The Profit-Maximizing Sales Volume

As we have noted, under the present circumstances management's decision problem is to choose the optimal sales volume *given* the market price of $X$. Since marginal revenue is price for a pure competitor, the decision rule for profit maximization is to choose that volume at which marginal cost is equal to price. Mathematically, this rule may be derived merely by differentiating the profit function and equating the result to zero. The firm's profit function is

$$\Pi(x) = R(x) - C(x)$$
$$= P^0 x - C(x) \tag{8-4}$$

Differentiating and equating to zero yields the rule

$$d\Pi/dx = P^0 - dC/dx = 0, \text{ which implies } P^0 = dC/dx \tag{8-5}$$

Volume must be chosen such that marginal production costs are equal to the market price.

In Figure 8-2, marginal cost is equal to price at *two* production rates, $x'$ and $x^*$. The profit-minimizing volume is $x'$, while $x^*$ is the profit-maximizing volume. To see that sales level $x'$ minimizes profits, note that at $x'$ *any* increase in sales (from $x'$ up to $x^*$) leaves the firm better off because increases in sales in this region add more to revenue than to cost. Also, any sales level less than $x'$ is better for the firm than the rate $x'$. Since all sales volumes lead to higher profits than $x'$, $x'$ is the profit-minimizing volume and may be ignored.

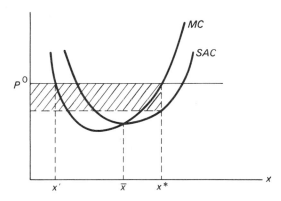

**FIGURE 8-2**

Profit
maximization:
the pure
competitor

One important fact can be learned from comparing the production rates $x'$ and $x^*$: *The profit-maximizing volume is always in a region of increasing marginal costs.* If we find a volume where price and marginal costs are equal but marginal costs are falling, then profits are minimum at that volume and it is of no interest. In other words, profit maximization implies that the plant must be utilized at a level where there is some "pressure on capacity." The shaded area in Figure 8-2 is the level of profits associated with the profit maximizing volume $x^*$.

In Figure 8-3 we have reproduced Figure 8-2 along with two associated graphs. The top panel contains total revenue and total cost functions, the middle panel contains average and marginal cost and revenue functions, and the bottom panel contains the profit function implied by the upper panels. Five volumes are of interest and are denoted as $x'$, $x''$, $x^*$, $x'''$ and $\bar{x}$ in the figure. The volumes $x''$ and $x'''$ are points of zero profit, so-called breakeven volumes. Clearly, the conditions $R = C$, $P^0 = C/x$, and $\Pi = 0$ all mean the same thing. The points $x'$ and $x^*$ are production rates at which the *slope* of the total cost function is equal to the *slope* of the total revenue function. This is another way of saying that marginal costs are equal to price or that $d\Pi/dx = 0$ at these volumes. As we saw, $x'$ is the profit-minimizing volume.

Referring now to the volume $x^*$, notice that any volume other than $x^*$ lowers profits, since at volumes less than $x^*$ marginal revenue is greater than marginal cost, and for volumes larger than $x^*$, marginal cost is greater than marginal revenue. Hence $x^*$ is the optimal volume.

One more point deserves mention: The production rate that maximizes

**FIGURE 8-3**

Revenue, cost,
and profit
functions:
the pure
competitor

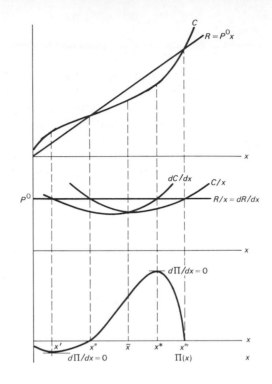

profits is *not* the production rate that minimizes unit costs. (The production rate that minimizes unit costs is denoted as $\bar{x}$ in Figures 8-2 and 8-3.) But if costs are minimum at $\bar{x}$ and not at $x^*$, how could profits be maximum at $x^*$? Can you provide an intuitive explanation?

### Economic Profits: A Measure of Market Performance

The shaded area in Figure 8-2 is the *economic profit* earned by the firm at the profit-maximizing production and sales level. It is economic profit and not accounting profit because opportunity costs must be included in costs if cost curves are to reflect the full cost of production. The interpretation of positive economic profits is that the resources (all factors including management) under the control of the firm are earning more than they could earn in any alternative activity. As a practical matter, the question of how much the resources under the control of the firm could earn in their "best alternative employments" is very difficult to answer, to say the least. An often adequate first approximation can be obtained by calculating average accounting returns in the industry in which the firm is located and then using this figure as the rate of return associated with zero economic profits. This procedure compares the firm in question to other firms with similar resources and in similar risk environments. Very often alternatives within the industry will be among the firm's best alternatives, since this is where management's expertise lies and where the firm's technology is specialized. For example, if the return on invested capital in a certain industry hovers around 10 percent, then an estimate of economic profits can be obtained by noting that the "normal" return to firms in this industry is 10 percent. Therefore, firms earning 10 percent earn zero *economic* profits, while a firm earning

14 percent is earning 4 percent more than it could earn in the best alternative
use of its resources—economic profits are 4 percent of investment.

Keep in mind that for decision evaluation one is interested primarily in
economic profits, since it is the return to a decision *relative* to the best alternative
that matters. Economic profits are the yardstick with which firm performance
is measured and upon which firm decisions must be based. The fact that a firm
earned fifty thousand, five hundred thousand, or even five hundred million
dollars by itself says little. The important question in evaulating performance is
whether the resources under management's control earned more or less than
they could have earned elsewhere. If the rate of return is higher elsewhere in
the industry (i.e., if economic profits are negative), then aside from extenuating
circumstances, management has done poorly. Analogously, the decision to
enter a new market is made on the basis of whether the return in that market
is higher than that in alternative uses of the firm's resources. The level of
accounting profits associated with entering the market is of interest *only* insofar
as it is an indicator of economic profits.

### Fixed Costs and the Production Function

If we call the profit-maximizing output rate $x^*$, then we saw in Chapter 7
that if price is less than average variable cost, $x^* = 0$, and if price is greater
than average variable cost, $x^* > 0$ and is determined by the marginal revenue–
marginal cost condition. In Figure 8-4, $x'$, $x^0$, and $x^*$ are the profit-maximizing

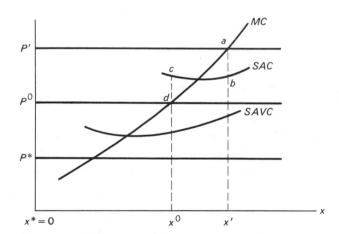

**FIGURE 8-4**
Profit-
maximizing
production
rates at
various prices

output rates associated with market prices $P'$, $P^0$, and $P^*$, respectively. The
profit-maximizing action when price is $P^*$ is to shut down, since the firm need
never lose more than its overhead costs. At the price $P^0$ the optimal policy
implies a loss (*cd* per unit produced), but a loss smaller than that incurred
if the plant were closed down. At price $P'$ the firm earns a profit of *ab* per unit
produced.

Our goal in this section is to come up with a method of finding the functional relationship between the profit-maximizing volume and the "current" market price. Such a relationship is precisely the decision rule of interest to the firm, since it would give the optimal volume as a function of market price. So once this rule is derived, the optimal volume could be calculated merely by "plugging in" the existing price. The first step in deriving this rule is to reexamine the relation between market prices and firm decisions. In particular, we must know the quantity firms will want to sell at different market prices. The schedule of the quantity of output a firm is willing to supply at various prices is called the firm's *supply function*. In Figure 8-5 the supply decisions of a profit-maximizing

**FIGURE 8-5**

The supply
schedule of a
profit-
maximizing
price-taker

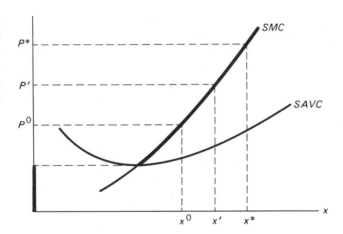

firm are shown for several different market prices. When price is $P^0$ the firm will supply $x^0$; when price is $P'$ the firm will supply $x'$ units, and so forth. These points, $(P^0, x^0)$, $(P', x')$, $(P^*, x^*)$, are indicated in the figure and are points on the firm's supply function. Clearly, quantity supplied is a function of market price and *the firm's supply function is that portion of the marginal cost function that lies above average variable cost*. If price is less than variable unit costs, the firm will close down. Given a price greater than average variable cost, the firm's marginal cost function determines the amount the firm will supply. Since factor prices and firm production technology are parameters in firm cost functions, these same variables will be parameters in firm supply functions. Notice that firm *supply functions will be positively sloped*, since, as we have seen, the profit-maximizing output is always in a region of rising marginal costs.

The relationship between the optimal volume and market price we set out to find is the firm's supply function. The only thing missing is how to actually calculate this function. If we could put the discussion of the preceding paragraph into mathematical terms, we will have accomplished our task.

To begin, keep in mind that in general production costs are a function not only of the production rate but also of factor costs and firm production technology. We expressed this earlier by writing $C = C(x, w_1^0, w_2^0, \tau^0)$, where

$w_1^0$ and $w_2^0$ are the given factor costs and $\tau^0$ reminds us that the cost function

depends upon a given production function.

Formally, the volume decision of a profit-maximizing price-taker is determined by choosing $x$ so that

$$P = \frac{dC(x, w_1^0, w_2^0, \tau^0)}{dx} \text{ whenever } P \geq \min \frac{D(x, w_1^0, w_2^0, \tau^0)}{x}$$

and                                                                                (8-6)

$$x = 0 \text{ whenever } P < \min \frac{D(x, w_1^0, w_2^0, \tau^0)}{x}$$

In this expression we have taken the extra effort to explicitly represent all influences on costs. Of course, nothing is new except the messy notation. Equation (8-6) says that for a given technology and given input prices, volume is chosen to equate marginal cost to market price as long as market price is at least as large as minimum average variable costs. If not, the profit-maximizing volume is zero.

The firm's supply function is the relationship between the volume a firm is willing to produce and market price. Clearly this is the information that is contained in (8-6). To be able to write the supply function we need only solve (8-6) for $x$ (as a function of $P$ and the given values of $w_1$, $w_2$, and $\tau$). Symbolically, the solution of (8-6) for $x$ may be written as

$$x = g(P, w_1^0, w_2^0, \tau^0) \text{ whenever } P \geq \min D/x$$
$$x = 0 \text{ whenever } P < \min D/x$$                     (8-7)

where the function $g$ is the supply function. To be more concrete, we derive the supply functions associated with several common cost functions in the next section.

### Supply Functions Associated with Common Cost Functions

In this section we investigate the properties of supply functions when variable cost functions are (i) power functions, (ii) linear functions, and (iii) quadratic functions.[1] In each case we will see that certain conditions must be met or a supply function cannot be obtained.

CASE. If the firm's variable cost function is a power function with parameters $a$ and $b$ (see equation (6-8)), then

$$D(x, w_1^0, w_2^0, \tau^0) = ax^b, \qquad a,b > 0$$              (8-8)

Marginal and average variable cost functions are

$$dD/dx = abx^{b-1}$$                                        (8-9)

and

$$D/x = ax^{b-1}$$                                           (8-10)

---

[1] Recall that the firm's total cost function $C(x)$ is not needed in the volume decision.

Since the optimal volume is determined by equating marginal costs and market price, the supply function is then obtained by solving

$$P = abx^{b-1} \tag{8-11}$$

for $x$. We then have

$$\begin{aligned} x &= (P/ab)^{\frac{1}{b-1}} \quad \text{whenever } P \geq \min D/x \\ x &= 0 \qquad\qquad \text{whenever } P < \min D/x \end{aligned} \tag{8-12}$$

Equation (8-12) is equation (8-7) for the case when variable costs are given by a power function. It must be remembered that the supply function given as (8-12) is valid only for one particular production technology and a given set of input costs. Input costs and the production technology are reflected in the parameters $a$ and $b$ of the cost function. Changes in either input costs or the production function imply changes in $a$ or $b$ or both.

Notice that supply functions in general and equation (8-12) in particular are the decision rules needed for optimal volume determination for a price-taker. These decision rules depend only upon the estimated parameters of the firm's cost function. Once $a$ and $b$ have been estimated, equation (8-12) yields the profit-maximizing volume for any market price, $P$.

But unfortunately this is not the end of the story. If one blindly used equation (8-12) to determine volume, there could be a problem. To see this, consider the case where the variable cost function is estimated and $b < 1$. (Remember from Chapter 6 that $a$ and $b$ must both be positive numbers for the cost function to make sense.) In these circumstances $1/(b-1) < 0$, and hence $x$ increases as $P$ decreases. The quantity the firm is willing to supply increases as price falls! Obviously, something is wrong.

If $b < 1$ the marginal cost function is falling throughout the production range. Several volumes determined by using equation (8-12) are shown in Figure 8-6. When price is $P^0$, volume is $x^0$, when price is $P'$, volume is $x'$, and

**FIGURE 8-6**

The breakdown of the supply function when incremental costs are falling

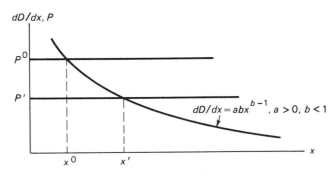

so forth. Sure enough, the lower the price, the higher the volume. The problem here is that the points shown in Figure 8-6 are not points of maximum profit. In fact, as we saw earlier, these are points of minimum profit! Therefore equation (8-12) is not a supply function when $b < 1$, since it is not the relationship between market price and the optimal volume.

We could have checked this much more precisely and easily by merely calculating the slope of the supply function, $dx/dP$. (Recall that the supply function of a price-taker *must* be positively sloping.) Using (8-12) we have

$$dx/dP = \left(\frac{1}{b-1}\right)(P/ab)^{\frac{1}{b-1}-1} \qquad (8\text{-}13)$$

Notice that if $0 < b < 1$ then $dx/dP < 0$ and (8-12) is not a supply function, since supply functions must have positive slopes to be consistent with profit maximization.

Could the situation we have been discussing ever occur in the world? This is tantamount to asking whether it is possible to obtain an estimate of the firm's cost function in which incremental costs fall. The answer to this question is often yes if observations on costs and production are not available over a wide range of production. In any limited production region marginal costs may be falling. But as we know, this behavior of costs cannot persist throughout, since pressure on capacity must eventually cause rising marginal costs. This point is illustrated in Figures 8-7 and 8-8. Figure 8-7 depicts the firm's actual

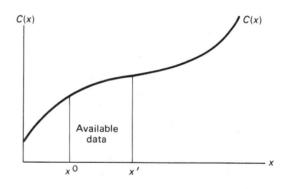

FIGURE 8-7
The production cost function of a hypothetical firm

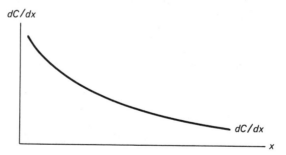

FIGURE 8-8
The estimated marginal cost function using available data

production cost function. Assume that data are available only on production rates between $x^0$ and $x'$. If so, the estimated marginal cost function will be of the form shown in Figure 8-8 even though the true cost function exhibits decreasing and then increasing incremental costs. If no observations are available on costs at production rates associated with rising marginal costs one thing is certain: Current production policy is inconsistent with profit maximization, since profit maximization demands utilization of capacity at a rate high enough to cause incremental costs to rise.

CASE II.  If variable costs are estimated to be linear, the same types of problems arise. To see this, assume

$$D(x) = ax, a > 0 \qquad \text{(8-14)}$$

where $a$ is a parameter (average variable costs). Equation (8-14) is a special case of the cost function in which variable costs are a power function ($b = 1$). Since $b$ is not greater than one, no supply function exists. Examination of Figure 8-9 makes it clear why this is so. Namely, at no point is there a volume at which incremental costs are equal to price. Incremental costs are $a$ and only by accident are equal to market price. Even if $a$ happens to equal the market price, there is not unique profit-maximizing volume.

**FIGURE 8-9**

The case of
linear costs:
no supply
function exists

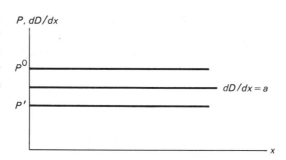

Again, the problem is similar to Case I. Here the firm estimates variable costs to be proportional to volume. This is quite plausible in many firms over a considerable region of production. But it cannot be true over all production rates. And it is precisely at these "high" production rates, at which marginal costs are rising, that profit maximization requires the price-taker to operate.

CASE III.  Finally, suppose the variable cost function confronting the firm is of the sort

$$D(x) = ax + bx^2 \qquad \text{(8-15)}$$

The supply function here is determined by solving

$$P = a + 2bx \qquad \text{(8-16)}$$

for $x$. Therefore

$$x = \frac{P - a}{2b} \quad \text{whenever } P \geq \min D/x$$
$$x = 0 \qquad \text{whenever } P < \min D/x \qquad \text{(8-17)}$$

is the supply function. Since

$$dx/dP = 1/2b$$

the requirement for (8-17) to be a supply function is $b > 0$, that is, marginal cost must be rising.

EXAMPLES. To illustrate the concepts we have been discussing we next

derive two different supply functions. First consider a firm whose variable cost function has been estimated to be

$$D(x) = .005x^{1.5} \qquad (8\text{-}18)$$

The supply function is then $x = (P/.0075)^{1/2}$, or

$$x = 133.3\sqrt{P}, \; P > 0 \qquad (8\text{-}19)$$

Since $b = 1.5 > 0$, (8-19) is indeed a supply function. A firm with this supply function will find it profitable to undertake some production no matter how low the price. This follows from the fact that average variable costs are minimum at $x = 0$ and $D/x = 0$ at this point. If $P = \$100$, the profit-maximizing volume is 1,333 units, while if price is \$144, the corresponding volume is 1,600 units.

Next, consider the estimated variable cost function

$$D(x) = 1.4x + .01x^2 \qquad (8\text{-}20)$$

The supply function is then $x = \dfrac{P - 1.4}{.02}$, or

$$\begin{aligned} x &= 50P - 70 \quad \text{whenever } P \geq \$1.40 \\ x &= 0 \qquad\qquad \text{whenever } P < \$1.40 \end{aligned} \qquad (8\text{-}21)$$

Note that if price falls below \$1.40, the firm will no longer produce this product. The reason is that the lowest permissible price consistent with profit maximization is that price where average variable costs are minimum. But average variable costs are minimum where marginal costs and average variable costs are equal. Thus, $1.4 + .02x = 1.4 + .01x$ yields the volume corresponding to minimum average variable costs. Solving gives $x = 0$. Average variable costs at $x = 0$ are \$1.40 (see Figure 8-10). Hence \$1.40 is the minimum price at which the firm will produce $X$.

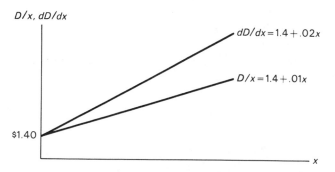

$D/x, dD/dx$

$dD/dx = 1.4 + .02x$

$D/x = 1.4 + .01x$

\$1.40

$x$

**The Determination of Market Price**

FIGURE 8-10

Average variable and marginal cost functions when $D(x) = 1.4x + .01x^2$

We noted in Chapter 7 that the market price that the firm takes as a parameter for decision making is determined by the interaction of demand and supply forces, or more precisely, by the intersection of market demand and supply functions (see Figure 7-1). Market supply functions are the sum of the quantities each firm in the market would be willing to sell at each price. The summation process is illustrated in Figure 8-11 for the case of two firms. The notation $S_1$ and $S_2$ is used to indicate the supply functions of firms one and two, with $x_1$ and $x_2$ denoting the quantities supplied. This notation is used only in this section and should not be confused with our previous usage in which $x_1$ and $x_2$ represented quantities of two different commodities $X_1$ and $X_2$. Here $x_i$ is the amount of commodity $X$ produced by firm $i$. The schedule $S$ in Figure 8-11 is the sum of $S_1$ and $S_2$ at every price and is market supply if all firms are included in the summation. At a price of $P^0$ firm one would supply $x_1^0$ units and firm two would supply $x_2^0$ units. The sum $x_1^0 + x_2^0$ is the point on $S$ at the price $P^0$. Other points on the market supply function are obtained in the same manner.

**FIGURE 8-11**

Adding individual firm supply functions to obtain the market supply function

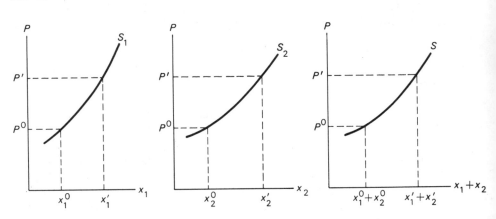

If we bring together the market demand function ($D$) and the market supply function ($S$), Figure 8-12 results. The only price that is consistent with the desires of both buyers and sellers is $P^*$, the market clearing price. At this price $x^*$ units will be bought and sold. The quantity $x^*$ is the sum of all firm sales at price $P^*$. At prices higher than $P^*$, sellers will want to sell more than buyers will buy. There is excess supply and price will fall. At prices below $P^*$ buyers will want to buy more than sellers are interested in selling. There is excess demand and price will be bid up. The price $P^*$ is the only price that is consistent with the desires of *both* buyers and sellers.

**FIGURE 8-12**

Market price determination in a market of price-takers

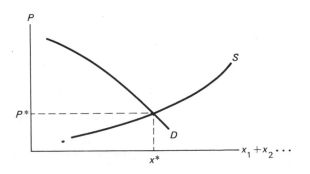

• *The Effects of Changing Market Conditions.* We have seen that the profitability of firm operations depends upon market "conditions" as given in market demand and supply functions. More carefully, market price is determined by the intersection of demand and supply, and shifts in demand and/or supply functions cause changes in market price, which in turn affects firm profitability.

To see the relation between what we have termed "market conditions" and the level of market prices, we need only recall the influences on demand and supply other than product price. In particular, the prices of inputs, the type of technology being used, and the number of producers in the market are a given set of "market conditions" that lie behind the market supply curve. On the demand side, the level of business activity, prices of substitutes, the size of the market, the level of advertising outlays, and so forth, are a given set of conditions that determine the characteristics of the market demand function. Changes in any of these "market conditions" shift demand and supply functions and hence change market price. For example, a downturn in business activity will shift market demand down for normal goods and up for inferior goods. Therefore, producers of normal goods should expect falling prices in these periods, all else being equal, while producers of inferior goods will experience increasing prices. If a tariff on a substitute is raised, the effect is the same as an increase in the price of a substitute. Demand will shift to the right and hence market price increases, the magnitude of the increase being determined by the size of the tariff increase and the closeness of the substitute. Analogously, rising input prices shift market supply functions upward and bring about increases in the price of $X$, while increases in the number of firms in the market or decreases in the effective size of the group of potential buyers will have the opposite effect.

### Optimal Volumes Under Price Control

Until now we have directed our attention to firms that either have no pricing power whatever or have so little pricing power that for all practical purposes the firm is a price-taker. (The latter implies the existence of many high-quality substitutes.) We now take up the decision problem confronting a firm facing a downward-sloping demand function, that is, a firm with pricing power, but which is constrained to price either no higher than $\bar{P}$, a price ceiling, or no lower than $\underline{P}$, a price floor. The prices $\bar{P}$ and $\underline{P}$ are determined outside the control of management and must be taken as parameters in firm decisions. Typically, price ceilings and floors are set by governments with the intention of "restricting price inflation" and "preventing ruinous price competition," respectively.

To be able to analyze the firm's problem in this context, it is necessary to know how price-makers choose price and volume if no pricing constraints are present. Our intention here is to provide only enough of the bare bones of the pricing-volume decision to permit analysis of the problem posed by price controls, since pricing and volume decisions of price-makers are discussed in detail in Chapters 9 and 10.

We saw in the preceding chapter that profit maximization implies choosing price and/or volume so that marginal revenue is equal to marginal cost. We also know that firms whose demand functions are not infinitely elastic have marginal revenue functions that lie everywhere beneath the demand function. Hence, marginal revenue is not equal to price for these firms. Management's pricing-volume decision problem in this case is depicted graphically in Figure 8-13. The symbols *MR, MC,* and *AR* represent marginal revenue, marginal cost, and average revenue. Price is chosen such that the sales volume at the chosen price equates marginal revenue and marginal cost. The profit-maximizing price and volume are shown as $P^0$ and $x^0$. Profit is lower at every other price.

**FIGURE 8-13**
The optimal
price and
volume:
no pricing
constraint

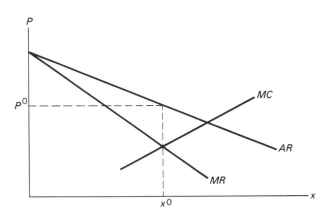

• *Price Ceilings.* We now turn our attention to determining the effect of price controls on the volume decision of the firm pictured in Figure 8-13. The existence of *effective* price controls implies that the firm has only a volume decision, even though the demand function is downward sloping. In this situation volume is chosen so that profits are as large as possible given the existing controls on pricing. The volume decision problem for a firm under a price ceiling is displayed in Figure 8-14. Management of the firm desires to do as well as possible given this constraint. As before, the firm would like to price at $P^0$ and sell $x^0$ units, but the price ceiling prevents this.

Two possibilities are shown: One arises if the ceiling is $\bar{P}_a$, the other if the ceiling is $\bar{P}_b$. (Notice that if the ceiling price is $P^0$ or higher it is irrelevant, since a profit-maximizing firm will not price above $P^0$). First, let us ask what the profit-maximizing volume is if the price ceiling is $\bar{P}_b$. To answer this question, observe that the *effective* average revenue function facing the firm is $\bar{P}_b$ until $\bar{P}_b$ crosses the demand function, $D$, at volume $\bar{x}_b$. At volumes larger than $\bar{x}_b$, firm average revenue and firm demand are once again the same. (See Figure 8-14.) In other words, at volumes smaller than $\bar{x}_b$ revenue per unit sold is merely the ceiling price. But volumes larger than $\bar{x}_b$ cannot be supported at a price as high as $\bar{P}_b$. And so once prices lower than the ceiling price are considered, firm revenues per unit are once again given by the demand function. The marginal revenue function associated with this average revenue function is merely $\bar{P}_b$ up to volume $\bar{x}_b$ (average and marginal revenues are equal when average revenue is constant) and the "regular" marginal revenue function, *MR*, for larger volumes. Therefore, given the price ceiling $\bar{P}_b$ it pays the firm to sell more than $x^0$,

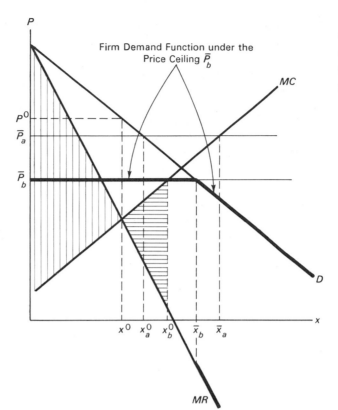

FIGURE 8-14

The optimal

volume:

the case of

a price ceiling

Firm Demand Function under the Price Ceiling $\bar{P}_b$

the profit-maximizing volume without the ceiling. The reason for this is that marginal revenues implied by the ceiling are greater than marginal costs at $x^0$ and at all other larger volumes until $x_b^0$, where marginal revenue and marginal cost are equal. Thus $x_b^0$ is the profit-maximizing output, given the price ceiling $\bar{P}_b$. Of course, profits will not be as large as when there is no ceiling. If there is no ceiling, profits are the vertically shaded area left of $x^0$ in Figure 8-14. Do you see why?[2] The reduction in profits caused by the ceiling $\bar{P}_b$ is shown as the horizontally shaded area.

Although it may seem as if the firm's decision problem is solved when volume is chosen to be $x_b^0$, difficulties remain. At a price of $\bar{P}_b$ buyers will want to buy $\bar{x}_b$ units of $X$, but the firm finds it in its interest to sell only $x_b^0$ units. There is excess demand of $\bar{x}_b - x_b^0$ at the ceiling price $\bar{P}_b$. Either buyers who want to buy must be turned away or the firm must increase its production to $\bar{x}_b$. Since profits will decrease if the latter action is taken, the firm will be most reluctant to do so. The price ceiling has caused a shortage, and the necessary conditions for appearance of a black market are present.

As far as the firm is concerned, it may seem that the decision rule for profit maximization in the presence of a price ceiling is simple: Merely choose the volume at which marginal production costs are equal to the ceiling price. We

[2]Hint: $\Pi(x^*) = \int_0^{x^*} (MR - MC)\, dx$. Intuitively speaking, what does this mean?

saw that there could be excess demand at this volume, but the rule still provides maximum profit. Or does it? Return once again to Figure 8-14, but this time observe the decision problem if the ceiling price is $\bar{P}_a$ instead of $\bar{P}_b$. If volume is chosen to equate marginal production costs to $\bar{P}_a$, the firm would choose volume $\bar{x}_a$. But at this price buyers will only buy $x_a^0$ units. Therefore, if this decision rule were adopted the firm would produce more than buyers will buy at the price $\bar{P}_a$, and hence inventories would increase by $\bar{x}_a - x_a^0$. The problem here is that $\bar{x}_a$ is *not* the profit-maximizing volume, since $\bar{P}_a$ is not marginal revenue beyond the volume $x_a^0$. This follows from the fact that firm average revenue is $\bar{P}_a$ only until $x_a^0$ and hence the marginal revenue function in this case is $\bar{P}_a$ until $x_a^0$, after which it is the original marginal revenue function $MR$. The optimal volume is then $x_a^0$, since marginal revenue is greater than marginal costs at volumes lower than $x_a^0$ and less than marginal costs at volumes higher than $x_a^0$. At volume $x_a^0$ all demands are met and the firm is as well off as possible given the price ceiling. Can you find the difference between profits with and without the ceiling price $\bar{P}_a$?

• *Price Floors.* Figure 8-15 depicts the firm's problem if a price floor of $\underline{P}$ is in effect. Given that the minimum price that may be charged is $\underline{P}$, the firm is interested in the profit-maximizing policy. The policy is straightforward: If the unconstrained profit-maximizing price is greater than $\underline{P}$, the price floor is irrelevant. This situation occurs if marginal costs are $MC_a$, in which case

**FIGURE 8-15**

The optimal

volume: the case

of a price floor

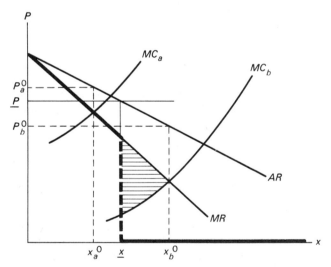

$P_a^0 > \underline{P}$ is the profit-maximizing price. If not, the price floor is the profit-maximizing price. To see this, observe that the marginal revenue function facing the firm is the regular marginal revenue function until volume $\underline{x}$, after which marginal revenue is *zero*. (See Figure 8-15.) This is the case because no price lower than $\underline{P}$ may be set, and hence it is not possible to sell more than $\underline{x}$. Given the demand function $AR$, additional units cannot be sold. As the figure indicates, if marginal costs are $MC_b$ the firm would like to price below the price floor at

$P_b^0$, but since it cannot, the marginal revenue function behaves as just stated and marginal revenue is greater than marginal cost at volumes less $\underline{x}$ and less than marginal cost at volumes greater than $\underline{x}$. Thus $\underline{x}$ is the optimal volume and is all the firm can sell at the price $\underline{P}$. So we see that if the price floor is binding on the firm, the optimal policy is to sell as much as possible at the floor price. The shaded area shows the reduction in profits (relative to unconstrained profits) caused by the price floor when marginal costs are $MC_b$. Clearly, a price floor discriminates against low-cost firms.

• *"Don't Rock the Boat" Policies.* We now briefly examine the consequences of a management policy that dictates taking current market price as given even though the firm has the power to change price. In these circumstances management wants for some reason to "leave well enough alone" and chooses the best volume at the existing price. This decision problem is shown in Figure 8-16

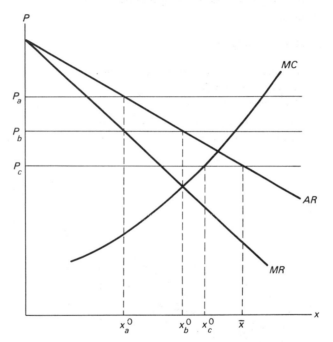

**FIGURE 8-16**
Optimal
volumes:
"don't rock the
boat" policy

for three different "existing market prices," $P_a$, $P_b$, and $P_c$. At each of these prices, the firm's marginal revenue function is the existing price until that volume at which no more buyers exist, that is, until the price line crosses the demand function. At volumes larger than this, marginal revenue is zero, since no more can be sold at the existing price, and by hypothesis the firm will not change this price. The same type of marginal revenue–marginal cost arguments we used in the preceding section lead to $x_a^0$, $x_b^0$, and $x_c^0$ as optimal volumes under the "don't rock the boat" policy. Note that the "existing price" $P_b$ happens to be the profit-maximizing price. Also note that if the existing price is low enough, for example, $P_c$, the problem of excess demand again arises. (Excess demand is $\bar{x} - x_c^0$ in the figure.) If the firm chooses to produce $x_c^0$, the profit-maximizing volume when the existing price is $P_c$, it will be forced to ration its output in some manner or adopt a first-come, first-served policy—a situation that will usually cause problems over the long haul.

• *Summary.* The policies discussed in the preceding three sections arise from a common source: The price management may choose is constrained to be either less than (in the case of a price ceiling), greater than (in the case of a price floor), or equal to (for "don't rock the boat" policies) a given fixed price. A review of the three cases will show that if price controls are binding or if the firm adopts a "don't rock the boat" policy, then the implied decision rule is either (i) sell as much as possible at the fixed price or (ii) don't fulfill total demand at the fixed price and choose volume such that marginal costs are equal to the given price. In the latter case, production is less than demand, and a method of allocating the limited production is needed. Whether (i) or (ii) is the profit-maximizing policy depends upon both the level of the "fixed" price and the level of marginal costs.

### Breakeven Analysis

In this section we return to the price-taker's problem of determining the profit-maximizing sales volume. We once again focus on firms that are very small relative to the markets in which they sell and for whose product there exist numerous close substitutes. This time breakeven charts will be utilized in the analysis. Figure 8-17 shows the breakeven chart that is appropriate for

**FIGURE 8-17**

Breakeven
analysis for a
given market
price

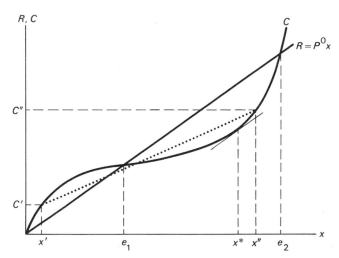

analyzing the volume decision. Of course we have seen this figure before (Figure 8-3), since a breakeven chart is merely a graph of total revenue and total cost functions. In the chart, the slope of the revenue function is constant and equal to market price, which clearly points out that a breakeven analysis under the present circumstances is *not* a pricing analysis. In general, firm cost functions will not be linear, and in particular *cannot* be linear at "high" production rates. The cost function in Figure 8-17 is for a firm whose marginal costs first decline and then rise. If this is the case, there will be more than one breakeven sales volume. In the figure, volumes $e_1$ and $e_2$ both generate the revenues necessary to cover costs. Of course, neither volume is optimal in any sense. At $e_1$ volume is "too small," and at $e_2$, "too large." The profit-maximizing volume is $x^*$, where the slopes of the revenue and cost functions are equal and hence the difference between revenue and cost is maximum. As we know, the volume where the slope of revenue and cost functions are equal is the volume where price equals marginal cost.

The only requirement for a breakeven analysis in the case of a price-taker is an estimate of the firm's cost function, at least in the "relevant" production region. It is for this reason that cost functions used in breakeven charts are sometimes *assumed* to be linear. Under this assumption, variable costs are proportional to the output level, and hence marginal cost is constant and equal to average variable cost. It is, of course, possible that unit variable costs are constant over some region of production. If not, the nonlinear cost function may be approximated with a linear function over some "standard" output region. The question here is the extent of the error introduced into firm decisions by the approximation. Obviously, the more nonlinear the cost function over the region, the poorer the approximation and the larger the error. For example, if plant volume is "usually" between $x'$ and $x''$ in Figure 8-17, one may calculate costs at these two volumes, $C'$ and $C''$ in the figure, and use the slope of the line connecting these points as an approximation to marginal and average variable costs over this region. Say the slope of this line (the broken line) is $\bar{a}$. Then $C \sim \bar{a}x + b$ between volumes $x'$ and $x''$ and the breakeven chart in Figure 8-17 is "approximately" the chart shown in Figure 8-18 over this range.[3]

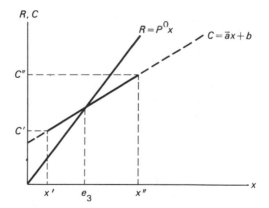

The volume $e_3$ is an *estimate* of the volume $e_1$ shown in Figure 8-17. As we have noted, whether or not the estimate will prove to be adequate depends upon how "severely" nonlinear $C(x)$ is over the region in question.

Even if costs are linear in the "standard production region," a linear breakeven analysis leaves the single most important decision problem without a solution. That problem is finding the optimal sales volume. Say that market price is

[3]The symbol $\sim$ means approximately.

$P^0$; then the breakeven point $e_3$ is given by solving $P^0 x = \bar{a}x + b$ for $x$, and $e_3 = b/(P^0 - \bar{a})$. Volume must be this large to break even, but $e_3$ is certainly not the profit-maximizing volume. Figure 8-18 provides no insight into answering this question. In fact, if one blindly uses this chart, one concludes that the larger the volume, the better off is the firm, since according to Figure 8-18 profit increases linearly with volume throughout the entire production region. This is true only if marginal costs are constant (and less than $P^0$) throughout the entire production region. But since capacity is fixed in any given production period, costs *must* eventually rise and hence the profit rate *must* eventually fall.

In one very important case, "increasing volume to the limit" is the optimal policy. This is in a firm in which costs are linear until capacity, at which time they "shoot up" vertically. Such a cost function is shown in Figure 8-19 where

**FIGURE 8-19**
Optimal
volume at
plant capacity

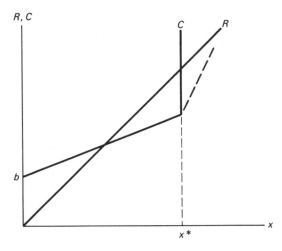

$x^*$ is both plant capacity and the optimal sales volume. The importance of this case lies in the fact that while few if any firms will have vertical cost functions at capacity, many find unit variable costs approximately constant until "close" to capacity after which costs soar. In such a situation, the optimal volume is roughly that volume at which costs begin shooting up. In a problem at the end of the chapter, you are asked to develop this point more concisely. Specifically, exactly how fast do costs have to increase before it does not pay to further increase volume? To get you started thinking, if the vertical portion of $C$ in Figure 8-19 is replaced with the broken line, the optimal volume remains $x^*$. Why? (Of course, $x^*$ is no longer maximum plant capacity.)

1. Consider a not so hypothetical case where the accounting department of a firm calculates profits to be $60 per unit of production and predicts, on the basis of a newly received order for 200,000 units, an increase in profits of $12 million. Under what conditions is such a calculation justifiable?

2. In trying to reach a decision as to whether or not to begin production of a new item, say $X$, a small firm has a production cost function estimated. Using

the estimated function, management is able to calculate the profit-maximizing volumes associated with what it deems to be the "most likely" range of prices for $X$. This procedure gives management some "feel" for the variability of volume over the likely range of market prices. The estimated cost function is

$$C(x) = 112,130 + 100x + 1.2x^2$$

and the range of prices for $X$ is thought to be $890 at minimum and $1,000 at most.

a. Over what interval will the optimal volume vary?

b. Calculate the supply function of this firm.

3. When asked to provide a cost estimate for the firm's marketing research department, the production manager forwards the following information:

$$\text{Direct Costs/Unit of Production} \begin{cases} \$5, & x \leq 10,000 \\ \$6, & 10,000 < x \leq 15,000 \\ \$8, & 15,000 < x \leq 20,000 \\ \$11, & 20,000 < x \leq 25,000 \\ \$16, & 25,000 < x \leq 30,000 \end{cases}$$

(a) If the current market price for $X$ is $9.80, what is the profit-maximizing volume? Use marginal revenue and marginal cost functions to get your answer. (b) Calculate gross profits at the profit maximizing volume.

4. In problem 2, Chapter 6, you found that variable costs of producing some item $X$ were given by $D = 1.63x^{2/3}$. Say that the item sells for $1.20/100 unit lot and that the cost function $D$ behaves according to the equation given until "capacity" at 9.5 million units. At this point, marginal costs for all practical purposes rise vertically. What is the profit-maximizing volume? If price is $1.20/1000, what is the optimal volume? Careful.

5. If the cost function for producing $X$ is estimated to be $C(x) = 101,212 + 2.1x + .002x^2$ and marketing managers decide to "leave well enough alone" and not change the price of $X$ from its established level of $149.95, what is the optimal volume? The volume you calculated is optimal *only* if a certain condition is met. What is this condition?

6. Referring to Figure 8-19 in the text, devise a decision rule for determination of the optimal volume. More specifically, consider a firm with a cost function that is linear until capacity at which time costs increase rapidly. Write a rule for determining the optimal volume. Draw a graph of your rule, using marginal revenue and marginal cost functions.

7. Consider once again the firm of problem 2 above with cost function

$$C(x) = 112,130 + 100x + 1.2x^2$$

a. Calculate the volume where profits are maximum if the price of $X$ is $950.

b. Calculate the volume that "optimizes costs," if this is taken to mean the volume where total costs per unit are minimum. Contrast this volume with the profit-maximizing volume, using a simple graph.

8. In this problem you are asked to think about the market for gasoline over a period of time in which refining capacity is fixed. Assume that industry refining capacity is being fully utilized, i.e., the industry supply function for gasoline is completely inelastic (vertical), and that due to political problems abroad, foreign supplies of gasoline are reduced from 10 to 14 percent, causing domestic shortages of the same magnitude. Taking "current" gasoline prices as $0.38 per gallon and using the results of a Department of Transportation study that estimated the price elasticity of demand for gasoline to be —.21, answer the following questions:

a. How much will the price of gasoline have to rise to eliminate the shortage?

b. What would be the effect of a government policy that prohibits prices higher than $0.50 per gallon?

c. If the industry supply function for gasoline is not perfectly inelastic, what will be the effect on the prices you calculated in part a?

# Price-Makers: The Case of Pricing Autonomy

In this chapter we investigate decision problems for a wide class of firms that have one common characteristic: Optimal decision strategies need not take into account the responses of other firms to the firm's own policies. Our focus will be on the decision problems of firms that possess *pricing autonomy*. Firms possessing pricing autonomy need not consider the reactions of other firms when designing their own optimal pricing policies. Such a situation occurs for one of two reasons. Either the firm is the only seller of a particular product, or the firm is one of many firms selling highly (but not perfectly) substitutable products. Obviously, in the former case, the firm need not concern itself with the actions of rival firms—there are none. In the latter, a large enough number of producers will mean that any one seller is so small relative to the market as a whole that the seller's decisions have no perceptible effect on other sellers. In Chapter 7 these two types of markets were labeled *monopolistic* and *monopolistically competitive*, respectively. We begin our discussion by reviewing the characteristics of these markets, after which the pricing decision is analyzed in some detail. The goal of our analysis is to derive rules that can be used to calculate the profit-maximizing price

### Monopoly

We have defined *monopoly* to be a market in which there exists but one seller of a specific product. Management's decision problem in this setting is choosing the price and sales volume that maximizes profits. Because the commodity in question has no substitutes, the seller's optimizing decisions obviously need not account for the reactions of competitors.

Since a monopolist has no competitors, strange statements are often made about the level of monopoly profits. The following proposition illustrates this point. Say for a fee of one hundred dollars you are offered a license to be a monopolist in some unspecified market. Would you take the offer? Hopefully not, since the profitability of monopoly, like that of any other market situation, depends upon the level of demand and costs. If demand is "too low" or production costs "too high" so that unit costs are not covered, the monopolist suffers losses. If average variable costs are not covered at the profit-maximizing price, then the monopolist will exit the market in the short run. And over the long haul, price must at least cover average total cost if the firm is to remain in business.

Economists are interested in studying the decision problems of monopolists, not because monopoly is a widely observed market phenomenon, but because in industries where there are but a few firms, firm decisions often closely approximate those that would be taken by a monopolist. Markets with one or only a few sellers exist because effective barriers to the entry of new firms exist. The more important barriers to market entry are discussed next.

• *The Causes of Monopoly: Barriers to Market Entry.* If earnings in a purely competitive industry rise above what the resources used in the industry could earn in alternative employments, owners of similar resources will be attracted to invest in that industry. In other words, purely competitive industries generating positive *economic* profits will find new firms entering the industry. Likewise, negative economic profits imply the exit of some portion of the existing firms. In monopolistic markets the same situation occurs whenever economic profits are negative—the monopolist will cease production. But here the symmetry between competitive and monopolized industries vanishes. If a monopolist earns positive economic profits (inputs are earning more than they could earn in alternative uses), by definition there will be no new firms entering the market. The reason other firms do not enter are called, appropriately enough, barriers to entry. The major barriers to entry in monopolistic markets follow:

i. **Control over an Essential Input by One Firm**—if one firm owns or controls an essential raw material or piece of technology, entry by other firms is precluded.

An example of a raw material entry barrier was Alcoa's ownership of the only known supplies of bauxite (aluminum ore) prior to World War II. In addition, patents on pieces of capital equipment can for a time effectively bar market entry.

ii. **Economies of Scale**—if unit costs fall with plant size over all production rates, then one firm can produce total market supply at lower cost than any number of smaller firms.

This situation is depicted in Figure 9-1, where $D$ is market demand and $LAC$ is the long-run average cost function of one firm. It is important to realize that economies of scale are not a barrier to market entry unless they are significant *relative to the size of the market*. After all, there may be economies of scale in purely competitive markets, but they are insignificant relative to the size of the market and hence are not barriers to entry. Also, keep in mind that here "economies of scale" refer to long-run cost functions—the behavior of costs when plant capacity is variable.

Cost and demand configurations like those depicted in Figure 9-1 lead naturally to one firm in the market, a circumstance that is often termed *natural monopoly*. If two firms, each with the production possibilities given by *LAC*, were to "split" the market "fifty-fifty," then *D'* would be the 50 percent market share demand function confronting each firm. Costs of production would rise appreciably, possibly forcing both firms to leave the market.[1]

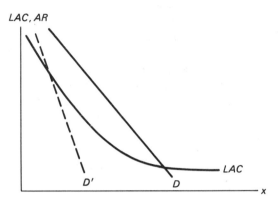

LAC, AR

D'    D

LAC

x

**FIGURE 9-1**

Significant economies of scale relative to the size of the market

   iii.  **Government-Imposed Barriers**—these barriers take the form of licensing, patents, and outright prohibition, as in the case of utilities.

The traditional reason for a governmental grant of monopoly rights in a market is the existence of technological conditions such that there are significant economies of scale relative to the size of the market. In this circumstance, one large firm will be able to supply total market demand at lower cost than any combination of smaller firms. Situations of this sort automatically lead to a dilemma, since two factors are working at cross-purposes: One firm can produce market supply most economically, but the lack of competition raises problems as to the price that will be chosen if the firm acts in its own interest. This gives rise to the possibility of governments' granting one firm monopoly rights in a market and then regulating the firm's price decision. We will explore this topic more fully below.

   iv.  **Absolute Cost Barriers**—in some industries, the cost of establishing a competitive operation effectively bars most entry.

For example, the sheer magnitude of the financial capital requirement in the steel or automobile industries makes it difficult for even the largest modern corporations to set up an effective competitive operation. Absolute cost barriers often go hand in hand with barriers caused by economies of scale.

[1] Electric utilities are classic examples of natural monopolies due to substantial economies of scale in the generation and distribution of power, although a portion of the technical economies realized by utilities is undoubtedly offset by managerial diseconomies associated with vast organizations.

The salient attribute of *pure* competition is the fact that the market price is treated as a parameter as far as managerial decisions are concerned. One of the requirements underpinning parametric prices is the condition that all firms in the industry produce the identical product. We saw in Chapter 7 that if this assumption is relaxed so that each firm within the industry produces a slightly different or *differentiated* product, and the "large number of firms" and "free entry" conditions of pure competition are retained, we have the market structure that economists call monopolistic competition.

The name *monopolistic competition* comes from the fact that these markets contain an important element of both monopoly and of competition. The competitive element derives from the "large number of sellers" condition and is especially important from a decision-making perspective. Practically, this condition implies that firm decisions need not account for the reactions of rivals. In other words, the existence of many firms in the industry ensures decision-making autonomy for the individual firm and thereby considerably simplifies market decisions.

The element of monopoly in "monopolistic competition" derives from the fact that each firm is the only seller of its particular product. Each firm has been able to slightly differentiate its own product, but unlike monopoly, the products of other firms in the industry are close substitutes. These two conditions imply that firm demand functions will be quite elastic, but not perfectly so; which in turn implies that the firm will have some control over price. But since differentiation is only "slight" (there are close substitutes), pricing options are limited.

From the point of view of management, monopolistic competition poses no decision problems that are *conceptually* different from those of a monopolist. The optimal price and volume are determined by the same decision rule, and, as we have noted, the large number of firms makes it unnecessary to include the "reactions of rivals" in the computation of these decisions.

## THE PRICING DECISION—
## THE CASE OF PRICING AUTONOMY

The primary difference between the pricing decision of a monopolist and that of a monopolistically competitive firm lies *not* in the pricing rule implied by profit maximization, since this rule is general and applies to all markets. Instead, the primary difference in pricing behavior arises from the fact that managers in monopolized industries are usually able to exercise far more control over price than are their counterparts in monopolistically competitive industries.

In general, management's "control over price" in any given market varies inversely with the absolute size of the price elasticity of demand in that market. As $\eta$ decreases in absolute value the sensitivity of sales to changes in price decreases, and hence sales volumes are less affected by price changes the closer is $\eta$ to zero. Obviously, if sales are relatively unaffected by increases in price, the firm possesses some degree of *market power*. On the one hand, is a product produced by a monopolist for which, by definition, there are no substitutes. On the other hand, a firm in a monopolistically competitive market is exposed to many close substitutes. Everything else being the same, we would expect $\eta$ to be smaller in absolute value in the monopolist's market than in the monopolistically competitive market.[2] That is, everything else being the same, firms in monopolistically competitive markets will have less control over price (less market power) than will firms in monopolistic markets.

Although the *extent* of management's pricing prerogatives may vary greatly between monopoly and monopolistic competition due to the difference in the number of substitutes in these markets, the *structure* of the pricing decision is identical in each case, that is, the pricing decision rule is the same in either market. The purpose of our analysis in the remainder of this chapter is to derive rules for determining optimal prices (and volumes) under various assumptions about the characteristics of demand and costs. We will see that the extent to which price may be raised above costs varies inversely with $|\eta|$ and therefore, ceteris paribus, monopolistic competitors will be unable to price much above costs while monopolists will usually have more discretion.

### The Optimal Price

One decision problem of particular interest to management is the choice of the price that maximizes profit. It has at times been alleged that management should set price "as high as possible." As it stands, this statement is nonsense, since demand functions are downward sloping and every increase in price brings about a decrease in sales volume. Clearly, price could be set high enough to drive volume to zero. Apparently, the "high as possible" dictum is at best an inaccurate strategy. How high should price be, then? Abstractly, the answer is straightforward: Increases in price, *ceteris paribus*, decrease sales. (The magnitude of the decline is determined by the price elasticity of demand.) Increases in price also reduce production costs due to the smaller volume. Price should be increased as long as the increases reduce costs (via a smaller volume) more than revenues. If price is at a level such that a price reduction (volume increase) would add more to revenue than to costs, then price is too high. This is illustrated in Figure 9-2, where prices higher than $P^0$ are "too high" and prices lower than $P^0$ are "too low"; $P^0$ is the profit-maximizing price. At $P^0$ sales volume is $x^0$ and marginal revenue and cost are equal.

Although price-takers and price-makers have the same "marginal revenue equals marginal cost" decision rule, the implications of this rule are quite different whenever marginal revenue is not price. In Figure 9-2 the price $P^*$ is the price at which marginal production costs are equal to price. The sales volume at this price is $x^*$. We see that profit maximization leads price-makers to select a higher price and hence a smaller volume than would be the case if the volume decision were made by a price-taker. This is a straightforward implication of profit maximization: Profit maximization demands that the firm's ability to

[2]The student should not infer from this discussion that the only determinant of the magnitude of $\eta$ is the number and quality of substitutes. This of course is not true, since all factors entering the demand function will influence $\eta$. For example, we saw in Chapter 2 that changes in the level of business activity and changes in advertising outlays caused $\eta$ to change.

FIGURE 9-2

The optimal
price:
price-takers and
price-makers

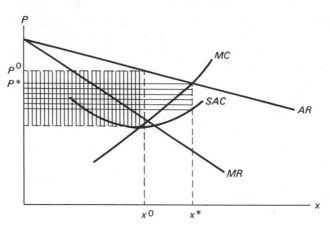

control price be used to enhance firm profitability. Profits associated with the price-maker's optimal price and volume are shown as the vertically lined area, while profits associated with the price-taker's optimal volume, given the same demand and cost conditions, are shown as the horizontally lined area. Algebraically speaking, profits at these volumes are given by $[AR(x^0) - SAC(x^0)]x^0$ for the price-maker and $[AR(x^*) - SAC(x^*)]x^*$ for the price-taker. The terms within the brackets are profits *per unit* at the volumes $x^0$ and $x^*$. Profits at volume $x^0$ are larger than at volume $x^*$. Can you prove this?

**Choosing Price *and* Volume**

One point implicit in our discussion should be made explicit: In general it is not possible to determine both price and sales volume. Profit maximization requires either choosing price and letting the market determine volume or choosing volume and letting price be determined as a function of the volume placed on the market. Figure 9-3 illustrates the consequences of attempting to choose both price and volume.

Assume that the profit-maximizing price $P^0$ is chosen, but instead of selling volume $x^0$, the firm decides to sell $x^*$ units. As the figure indicates, and as management will soon find out, it is not possible to sell $x^*$ units at a price as high as $P^0$. Either price must be lowered to $P^*$ or there will be an unplanned increase in inventories of $x^* - x^0$ units. Both of these alternatives are inconsistent with profit maximization which requires that a volume of $x^0$ be sold at the price, $P^0$. Of course, $x^0$ units is just what buyers are willing to buy at this price.

Similar conclusions hold if the firm were to choose the profit-maximizing sales volume $x^0$ and at the same time set a price not equal to $P^0$, say $P'$. Reference to the demand function in Figure 9-3 makes it obvious that if $x^0$ units are placed on the market, it will not be possible to support a price as high as $P'$. If the firm insists on the price $P'$, only $x'$ units will be sold and unplanned inventory accumulation of $x^0 - x'$ will occur. Again, the profit-maximizing goals of the firm have been thwarted. Profit maximization requires choosing *either* price *or* volume as the decision variable and then leaving determination of the remaining variable to the demand function.

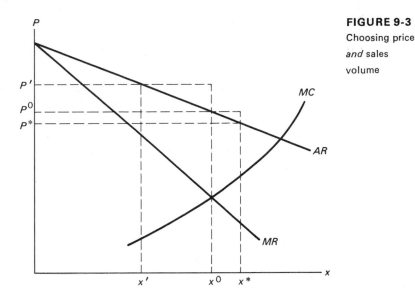

FIGURE 9-3

Choosing price
*and* sales
volume

**Pricing and Volume Policy**

In this section we turn our attention to deriving rules for calculating optimal volumes and prices. In principle our task is identical to that of the preceding chapter in which we determined the rule that related the optimal sales volume to existing market prices. As you recall, we labeled this rule the firm's supply function and found that it incorporated all the information needed for the volume decision confronting a price-taker. Also recall that the supply function contained the firm's production technology and a given set of input costs as parameters. Practically, this means that a change in any one of these parameters necessitates computation of a new supply function.

One particularly appealing aspect of the decision confronting price-takers was the very limited amount of information required to derive the supply function. All that was needed was an estimate of any *one* of the firm's total or variable cost functions.

In the course of our discussion of supply functions, we found that the price-taker's optimal volume depended *only* upon the price of the product (for given values of the parameters mentioned above). And it is at precisely this point that a major difference appears between the volume decision of a price-taker and the volume (or price) decision of a price-maker. A convenient way of contrasting supply decisions in these two types of market is to note that the extent of the demand information needed in the price-taker's decision is market price, while both price *and* the sensitivity of price to changes in volume are required for the price-maker's decision. Writing out the marginal revenue–marginal cost condition for optimal volume determination makes this point obvious:

$$x\frac{dP}{dx} + P = \frac{dC}{dx} \qquad (9\text{-}1)$$

Equation (9-1) reduces to the price-taker's profit-maximization rule if market price is a parameter in firm decisions (i.e., if $dP/dx = 0$). One arrives at the optimal volume by solving (9-1) for $x$. But unlike the case of the price-taker, the price-maker's optimal volume, say $x^0$, depends upon price, the nature of the marginal cost function, *and* the slope of the demand function, that is, on how rapidly price changes with volume. The optimal price, say $P^0$, is obtained by substituting $x^0$ into the demand function, that is, $P^0 \equiv g(x^0)$. Since $x^0$ depends upon the marginal cost function, we see once again that calculations for the optimal price and volume depend upon a given set of input costs and a given production technology. Changes in either change the form of the marginal cost function and hence change the solution to (9-1).

EXAMPLE.    Assume that the existing price of some commodity is $900 and that demand and cost functions have been estimated to be

$$P = 10{,}000x^{-1/2} \text{ and } C = 33.3x^{1.5} + 31{,}000 \tag{9-2}$$

Let us first check to see if the existing price is optimal by finding the optimal volume and the associated price. The optimal volume is given by solving the marginal revenue–marginal cost condition

$$5000x^{-1/2} = 50x^{1/2} \tag{9-3}$$

for $x$, which yields $x^0 = 100$. The profit-maximizing price is then

$$P^0 = 10{,}000(x^0)^{-1/2} = \$1000 \tag{9-4}$$

The existing price of $900 is too low.

Now consider the volume decision that would have been arrived at if the firm had taken the price of $900 as given and made a volume decision based upon this price. We showed earlier that the optimal volume in such a situation is given by equating marginal costs and the existing price *if* the volume so determined can be sold at that price.[3] Let us calculate the volume that equates marginal costs and price and then check to see if it is feasible. We then have

$$900 = 50x^{1/2} \tag{9-5}$$

which implies $x = 324$. To see if 324 units can be sold at a price as high as $900, we need only substitute $x = 324$ into the demand function. Doing this we find that 324 units can be sold only if price is lowered to $555.55. The optimal strategy is then to sell as much as possible at the price of $900. (Remember, this strategy is optimal *only* if the firm will not change the existing price.) Substituting $900 into the demand function, we see that approximately 123 units can be sold at that price.

It is interesting to compare the profits generated at the profit-maximizing price of $1,000 with those forthcoming when the $900 price is taken as a parameter in management decisions. Profits are given by

$$\Pi(x) = 10{,}000\sqrt{x} - (33.3x^{1.5} + 31{,}000) \tag{9-6}$$

[3] If you have forgotten the details of this "don't rock the boat" decision strategy, reread the appropriate section of Chapter 8.

At $P = 1000$ we found $x = 100$, and hence $\Pi(100) = \$35,700$. At $P = 900$, $x = 123$, which yields profits of $\Pi(123) = \$34,480$. Making decisions based upon the existing price of $900 costs the firm more than $1,200 in forgone profits. But once it is decided not to change price, the decision to produce 123 units yields more profit than any other volume.

### The Price Decision: Full Cost Plus A Markup?

Profit maximization implies that price be chosen such that sales at that price bring marginal revenue and marginal cost into equality. Are pricing decisions made in this manner? Are they made *as if* the marginal revenue–marginal cost rule were the decision criterion? That is, does a rule of thumb used by management lead to the same pricing decision as would be taken if the marginal decision criterion were used?

A pricing rule that is an alternative to the marginal criterion and has at times been held to be inconsistent with profit maximization is the so-called full-cost pricing rule. *The full-cost pricing principle specifies that price should be set equal to direct (variable) costs per unit plus a markup.* The markup includes contributions to both overhead and profits. That is, full-cost pricing requires $P^* = AVC + M$ where $P^*$ is the chosen price and $M$ is the markup.

An interesting question concerns how the markup is determined. Should it be 5, 10, 15, or 50 percent? Managers using full-cost pricing claim that the markup depends upon the "competitive position" of the product—the number and quality of substitutes primarily. In the discussion that follows we examine the determinants of this markup and analyze the relationship between pricing done in accordance with profit maximization and pricing done in accordance with the "full-costing" criterion.

Profit maximization implies that price should be set to equate marginal revenues and costs. Our work in this section is simplified if we use the fact that marginal revenue is $P(1 + 1/\eta)$, in which case the profit-maximizing price satisfies

$$P^0(1 + 1/\eta) = MC \qquad (9\text{-}7)$$

or

$$P^0 = \frac{MC}{(1 + 1/\eta)}$$

The optimal price depends upon marginal production costs and the price elasticity of demand.

If production costs are linear or approximately linear in the production region under consideration, marginal and average variable costs are equal and

$$P^0 = \frac{AVC}{(1 + 1/\eta)} \qquad (9\text{-}8)$$

Upon rearrangement,

$$\begin{aligned} P_0 &= AVC\,[\eta/(\eta + 1)] \\ &= AVC\,[1 - 1/(\eta + 1)] \\ &= AVC - \frac{AVC}{\eta + 1} \end{aligned} \qquad (9\text{-}9)$$

*If costs are linear, profit maximization implies that price should be set equal to average variable costs plus a markup* which varies inversely with the product's price elasticity of demand.[4] In other words, if unit direct costs are approximately constant, profit maximization implies using the same type of pricing rule that is used in the "full-costing" approach to pricing! More importantly, we have shown precisely how the markup on a product is determined, with both the level of unit costs and the price elasticity of demand determining the extent of the markup. Since the profit maximizing markup varies inversely with $\eta$, we will find small markups in highly competitive product lines, while products for which there are few good substitutes will provide more substantial profit contributions.

We now see that for the important case of linear costs, profit maximization implies pricing at average variable costs plus a markup that is a multiple of these costs. As an example, assume that variable costs are four dollars per unit and that

$$\eta = -1.5 \text{ , then } M = 2AVC = \$8 \text{ and } P^0 = \$12 \text{ , or if}$$
$$\eta = -2 \text{ , then } M = AVC = \$4 \text{ and } P^0 = \$ 8 \text{ , or if}$$
$$\eta = -3 \text{ , then } M = 1/2AVC = \$2 \text{ and } P^0 = \$6.[5]$$

One major difference between the decision problem confronting price-takers and that confronting price-makers is implicit in the discussion of this section. The difference centers on the nature of incremental costs. We found that profit maximization on the part of a price-taker demanded "heavy" utilization of capacity in the sense that volume had to be high enough to cause rising incremental costs due to "pressure on capacity." For a price-maker no such condition exists, with the consequence that constant unit direct costs are fully consistent with profit maximization.[6] This is an especially welcome result, since linearity of costs greatly simplifies the pricing decision. As the above example illustrates, to determine the optimal price, all that is needed in this case is direct costs per unit and an estimate of the sensitivity of sales to percentage changes in price.

### Breakeven Analysis: A Pricing Analysis

A breakeven analysis for a price-making firm is automatically a pricing analysis if the firm's revenue function is appropriately specified. A typical breakeven chart is shown in Figure 9-4, in which $R$ and $C$ represent total revenue and total costs, respectively. As before, two breakeven volumes are indicated, neither of which, of course, is in any sense optimal. The optimal volume is $x^0$, since the difference between the functions $R$ and $C$ is maximized at the volume where the slopes of these functions are equal. The associated price is $P^0$. Calculation of $P^0$ from the chart is immediate by noting that at volume $x^0$, revenue is $R^0$ and hence $R^0/x^0 = P^0$ is the profit-maximizing price.

[4] $-AVC/(\eta + 1)$ is positive, since $\eta < -1$ for profit maximizers.
[5] By equation (9-9), $M = -AVC/(\eta + 1)$.
[6] If marginal costs are *falling* fast enough, we could find a volume where $MC = MR$ but profits are not maximum. This point is discussed in the following section on breakeven analysis.

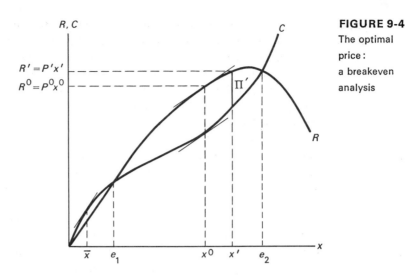

FIGURE 9-4
The optimal
price:
a breakeven
analysis

For price-makers, a breakeven analysis is a pricing analysis. The information in Figure 9-4 is the same information as that in Figure 9-2, but in a slightly different form. At price $P^0$ the marginal revenue associated with volume $x^0$ is equal to marginal cost. Why? Notice that marginal revenue is also equal to marginal costs at $\bar{x}$. At this volume, marginal costs are falling faster than marginal revenues and profits are minimum. Explain why profits cannot be maximum if marginal cost and revenue functions behave in this manner. Also draw a graph similar to Figure 9-2 to illustrate this situation.

To do the breakeven analysis we have just discussed, management will need two pieces of information—estimates of firm cost and demand functions. Although it is often tempting to use linear approximations to these functions, a linearized revenue function is valid *only* if the pricing decision has already been made. But if the pricing decision has already been made, the breakeven volume is of limited interest because calculation of the optimal price, by whatever means, implies the optimal volume. Breakeven calculations are irrelevant. This argument does not apply to price-takers. As we have seen, in such cases revenue functions *are* linear, and assuming costs to be linear gives management a breakeven chart that can be used to estimate minimal volume requirements. But as we have also seen, such calculations yield no information as to the profit-maximizing volume.

### Sales Maximization as a Managerial Objective

Up to this point we have assumed that pricing and volume decisions are taken with the objective of maximizing firm profits. And for owner-operated or closely held firms, this would seem to be the only reasonable assumption about firm goals. But consider for a moment the case of many modern corporations where firm ownership and firm control are only nebulously connected. The incentive structure facing managers of such corporations may lead to behavior inconsistent with profit maximization. More specifically, there is evi-

**211**

dence that in some firms managerial rewards are tied more to firm growth and market share than to the absolute level of profits. Since growth and market share are closely related to sales volume but not necessarily to profits, the interests of shareholders and managers may be inconsistent. Owners are interested in maximum profits, while managers may be interested in maximizing volume *as long as some minimal profit level is attained*. (This profit level may be management's views as to the smallest return that will be tolerated by major stockholders.) Therefore, if managerial rewards are a function of a variable that is closely tied to sales volume (growth or market share) rather than directly to management's ability to increase profits, management will have different goals than owners and these goals may be reflected in the pricing decision. The pricing implications of a decision to maximize volume, given a minimal profit level, rather than profits are shown in Figure 9-4. If management desires maximum volume, given only that profits be no smaller than $\Pi'$, then the optimal price is $P'$ with associated volume $x'$. As would be expected, this goal will usually imply a lower price, lower profit, and higher volume than profit maximization.[7] Clearly, it is in the interest of firm owners that managerial rewards be tied to the level of profits and not to sales volumes.[8]

## PRICING IN MULTIPLE MARKETS: PRICE DISCRIMINATION

We next consider the problem of choosing the optimal price if the firm sells the *same* product in several *different* markets. Notice that the statement of the problem implies the various markets are in some sense *separate*. If the product (a good or a service) can pass freely between markets, there is really only one market, since it will not be possible for the firm to sell the product at different prices. Inevitably, low-price buyers would sell to buyers in the higher-priced market, undercutting the firm's price.[9]

Examples of an identical product being sold in different markets at different prices are easy to find. Japanese television sets commonly sell at lower prices in the United States than in Japan. This is possible only because of import restrictions which make it impossible for an American buyer to purchase the lower-priced sets and then resell them in Japan below the going price. Doctors often charge fees that are a function of the income of the patient. High-income patients pay higher fees than do patients with lower incomes. The low- and high-income markets for medical services are separate by the very nature of the product. Low-income patients cannot buy "extra" medical service and resell

[7] Profit maximization and sales maximization given a minimal profit constraint will imply the same price (i) if the minimal profit is unattainable, and (ii) if minimum acceptable profits are maximum profits.

[8] There are exceptions to this statement, of course. For example, profit maximization over the long haul may imply the substitution of growth for profits for some period of time.

[9] In this section we are speaking of price differences in excess of any differences in the cost of servicing the various markets. If price differences merely reflect cost differences, the pricing problem is the same as those we have been studying. The unique attribute of the present problem is that the focus is on setting prices to take advantage of differences in buyers with respect to their "willingness to pay" and hence their evaluation of the relative worth of the product. We will see that "willingness to pay" is reflected in the demand elasticities of buyers.

it at a profit to higher-income patients.[10] One last example: Gas and electric utilities charge substantially higher rates to residential power users than to industrial users. Why are residential and industrial power markets separate in the sense we have been speaking of?

### The Optimal Price and Volume

Given that the firm has several *separate* markets, it will usually pay to set different prices in the various markets—prices that reflect differences in the price elasticities of demand between markets. To see the relationship between optimal prices and demand elasticities, the decision rule for determination of optimal prices must be derived.

To do this, call $P_i$ the price of some commodity $X$ in market $i$ and $x_i$ the associated volume. If there are $n$ separate markets, total production will be denoted $x \equiv x_1 + x_2 + \cdots + x_n$. The firm's profit function is then[11]

$$\begin{aligned} \Pi(x) &= P_1 x_1 + P_2 x_2 + \cdots + P_n x_n - C(x_1 + x_2 + \cdots + x_n) \\ &= R_1(x_1) + R_2(x_2) + \cdots + R_n(x_n) - C(x) \end{aligned} \quad (9\text{-}10)$$

Profit-maximizing volumes for each of the $n$ markets can be found by partially differentiating (9-10) with respect to $x_1, x_2, \ldots$ and $x_n$ and setting the resulting equations equal to zero. That is,

$$\frac{\partial \Pi(x)}{\partial x_i} = \frac{dR_i(x_i)}{dx_i} - \frac{dC(x)}{dx} = 0, \ i = 1, 2, \ldots, n \quad (9\text{-}11)$$

Equation (9-11) tells us that marginal revenue in individual markets must be equal to "total" marginal production costs. It therefore follows that marginal revenues must be equal in each market. The intuitive reason for this conclusion lies in the fact that if marginal revenues were not equal in, say, two markets, profits could be increased by reshuffling sales volumes between the markets. For example, if marginal revenue is higher in market one than in market two, profits can be increased by raising price (decreasing volume) in market two and then lowering price in market one enough to sell the additional volume freed from the second market. Anytime marginal revenues are not the same, transferring volume from the market with the lower marginal revenue to the market with the higher marginal revenue will increase profits.

But as equation (9-11) indicates, pricing so that marginal revenue is equal in all markets is an incomplete decision rule, as it does not account for production costs. In any one market, if marginal production costs are not equal to marginal revenues, profits can be increased by changing price. This familiar concept implies that marginal cost be equal to marginal revenue in each market, which in turn is equal to marginal revenue in every other market.

[10]The American Medical Association attributes such fee schedules to the altruism of doctors. We will see later that the same fee schedules are implied by profit maximization. So, profit maximization is an alternative hypothesis (along with altruism) for explaining the behavior of physicians.

[11]Notice that the condition of separate markets is needed to write equation (9-10) in the form we have.

These calculations are shown graphically in Figure 9-5 for the case of two markets ($n = 2$). The function labeled $MR_1 = MR_2$ in the third panel is the horizontal sum of the two marginal revenue functions and is obtained by summing sales in the two markets at all points of equal marginal revenue. For example, the point $x_1' + x_2'$ on the function $MR_1 = MR_2$ generates incremental revenues of $r$ and is obtained by adding the sales volume that produces a marginal revenue of $r$ in market one, $x_1'$, to the sales volume that produces the same marginal revenue in the second market, $x_2'$. All such points would trace out the function $MR_1 = MR_2$. The intersection of this function with $MC(x)$ yields the profit-maximizing *total* volume which is labeled $x_1^0 + x_2^0$. The number $x_1^0 + x_2^0$ gives no clue as to how the total volume is to be distributed between markets.

**FIGURE 9-5**
Optimal
pricing in two
separate
markets

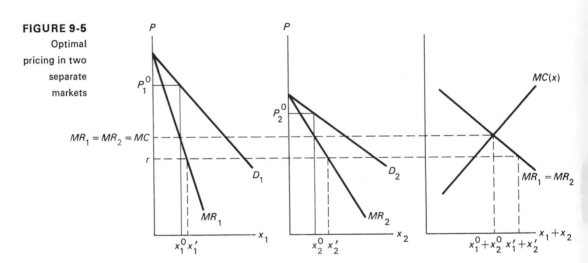

Or, analogously, it does not give the prices to be charged in the two markets so that profits are maximum. These calculations must utilize the information in individual market demand functions. Graphically, this is done by bringing the point where $MC(x) = MR_1 = MR_2$ across to intersect the respective marginal revenue functions and reading off the optimal prices and associated volumes. These are the points where $MR_i = MC$, as required by equation (9-11). Since the graphical calculation of these prices and volumes is rather complicated, it is probably worthwhile to present examples here that indicate the value of this pricing model.

### Pricing in Two Separate Markets—Examples

Suppose that direct costs are \$4 per unit over the relevant production region (that is, $C = 4x + b$), and that "marketing" is asked to make an estimate of the sensitivity of sales to percentage changes in price in each of the firm's two markets. Based upon past pricing experience, marketing managers feel that each percentage change in price in market one will lead to a change in sales of around 2 percent and in market two the sales response would be around 3 percent.

Calling $\eta_i$ the price elasticity of demand in market $i$, the optimal prices are given by

$$P_1^0 = MC/(1 + 1/\eta_1) = 4/(1 + 1/-2) = \$8$$
$$P_2^0 = MC/(1 + 1/\eta_2) = 4/(1 + 1/-3) = \$6$$

The prices of $\$8$ and $\$6$ are only as good as the marketing manager's estimate of $\eta_1$ and $\eta_2$. The better the estimates, the closer the prices to the optimal prices.

In this example, the implicit assumption underlying the marketing manager's estimates is that price elasticities are more or less constant over the sales volumes of concern. This could very well be a reasonable assumption. If management did not want to make that assumption, demand functions would have to be estimated in the two markets. Say these estimates are $P_1 = 14 - x_1$ and $P_2 = 10 - 2x_2$. Revenue functions are then $R_1(x_1) = 14x_1 - x_1^2$ and $R_2(x_2) = 10x_2 - 2x_2^2$, with marginal revenue functions given by $dR_1(x_1)/dx_1 = 14 - 2x_1$ and $dR_2(x_2)/dx_2 = 10 - 4x_2$. The profit-maximizing sales volumes are then obtained by equating marginal cost and marginal revenues in each market. Therefore $\$4 = 14 - 2x_1$, $\$4 = 10 - 4x_2$, and optimal volumes (in thousands) are $x_1^0 = 5$ and $x_2^0 = 1.5$. The profit-maximizing prices are obtained by substituting the optimal volumes into the estimated demand functions. In market one, $P_1^0 = \$9$, and in market two, $P_2^0 = \$7$.

### Prices and Price Elasticities—The Implications of Profit Maximization

In the first example, $\eta_1 = -2$ and $P_1^0 = \$8$, $\eta_2 = -3$ and $P_2^0 = \$6$. The optimal price is higher in the market with the less elastic demand. In the second example, $\eta_1 = (-1)(P_1^0/x_1^0) = -(9/5)$ and $P_1^0 = \$9$; $\eta_2 = (-1/2)(P_2^0/x_2^0) = (-7/3)$ and $P_2^0 = \$7$. Again, price is higher in the market with the less elastic demand. Are these instances of a general implication of profit-maximizing behavior, or are they merely coincidences? To check, recall that profit maximization implies that prices be chosen such that marginal revenues are equal in all markets. If there are but two markets

$$P_1(1 + 1/\eta_1) = P_2(1 + 1/\eta_2) \qquad (9\text{-}12)$$

Now assume $|\eta_1| < |\eta_2|$. It then follows that $(1 + 1/\eta_1) < (1 + 1/\eta_2)$, and therefore $P_1 > P_2$. *Profit maximization implies that price should be highest in the market with the least elastic demand.* As a corollary, we might note that if $\eta_1 = \eta_2$, then $P_1 = P_2$ and it does not pay to practice differential pricing.

We now have a prediction about the pricing behavior of profit-maximizing firms that face separate markets. It is interesting to check this prediction against observed behavior. If gas and electric utilities maximize profits (albeit under constraint), then according to our analysis we would expect to see the highest rates in markets with the least elastic demands. In other words, everything else being the same, rates should be highest in markets where there are the fewest substitutes for utility-generated power. Are there more substitutes for utility-generated power in industrial or residential markets for power?

If medical doctors are profit maximizers, we would expect to find higher fees in markets where the demand for medical services is least elastic. Fees are generally higher for high-income patients than for low-income patients. Would you expect patients with high income to have more elastic or less elastic demands for medical services than patients with low incomes? Hint: Which group is more likely to view "everyday" medical service (treatment for influenza, colds, etc.) as a necessity? As a luxury? What does this imply about demand elasticities?

## REGULATION OF MONOPOLY

In this final section we turn to the problem of regulating a firm that has been granted a monopoly in a specific market. Recall that industries in which long-run average costs are falling for all feasible levels of market demand were termed *natural monopolies*. They are "natural monopolies" because a single firm can supply the entire market at lower costs than any number of smaller firms, and the unfettered working of market forces will eventually result in an industry with but one firm.

Natural monopolies have two conflicting attributes. First, one firm is more efficient than any number of smaller firms. So, as a matter of public policy, it is often deemed in the public interest to allow one firm to be sole producer of the commodity or service in question—which gives rise to the second attribute. A profit-maximizing monopolist will usually earn positive economic profits, that is, a return on resources under its control in excess of what those same resources could earn in similar market conditions where industry entry, and hence competition, is possible. Such a return is *not* a return generated by excellent managers or superior factors of any kind. It is a return that is due, not to market performance, but to the fact that the firm has no competitors and cannot have competitors.

In such situations, governments sometimes allow one firm to monopolize the market. In return, the firm relinquishes its pricing decision to a regulatory body which uses price as a means of regulating the rate of return earned by the monopolist. The monopolist agrees to supply market demand at the regulated price.

### The Regulated Price

What should be the price of, say, a kilowatt hour of electric power? Can any general principles aid the regulatory agency in rate (price) setting? As a first step toward an answer to this question, note that the agencies regulating public utilities are usually charged with setting rates in such a manner that the firm in question earns a "fair" rate of return. In a market economy, a "fair" rate of return is usually deemed to be that return that the firm's inputs (including management) could earn in alternative employments at comparable risks. Although this return is theoretically well defined, it must obviously be an educated guess on the part of the regulatory agency. If "similar" factors in "similar" markets earn, say, 9 percent on invested capital, 9 percent is a good estimate of the rate of return that would be determined in the regulated industry if market entry were not barred.

The last statement is another way of saying that an *accounting* return of 9 percent in the industry in question yields zero *economic* profit. If price were set

so that the firm earned a 9 percent return, then (given 9 percent was a good estimate) the monopolist would earn only what it could earn in its best market alternative. This, in a nutshell, is the rate of return that regulatory agencies are charged with calculating and then implementing by setting the appropriate rate.

Figure 9-6 pictures the profit-maximizing decisions of a monopolist with and without regulation. Without regulation, the firm would charge price $P^0$ and

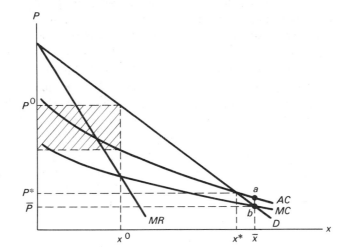

**FIGURE 9-6**
The regulated
monopolist

supply volume $x^0$. Economic profits associated with this decision are given by the shaded area. It is a simple matter to calculate the regulated price once it is decided what the firm's inputs could earn in their best alternative. This return is the opportunity cost of using the inputs under the monopolist's control and, when added to direct production costs, yields the total cost functions we have used throughout. Therefore the regulated price will be $P^*$, which results in zero *economic* profit and is the appropriate price for the regulatory body to set.

An alternative method of calculating the regulated price is to use marginal cost instead of average cost, as we have done. Both methods have advantages. A discussion of the advantages of marginal cost pricing would take us too far afield in a book of this type. But one point is easy to see and of considerable interest. Notice that if the regulatory agency chooses the regulated rate to equate marginal costs and price, the rate becomes $\bar{P}$ (in Figure 9-6) with the associated volume $\bar{x}$. Such a rate-setting policy will require that the regulated firm receive a *subsidy* of $(a - b)\bar{x}$, since economic profits are negative in this amount.

1. A certain firm has ten different products in a product line. The price of each product is determined by adding a 30 percent markup to direct costs per unit. Comment on this pricing policy. Is it consistent with profit maximization?

2. Does a change in the level of advertising outlays have any effect on the firm's breakeven chart? Explain.

3. Consider a firm whose average variable costs are approximately constant to capacity. At the profit-maximizing sales volume, the price elasticity of demand is estimated to be $-1.5$. The firm experiences an increase in demand and estimates the price elasticity to be $-2.2$ at the new profit-maximizing price. Will the new price be lower or higher than the former price? Show why. You may assume the increase in demand does not "press" plant capacity.

4. Two books have identical production costs. The first is a *Principles of Economics* textbook, the second a specialized monograph in mathematical economics. The publishing firm prices the former at $10.95 and the latter at $17.95. Make a case supporting the publisher's claim that these are the profit-maximizing prices. Explain why profit maximization would imply such a large difference in the prices of books that have the same production costs.

5. The variable costs per unit (direct costs) of producing a particular textbook are constant at $8.50. Market research indicates that each percentage increase in price will result in about a 3 percent decrease in sales. What is the profit-maximizing price?

6. Consider the problem of determining the profit-maximizing price and volume when the only information available is sales estimates provided by an experienced marketing executive and the fact that direct production costs are $12 per unit. The sales estimates are as follows:

| Price (dollars) | 40 | 38 | 36 | 34 | 32 | 30 |
|---|---|---|---|---|---|---|
| Estimated sales (thousands of units) | 20 | 22 | 24 | 26 | 28 | 30 |

a. Calculate and graph the marginal revenue function associated with these estimates.

b. Is there enough information here to determine the optimal price? Use the graph from part a as a decision aid.

7. In problem 4a, Chapter 6, you found the variable cost function to be $D(x) = .92x$ when $w_1 = \$3$ per unit and $w_2 = \$4$ per unit.

a. If the demand function for $X$ is estimated and turns out to be $x = 19,500 - 10,000P$, calculate the profit-maximizing price.

b. If the price of factor two increases to $16 per unit, what is the profit-maximizing price?

8. In problem 4d, Chapter 6, you calculated the variable cost function for production of $X$ when the amount of $V_1$ was limited to 180 units. Graph the marginal cost function and the marginal revenue function associated with the demand function for $X$ given in Problem 7 (part a). Find the profit-maximizing volume and price under these conditions.

9. Suppose the marketing research department of a large firm estimates the demand function for a particular product to be

$$x = 1.6P^{-2.0}A^{1.0}Y^{.5},$$

where

$x$ = sales of $X$
$P$ = price of $X$
$A$ = advertising expenditures
$Y$ = Index of Industrial Production

a.  If unit costs are constant at \$2.50 per unit up to 100,000 units, what is the profit-maximizing price, given advertising expenditures are \$125,000 and $Y = 144$?

b.  Several older marketing executives are highly suspicious of the quantitative sales forecasting done in the marketing research department. They argue that price should be marked up by an amount that reflects "competitive pressures." They claim that recent pricing experience indicates that sales respond about 2 percent to every percentage change in price and that based upon this information the markup on unit costs should be 100 percent. Contrast this pricing decision with the price obtained in part a using the estimated demand function.

10.  Some oil companies sell gasoline to their own filling stations (who market it as brand-name gasoline) at a higher price, then they sell the same gasoline to independent filling stations who market it as an unbranded gasoline. Why is it in the interest of oil companies to sell to the independents at a lower price? Are the conditions needed to make this a profitable policy fulfilled?

11.  Amtex, Inc., produces some commodity $X$ for a national market in two different plants. Cost functions are estimated for each plant and are

$$C_1(x_1) = 904 + 1.5x_1^2$$
$$C_2(x_2) = 831 + x_2^2$$

Here $x_i$ denotes the quantity of $X$ produced in plant $i$. By definition, $x_1 + x_2 = x$, the *total* production. Demand for $X$ has been estimated to be related to price in the following manner: $x = 10,000 - P$.

a.  Without reference to the particular cost and demand functions facing Amtex, find the profit-maximizing decision rule for a multiplant firm. (Hint: Use an approach similar to that used to derive equation (9-11) in the text.)

b.  Use the decision rule derived in part a to determine the optimal production volume in each plant and the optimal price. (Notice that the "low-cost" plant produces the largest share of total volume.)

12.  The demand function $x = 111.2 - 1.5P + .9Y$ has been estimated for the product $X$. The variable $Y$ is an index representing consumer disposable income. Several quarters ago, this index stood at 130 and the profit-maximizing price was calculated to be \$92.13. The firm's research unit estimates that the index should reach 150 this quarter. Given that unit production costs are approximately constant:

a.  Should the price of $X$ be changed?

b.  If so, what should it be?

c. Can you derive an expression relating changes in the disposable income index to the implied change in the optimal price? (This expression tells the decision maker how price should be altered per unit change in $Y$.)

d. Use this expression to calculate the profit-maximizing price at index values of 155 and 165.

13. "Marketing" estimates that a 1 percent increase in price will cause a 1.6 percent fall in sales of some product. Variable costs are approximately constant at $16.75 per unit. Based on this information, a decision is made to charge $32.95 for the product. Is that the profit-maximizing price? Explain.

14. In a number of university towns, college professors receive discounts from local bookstores, usually about 10 percent. Students are not given similar discounts. Assuming the bookstores are profit maximizers, what conditions are necessary before this differential pricing policy will be optimal?

15. Contrast the production volume that maximizes profits per unit of output to the volume that "optimizes costs." (As before, the volume that "optimizes costs" is taken to mean the volume where unit total costs are minimum.) Under what conditions are these two volumes the same?

# Price-Makers: The Case of Pricing Interdependence

Up to this point we have studied a class of pricing and volume decisions in which management did not have to concern itself with the effects of "other firm" decisions on the firm's own revenues. Although in many circumstances such an approach to firm decision making is warranted, there is one obvious exception: the case where there are but a small number of firms in a market selling highly substitutable products. When markets of this type were first introduced in Chapter 7 we labeled them *oligopolistic*, from the Greek meaning "few sellers." Fewness of sellers implies that *market decisions of sellers are mutually interdependent*.

Instances of *oligopoly* abound in the U. S. economy. The refining stage in the processing of most primary metals, and the manufacture of steel, cigarettes, automobiles, computers, and rubber, are but a few of many examples. In each case the production of a few firms is sufficient to satisfy much or most domestic demand, and in some cases, even much of world demand.

### Mutual Interdependence

From the perspective of firm decision makers, the crucial difference between oligopoly and all other market structures is that since there are only a few sellers, individual firms will be acutely aware of the decisions of rivals and the reaction of rivals to the firm's own policies. More technically, *demand functions of individual sellers are interdependent*. Demand interdependence and the resultant interdependence of decisions of all firms in a market present managers with formidable difficulties. To illustrate, consider the demand functions of the two firms in a two-firm oligopoly, $x_1 = f_1(P_1, P_2, Y, A_1, A_2)$ and $x_2 = f_2(P_1, P_2, Y, A_1, A_2)$, where the advertising expenditures of firm two have been included in the demand function facing firm one, and vice versa. If there are but a few sellers, changes in the advertising outlays of any one firm will affect the market shares of other sellers.

The effects of demand interdependence show up vividly if the demand functions for $X_1$ and $X_2$ are graphed. The demand curve for $X_1$ is then written $x_1 = \bar{f}_1(P_1)$, and that for $X_2$ is $x_2 = \bar{f}_2(P_2)$. Keep in mind that the price of $X_2$, "business conditions," and advertising expenditures are parameters in the demand curve for $X_1$, while the price of $X_1$, "business conditions," and advertising expenditures are parameters in $\bar{f}_2(P_2)$. Now consider what happens when the seller of $X_1$ decides to lower the price of $X_1$ from $P_1^0$ to $P_1^*$. Let us say that at the original price of $P_1^0$, firm two was selling $X_2$ at $P_2^0$. This situation is depicted graphically in Figure 10-1. At these prices, firm one is selling $x_1^0$ units and firm

FIGURE 10-1

Pricing
interdependence:
the case of
two firms

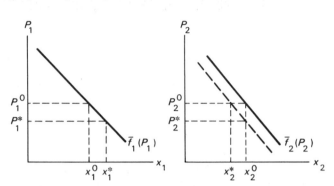

two is selling $x_2^0$ units. Under other circumstances, firm one could expect sales to increase to $x_1^*$ units when price is lowered to $P_1^*$. But, in oligopolistic markets, this usually does not happen, since firm one's decision to lower price to $P_1^*$ must, at one and the same time, be a decision to take a portion of firm two's market share. To see this, recall that $P_1^0$ is a parameter in $\bar{f}_2(P_2)$, that there are only two firms, and that $X_1$ and $X_2$ are substitutes. Any decrease in $P_1$ will *shift $\bar{f}_2(P_2)$ to the left* (shown as a broken line), and firm two suddenly finds that volume has decreased by $x_2^0 - x_2^*$. To regain the lost share of the market, the seller of $X_2$ will be forced to lower price to $P_2^*$, which will in turn shift $\bar{f}_1(P_1)$ to the left, reducing the newly gained market share of $X_1$. This in a nutshell illustrates the central characteristic of oligopoly—mutual interdependence of sellers. Rivals find that every time one of them lowers price, all others automatically respond to protect their share of the market.[1] An analogous argument shows that advertising policies of firms, like pricing policies, must also be mutually interdependent in oligopolistic markets.

### Mutual Interdependence:
### Differentiated and Homogeneous Oligopoly

It is possible to classify oligopolists as being either homogeneous or differentiated, depending upon the degree to which products are differentiated in given markets. If there is little product differentiation, the oligopoly is called

---

[1] Although market shares remain approximately the same after all price cuts, *total* market volume will have increased.

*homogeneous*; but if distinct product differentiation exists, the oligopoly is said to be *differentiated*.

As far as management is concerned, the importance of the distinction between homogeneous and differentiated oligopoly lies in its implications for decision making. In homogeneous oligopoly, decision interdependence of firms will be most acute, since products are virtually identical. Hence, even small price changes will have a dramatic effect on market shares. The more differentiated is the product of any one seller, the more that seller is insulated from the pricing policies of other sellers *and* from retaliation on the part of other firms when the firm in question lowers price. A product is perfectly "insulated" from the pricing policies of competitors only if all cross-elasticities of demand are nonpositive, that is, if the firm is a monopoly; or if there are such a large number of firms that the actions of any single firm has no perceptible effect on other sellers, that is, the firm is in a monopolistically competitive industry.

The concept of "product homogeneity" must be interpreted carefully. In the context of the present chapter, the word *product* should be taken to mean the entire "bundle of services" sold by the firm. This usage arises from the fact that producers of homogeneous products (in the narrow sense) often engage in substantial product differentiation in terms of the "bundle of services" that accompany the firm's product. Such firms spend considerable amounts of money to provide optimum delivery schedules, consulting service, and so forth, as well as the traditional wining and dining of buyers.

Another possibility for categorizing oligopolistic firms would be to distinguish between firms that produce goods for direct consumption by consumers and those that produce intermediate goods for use by other firms. The primary difference between these two classes of firms lies in the fact that product differentiation undertaken in consumer good oligopolies is often unlike that found in oligopolies producing intermediate goods. In a nutshell, buyers of intermediate goods are experts on the products they buy, and hence the informational advertising carried on by the producers of consumer goods is of limited value. For this reason producers of intermediate goods often differentiate their products by offering different "bundles of service."

### More on Mutual Interdependence

To see more precisely the nature of the decision interdependence of which we have been speaking, consider once again the same two-firm oligopoly discussed above. The primary market decisions open to firms are the pricing and advertising decisions. But as we have seen, in oligopoly, *individual firm revenues will depend upon the reaction of rival firms to the firm's own marketing policies*. To explore this relationship more thoroughly, write the demand functions of the two firms as

$$x_1 = f_1(P_1, P_2, Y, A_1, A_2) \tag{10-1}$$
$$x_2 = f_2(P_1, P_2, Y, A_1, A_2) \tag{10-2}$$

It is helpful to solve the demand function for firm two for $P_2$, after which equation (10-2) becomes

$$P_2 = g_2(P_1, x_2, Y, A_1, A_2) \tag{10-2'}$$

Equation (10-2′) tells us that the price firm two is able to charge for $X_2$ depends upon the price of $X_1$, the amount of $X_2$ being sold, business conditions, and the advertising outlays of the two firms.

For given advertising policies and business conditions, revenues of firm one depend upon the pricing policies of *both* firms. That is,

$$r_1(P_1, P_2) = P_1 x_1 \qquad (10\text{-}3)$$

where we have used a lowercase letter $r$ to denote revenue as a function of price. The quantity $x_1$ is given by equation (10-1). Using equation (10-1) and remembering that $P_2$ is a function of the price of $X_1$ by equation (10-2′), it is a simple matter to calculate the response of $r_1$ to changes in $P_1$:

$$\frac{\partial r_1}{\partial P_1} = x_1 + P_1 \left( \frac{\partial x_1}{\partial P_1} + \frac{\partial x_1}{\partial P_2} \frac{\partial P_2}{\partial P_1} \right) \qquad (10\text{-}4)$$

The *percentage* change in $r_1$ due to *percentage* changes in $P_1$ is given by

$$\frac{\partial r_1}{\partial P_1} \left( \frac{P_1}{r_1} \right) = 1 + \eta_{11} + \eta_{12} \left( \frac{\partial P_2}{\partial P_1} \right) \left( \frac{P_1}{P_2} \right) \qquad (10\text{-}4')$$

This expression clearly shows the problem management encounters when trying to come up with a consistent pricing policy. More specifically, the percentage response of firm revenues to percentage changes in the price of $X_1$ depends not only upon the price elasticity of demand for $X_1$ and the cross-elasticity with $X_2$ but also upon $(\partial P_2 / \partial P_1)(P_1 / P_2)$, the percentage response of $P_2$ due to a change in the price of $X_1$. Call this term $\theta_{21}$ and notice that it measures the amount of pricing interdependence between the seller of $X_1$ and the seller of $X_2$. More precisely, $\theta_{21}$ is the elasticity of $P_2$ due to changes in $P_1$. If $\theta_{21} = 0$, we are back to the case of pricing autonomy, and (10-4′) collapses into equation (7-6). For price-makers with pricing autonomy, the response of revenues to percentage changes in price depends only upon $\eta_{11}$ for *given* values of $P_2, P_3$, and so forth. And this is precisely the difference between markets with pricing antonomy and oligopolistic markets; in the latter management cannot take the prices of rivals to be invariant to management's own pricing decisions.

Although the size of the *reaction coefficient* $\theta_{21}$ is highly uncertain as far as management of firm one is concerned, the message of (10-4′) is clear—the pricing policy of firm one must "take into account" the change in the price of $X_2$ which is *induced* by a change in $P_1$. Fewness of sellers implies that the pricing policies of firms one and two are necessarily interdependent. To see just how uncertain the revenue effects of changes in price are, let us rewrite (10-4′) as

$$\frac{\partial r_1}{\partial P_1} \left( \frac{P_1}{r_1} \right) = (1 + \eta_{11}) + \eta_{12} \theta_{21} \qquad (10\text{-}4'')$$

and examine the terms more closely. First, we know that for profit-maximizing firms $\eta_{11} < -1$ (see Chapter 7, problem 11) and therefore $1 + \eta_{11} < 0$. Also, the fact that $X_1$ and $X_2$ are substitutes means $\eta_{12} > 0$. Although we would expect $\theta_{21}$ to depend upon the current goals of management of firm two, this

term will normally be positive (or possibly zero). Firm two will usually follow price changes instigated by firm one, or at the very least, not make price changes in response that are in the opposite direction. More concretely, price *reductions* by firm one will almost certainly be followed by firm two in the interest of preserving its market share, that is, $\theta_{21} > 0$ for price reductions. Price *increases* by firm one will usually be followed but at times may be ignored, that is, $\theta_{21} \geq 0$ for price increases. Hence, in general, $\theta_{21} \geq 0$. Using this fact and equation (10-4″) provides additional insight into the pricing problem facing management. The term $(1 + \eta_{11})$ is negative, whereas $\eta_{12}\theta_{21}$ is positive (or possibly zero) and hence the effects on firm one's revenues of a change in price are not known— *even if the demand function for $X_1$ were known*. This follows because $\theta_{21}$ is not known by management of firm one. Notice that not even the *direction* of change of revenue can be determined. For example, if the price of $X_1$ is lowered, firm one revenues will *increase* if firm two changes the price of $X_2$ by "relatively little," while if the change in $P_2$ is "relatively large," $r_1$ will *fall*.

The discussion of the preceding paragraph is important enough to deserve further amplification. The fact that the response of revenue (not profits) to price changes is unknown is overwhelming! In any other type of market, management can infer from the size of the price elasticity of demand what will happen to firm revenues as a result of a price change.[2] But not in oligopoly. Even if the demand function were known exactly (with certainty), the individual oligopolist will not know the revenue effects of a price change or even the sign of these effects.

The effect of so much uncertainty surrounding the outcome of pricing decisions provides a strong incentive for management to search for policies that will reduce that uncertainty. There are two obvious alternatives: (i) reach an accord with the other firms in the industry concerning pricing policy, or (ii) adopt a pricing policy designed not to provoke reaction from other firms. In the first instance we will say the firm *colludes* with rival firms; in the second we will say the firm adopts a *conservative* pricing policy. "Conservative pricing policies" are pricing policies that are constrained to that set of prices that will not provoke rival reactions.

### A Summary of the Pricing Problem In Oligopoly

We have seen that "fewness of sellers" in a market implies that sellers' demand functions are interdependent and hence decision makers cannot ignore the decisions of other sellers in the market. Indeed, any coherent pricing strategy must include some assumption about how rivals react to the pricing policies of other firms. Technically, if there are $n$ firms in a market ($n$ is "small"), then managers responsible for pricing policy in any single firm, say firm $j$, are forced to make some assumption about the reaction coefficients $\theta_{ij}$, $i = 1, 2, \ldots, n$, $i \neq j$. And as shown above, there is much uncertainty as to the size of these terms.

[2]The relationship between firm revenues and price was explored in Chapter 7.

At this point the student might legitimately ask how real-world oligopolists make pricing decisions if it is as difficult as we have implied. The answer has already been alluded to: Real-world oligopolists very often either collude with rival firms or adopt "conservative" pricing policies. Most of the remainder of the chapter will analyze firm decisions under one of these alternatives.

### Collusion Among Rivals

Collusion among rival firms spans the gamut from independent actions on the part of individual firms to highly detailed agreements between sellers concerning pricing and production policy of the type commonly found in cartels. Although collusive arrangements are illegal under the antitrust laws in the United States, they are not illegal in many other parts of the world.[3] Cartels are a common form of business organization in many European countries and in Japan.

In practice, it is often difficult to determine whether certain observed policies are evidence of collusion among firms or are merely the outcome of individual firms acting independently and rationally in their own self-interest. For example, in many industries in the United States, price is set by a "price leader" and is then adopted by all other firms. Whether these firms are following a well-planned collusive strategy or merely pursuing "conservative" pricing policies by adopting the "safe" price of the leader is often impossible to determine. After all, each firm knows that if all firms follow the price leader's policy, pricing reactions are eliminated, market shares are determinate, and firms are free to attend to other matters. Clearly, firms need not collude to reach such a decision.

Oligopolistic markets in which firm pricing policies are neither "conservative" nor collusive are usually characterized by periods of extreme price instability, at times culminating in "price wars." But often once a price has been established in these markets, there are extended periods of price stability due to a reluctance on the part of individual sellers to change a price once it has been established—a reluctance due primarily to the amount of uncertainty surrounding the effects of a price change. So in market situations like those just described, sellers have a tendency to vacillate from the ultimate in conservative pricing policies (seldom changing price once a price is established) to the aggressive, market share threatening type of pricing policy that can foment a price war.

Now let us consider the reaction coefficients $\theta_{ij}$ if firms within a market should (1) agree to collude on prices or (2) adopt a pricing policy explicitly designed not to provoke reactions from other firms. It is important to see that in either circumstance *the reaction of firm i to a change in $P_j$ is known*! For example, consider a simple case of price leadership where firm one is price leader and whenever firm one changes price other firms adopt the new price within a few days. This may occur because of a formal agreement or because "following the leader" is a "safe" (conservative) pricing policy. In either case

---

[3]Illegal cartellike arrangements do periodically come to light in the United States. A fairly recent example is the conviction of General Electric and several other large electrical contractors for price-fixing agreements. In this case a formal pricing scheme was discovered, the so-called phases of the moon formula, which established collusive behavior beyond a reasonable doubt.

$\theta_{i1} = 1$, for all firms $i$ and $\theta_{1j} = 0$, $j \neq 1$. This follows since a $y$ percent change in $P_1$ means a $y$ percent change in all other prices within a few days which in turn causes no reaction from firm one. *Pricing agreements and "conservative" pricing policies have the effect of reducing or eliminating the uncertainty generated by interdependent demand functions.* The stronger the collusive agreement, or the more "conservative" the firm's pricing policy, the more predictable is the reaction of rivals to price changes (i.e., the less uncertain are the $\theta_{ij}$).

We have briefly examined the roles of both "conservative" pricing policies and price collusion in oligopolistic markets and have found that without such policies there is much uncertainty surrounding the effects of price changes— uncertainty that cannot be decreased by estimating demand functions.[4] Consequently, no *general* strategies for optimal pricing exist (i.e., strategies that hold for all types of rival reactions). On the other hand, agreements between firms concerning pricing policies, or pricing policies carefully chosen not to provoke rival reactions, have the effect of determining the reaction coefficients, $\theta_{ij}$, and thereby make it possible for management to use pricing strategies similar to those analyzed in the preceding chapter. We next examine several pricing models that testify to this fact. Each model is based upon the intention on the part of management to maximize profits *given* some assumption about how rivals will react to price changes.

## PRICING IN OLIGOPOLISTIC MARKETS

### Cartels

A cartel is a group of firms organized via overt, formal agreements to act as a unit. A central association is appointed or elected from the management of participating firms, and individual firm pricing decisions and production quotas are surrendered to the association. The task of the association is to take decisions that maximize *industry* profits subject to the constraint that prices and production quotas be acceptable to all cartel members. If not, dissatisfied members may leave the cartel and jeopardize its existence.[5]

Clearly, if the goal of the cartel is to maximize *industry* profits, the price set would be the same price a monopolist would choose. Keep in mind that it is not possible for individual sellers to follow independent profit-maximizing strategies because of their mutually· interdependent demand functions, and the cartel arrangement is the second-best option.

The decision problem of the central association is depicted graphically in Figures 10-2a and 10-2b. Very little is new. The curve labeled $AR$ is the demand function for the entire market, and $MR$ is the associated marginal revenue function. To "price as a monopolist," it will be necessary to have a marginal cost function for the entire cartel output. This is obtained by summing the marginal cost functions of individual cartel members and is denoted $\sum MC$ in

---

[4] Estimation of demand provides no information about the $\theta_{ij}$'s, which are responsible for the type of uncertainty we have been discussing.

[5] With an agreement of this type $\theta_{ij} = 0$, $i \neq j$, since there are no pricing reactions of any kind.

FIGURE 10-2

Determination
of price and
production
quotas in a
cartel

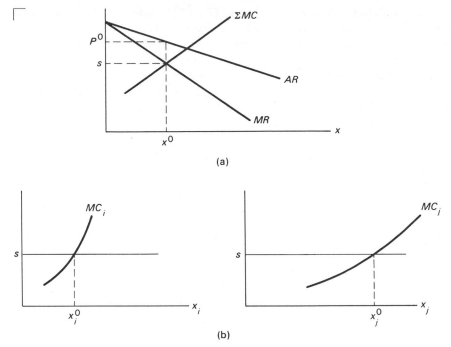

(a)

(b)

Figure 10-2a. The price that maximizes cartel profits is obtained via the familiar rule and is shown as $P^0$. The corresponding volume is $x^0$.

There remains one important problem, a problem often responsible for the dissolution of cartels: Production quotas must be determined in a manner deemed satisfactory by individual cartel members. Profit maximization implies that members should produce that volume such that *member* marginal cost equals *cartel* marginal revenue at the optimal volume, $x^0$. (Can you show why this is so?) Cartel marginal revenue at the profit-maximizing price is $s$ in Figure 10-2a. Given this information, the production quotas of all firms are determined. This process is depicted graphically for two member firms in Figure 10-2b. Since an estimate of each firm's cost function must be obtained by the central association before cartel price and volume can be determined, these same estimates will be used to set member firm's production quotas.

The major problem with determining quotas in this manner is clearly brought out in the same figure. Low-cost firms have high quotas, and high-cost firms have small quotas. So unless costs are similar, there could well be problems. The situation depicted in the figure is probably unstable, since firm $i$ may not stay in the cartel unless its quota expands relative to that of firm $j$. Possibilities include determination of quotas using historical market shares, existing firm capacities, or bargained quota allocations.

Firms enter into cartel agreements to eliminate the decision problems posed by the indeterminate demand functions confronting individual firms. Formation of a cartel accomplishes this famously. Instead of a market with a number of firms, each with a highly volatile share depending on the pricing policies of other firms, the cartel confronts a stable demand function and, as far as pricing is concerned, is in the enviable position of a monopolist. Even so, cartels have a difficult time staying intact because of differences among members concerning policy. Seldom is there disagreement about pricing policy, since the method used yields the largest "pie." But how to split up the "pie" is another matter.

Also, there is every reason for an individual member to "cheat" and sell below the established price, if it can be done without detection. For any one firm, demand will be extremely elastic at prices just beneath the cartel price, and hence a small price reduction will cause volume to soar. If there are but few firms in the agreement, such a tactic will be detected immediately. But the greater the number of firms, the more differentiated the products, and the greater the distance between firms, the more difficult it will be to detect price cuts and hence the greater the incentive for cheating. This will be especially true in periods of low demand. And even if partners to a collusion are able to detect the firm selling at lower prices, a difficult problem remains in countries where collusion is illegal. If collusion is illegal, detection of the low-priced firm does not mean the lower prices will cease, since legal sanctions cannot be exercised against the errant firm. In practice, policing of an illegal agreement requires great powers of persuasion or credible threats of retaliation.

### Price Leadership by the Low-Cost Firm

In a cartel, rivals behave as if they were one firm. In the case of price leadership, one firm sets price and other firms follow. There may exist an agreement between the firms involved, but as often as not, price leadership roles evolve with an industry as firms gradually and independently find it in their interest to adopt the "safe" policy of following the pricing leader. As we have mentioned previously, if all firms in an industry follow the price leader, the uncertainty surrounding reaction coefficients vanishes and policies based upon considerations similar to those studied in the preceding chapter may be undertaken. In this section we examine the case where the low-cost firm is the price leader, and in the next the case where the "dominant" firm is the price leader.

There will seldom be any doubt within an industry as to which firm has the lowest costs, since profit maximization implies, ceteris paribus, that relatively low costs will result in relatively low prices. The low-cost firm generally is the firm that, before its price leadership role, underpriced other firms in the industry and often fomented price wars, and because of its cost situation was in a position to outlast competitors in periods of price warfare.

Figure 10-3 shows the pricing problem confronting the low-cost firm when there are but two firms in the market *and* the firms agree to split the market "fifty-fifty." (Limiting consideration to two firms and a fifty-fifty split allows a relatively comprehensible graphical display of the problem.) The curve labeled $D$ represents total (market) demand, $d$ is the 50 percent market share demand function facing each of the firms, and $mr$ is the marginal revenue function associated with $d$. The cost functions of the two firms are subscripted to indicate their origin. Obviously, firm one is the low-cost firm and market price will be set to be $P_1^0$, the price that maximizes the profit from firm one's share of the

FIGURE 10-3

Price

leadership by

the low-cost

firm

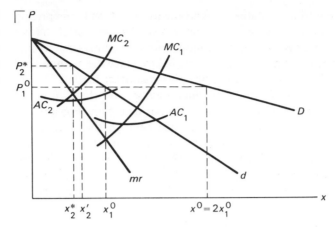

market. Since costs are not identical, a conflict of interest arises over this price. Firm two would like to price at $P_2^*$ and sell $x_2^*$ units but of cour⸱ ⸱annot, since firm one would capture the entire market if such a policy we⸱ followed.[6] In addition, firm two is in a cost position that will not allow it to precipitate a price war as a protest against firm one's pricing policy.

One other point is of interest here: Given the market price of $P_1^0$, firm two's profits would be highest at a volume of $x_2'$. (Do you see why?) But this volume is not consistent with the 50 percent market share the two firms have agreed upon. To maintain its share of the market, firm two must increase volume to $x_1^0$. This volume gives firm two one-half of the market, and implies market volume is $x^0 = 2x_1^0$, the total amount that will be demanded at the price $P_1^0$. Also, note that firm one could lower price below $P_1^0$ for a time and drive firm two out of the market. Whether this is advisable or not depends upon the antitrust laws in the economy in question.

### Price Leadership by the Dominant Firm

In many oligopolistic markets, one or two large firms are found along with a number of smaller firms, much like the steel industry in the United States. As in all oligopolistic settings, these firms will not find it possible to follow independent pricing strategies. One type of arrangement that is used occasionally with some success is termed "price leadership by the dominant firm." Under such an arrangement the dominant firm sets industry price, smaller firms sell as much as they desire at this price, and the dominant firm fills out the market.

As before, such a situation may be the outcome of a formal agreement among the firms involved, or it could gradually come into existence as individual firms adopt pricing schemes designed to minimize rival reactions. The evidence in the United States seems to favor the latter hypothesis in most cases.

---

[6]This statement presumes homogeneous oligopoly. If products are differentiated, firm two may not lose its entire market share.

Under the type of arrangement between firms we have described, there are two distinct decision problems—the volume decision of smaller firms, and the pricing decision of the dominant firm. The pricing decision problem of the dominant firm is to choose that price that maximizes dominant firm profits, *given* this arrangement with the smaller firms. Again, keep in mind that such an arrangement would never be entered into by either the small firms or the dominant firm if it were not for the highly unstable demand functions that confront individual firms without some type of arrangement among firms.[7]

Under the conditions outlined, small firms will choose volumes so that their individual profits are maximum at the price established by the dominant firm. And, since under these conditions each small firm will face a perfectly elastic demand function at this price, the volume decision rule for the $i^{th}$ small firm is $P^0 = MC_i$. That is, if $P^0$ is the price set by the dominant firm, the $i^{th}$ firm will choose that volume at which its marginal cost is equal to $P^0$. As we saw earlier, under these circumstances marginal cost functions are firm supply functions. Therefore, total small-firm supply is given by summing small-firm marginal cost functions. Notice that this is precisely the information the dominant firm needs to make its own pricing decision, namely, how much small firms will supply at various prices. Once this is known, the dominant firm can calculate the difference between market demand and small-firm supply, at different prices. Under the conditions outlined, this is the market share of the dominant firm as a function of price.

In Figure 10-4, $\sum MC_i$ represents the supply function of the smaller firms and $D$ is market demand. The curve $AR_d$ is the dominant firm's demand function

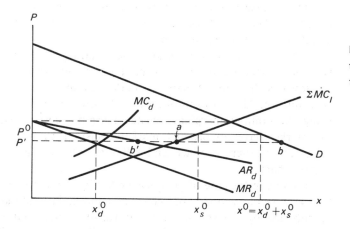

**FIGURE 10-4**

Price
leadership by
the dominant
firm

which is the residual between market demand and small-firm supply at every price. To calculate dominant firm demand at, say, price $P'$, note that small firms will supply the quantity, $P'a$, leaving a residual demand of $ab$. This volume

---

[7]It is important to remember that the "small" firms mentioned here are only "small" relative to the dominant firm; and they are price-takers only because of the arrangement we have been discussing. Without the arrangement, they are price-makers, albeit smaller than the dominant firm.

is the point on the dominant firm's demand function at price $P'$. All other points are found analogously.[8]

Given the residual demand function, the dominant firm's pricing strategy poses no new difficulties. If $MR_d$ represents the marginal revenue function associated with the dominant firm's demand function and $MC_d$ is dominant firm marginal cost, then the profit-maximizing price, $P^0$, is that price that generates the sales volume $x_d^0$. At this price, small firms will supply a total of $x_s^0$ units, making total volume $x^0 = x_s^0 + x_d^0$ as shown. Of course this is the amount that can be sold at the price $P^0$, since $P^0$ corresponds to the point $x^0$ on the market demand function. (Note that $x_d^0 = x^0 - x_s^0$ by definition.)

**A Summary of Pricing in Collusive Markets**

We have investigated three pricing models that have one common factor: In each there is an "understanding" among sellers in the market as to how market price is to be determined. As we have seen this need not, and often does not, imply collusion among the firms. As long as this arrangement is honored, the central problem of oligopolistic decision making is circumvented. That is, such arrangements eliminate the effects of mutual interdependence upon firm decisions.

In the case of the cartel, the central association will need an estimate of market demand and an estimate of the cost functions facing individual cartel members to determine market price and member production quotas. Once these estimates are obtained, the association's pricing decision is identical to that confronting a monopolist.

In the case where pricing is done by the low-cost firm with other firms following, there is only one pricing problem—that of the low-cost firm. In this situation, not only must high-cost firms agree to follow the low-cost firm's price, but there must also be an understanding as to the share of the market each of the sellers is to have. To price using this model it will be necessary for the low-cost firm to estimate its market share demand function and its own cost function. Given this information, the low-cost firm determines market price using the familiar marginal revenue–marginal cost criterion. Other firms in the market have no product market decisions to make. At the determined price, other sellers produce and sell that volume that corresponds to their market share.

Finally, in the case of price leadership by the dominant firm, the dominant firm will need an estimate of market demand and an estimate of how much will be supplied by the smaller firms at various prices. Given this information, the dominant firm's demand function can be computed. This and an estimate of the dominant firm's cost function provide enough information to determine the profit-maximizing price and both dominant firm volume and the combined volume of the small firms. Small firms will split up this latter volume in the manner discussed above. The only pricing decision is made by the dominant firm according to the familiar criterion. Small firms have only volume decisions to make, given the price set by the dominant firm.

[8]In the figure, $ab = P'b'$.

Up to this point we have discussed pricing models in which (1) there was collusion among sellers or (2) sellers followed "conservative" pricing policies of one sort or another. If neither of these circumstances prevails in an oligopolistic market, then independent actions on the part of individual firms create a persistent danger of price wars. For example, one firm may lower price in an attempt to increase profits. This action takes customers away from rivals, and rivals will often be forced to retaliate to stay in business. Such behavior can easily spread across the industry with disastrous consequences for one and all.

As we have seen, the market instability just described provides a strong incentive for either the formation of collusive agreements or the adoption of "conservative" pricing strategies. In some instances the latter strategy may amount to not changing price unless there is no other alternative. This phenomenon is an often noted characteristic of noncollusive oligopoly: A price once established tends to be maintained for extended periods of time even in the face of changes in demand and cost that in other markets would imply a price change on the part of the seller. It is interesting to note that in this situation rigid prices over extended periods of time are consistent with, and indeed implied by, profit maximization. We next present a model that predicts rigid prices in the face of changing demand and costs.

### The Kinked Demand Curve: A Model of Noncollusive Oligopoly

The model that follows is not a pricing model, as it takes the historical price as given. The purpose of the model is merely to demonstrate that in markets where no collusion exists, one may well find highly rigid prices even in periods of changing demand and cost conditions.

Consider an oligopolistic industry in which there are no formal agreements among firms, nor has the industry evolved to the point where self-interest on the part of individual firms has led to consistently "conservative" price policies. So for example, price leadership in any form is not present in the industry in question. Now let us consider the most likely effect of a price change instigated by any one firm. In these circumstances, we would expect to find that price cuts on the part of any one seller will be met with retaliatory price cuts on the part of other sellers designed to maintain, or even increase, market shares. Thus, for price decreases, individual sellers can expect to do little more than hold their own market shares. In other words, for price decreases, individual firm demand is quite inelastic (sales respond only minimally to price reductions). On the other hand, if one seller decides to increase price, under the circumstances there will most likely be few, if any, followers. Thus, for price increases, individual sellers will find demand very elastic, with "small" price increases causing "large" decreases in sales as customers leave for other firms.

This situation is shown in Figure 10-5, where $P^0$ represents the established price in the market. The firm's demand function will have a "kink" at this point

233

**FIGURE 10-5**

The kinked
demand curve:
a model of
noncollusive
oligopoly

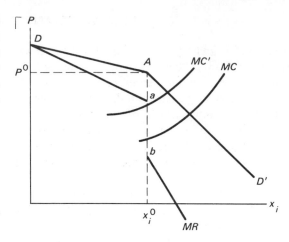

for the reasons given in the preceding paragraph. So, as far as the firm, say firm $i$, is concerned, its demand function is $DA$ for price increases and $AD'$ for price decreases. The importance of this demand curve lies in the associated marginal revenue function in which there is a discontinuity at the same volume as the kink. The marginal revenue function is labeled $DabM$. If the seller's marginal cost function is $MC$, volume will be $x_i^0$ at the established price. Note that this is the profit-maximizing volume, since marginal revenue is greater than marginal cost at lower volumes and less than marginal cost at higher volumes. But the unique attribute of this model is that substantial changes in cost, brought about by, say, increased factor prices, can result in no move to increase price (see $MC'$ in the figure), a conclusion brought about by the mutual interdependence of sellers and the lack of any coherent pricing strategy in the industry.

At this juncture, one point should be emphasized: The foregoing discussion does *not* imply that economists believe that managers draw diagrams like Figure 10-5 for decision making, or even that managers conceptualize the demand function as being of the form shown. Instead, the important point brought out in Figure 10-5 is that if there is no collusion in an oligopolistic market, then demand functions of sellers will be kinked at the established price and consequently it will not be profitable to change price over a wide range of costs. How managers come to terms with this fact is irrelevant. Our diagram is merely a simple means of depicting the implications of these demand conditions.

### Nonprice Competition

Because demand functions of sellers are interdependent in oligopolistic markets, and because the consequences of price cuts are highly uncertain, oligopolists often choose competitive techniques other than price cuts to increase sales. Most commonly, *nonprice competition* consists of quality and design changes, special service contracts, and advertising expenditures designed to increase both market share and customer loyalty. Increased expenditures on any one of these activities will usually result in "rightward" shifts in demand which allow the existing volume to be sold at an increased price or an increased volume to be sold at the existing price.

A major "plus" on the side of changes in these nonprice variables is that their effect on sales is fairly predictable, at least in direction. Price cuts constitute such a formidable competitive weapon in oligopoly that affected firms are usually forced to respond rapidly in what may be a self-feeding process of price cuts and retaliation resulting in lower profits for all. The reader should not conclude from this statement that nonprice competition cannot result in similar consequences. In fact, any selling activity, whether it be a design change or an increase in advertising outlays, if successful, will increase one seller's market share often at the expense of other sellers, forcing adversely affected sellers to retaliate. Therefore, the basic fact of oligopolistic life, mutually interdependent demand functions, means that all market decisions on the part of any one seller affect all other sellers in the market. But the major drawback of price cuts as a competitive weapon is the speed with which competitors can match the cut. Such competitive moves as advertising campaigns and design changes cannot be quickly matched and hence are more likely to be used to gain competitive advantage.

## PROBLEMS AND QUESTIONS

1. Consider an oligopolistic market with $n$ sellers. Derive an expression relating the percentage change in firm $i$ revenues due to a percentage change in $P_i$ to the various demand elasticities, $\eta_{ij}$, and reaction coefficients, $\theta_{ij}$. (Hint: The case where $n = 2$ is equation (10-4'') in the text.)

2. Consider a two-firm oligopoly in which firms compete primarily by means of advertising campaigns. Prices are seldom changed and then only after mutual consideration. Derive an expression showing the response of firm one revenues to changes in its own advertising outlays. This expression will include an "advertising interaction" term similar to the "pricing interaction" term $\theta_{21}$ in equation (10-4'').

3. Before a recent advertising campaign, the demand function for $X_1$ (in thousands of units) was estimated to be $x_1 = 9070 - 6.1P_1 + 2.2P_2 + .5Y + .09A_1 - .07A_2$. At present $P_1 = \$500$, $P_2 = \$450$, $Y = 150$, $A_1 = \$50,000$, and $A_2 = \$120,000$. During the campaign $A_1$ was increased to $\$60,000$ while $P_1, P_2, Y$, and $A_2$ remained unchanged.

a. Assuming the producer of $X_2$ did not change the price of $X_2$ during the campaign, show what has happened to the price elasticity of demand of $X_1$ as a result of the advertising campaign. Interpret this finding using the marketing concept of "product loyalty" where a "loyal" customer is one who is relatively insensitive to price changes.

b. Now assume the producer of $X_2$ decreases $P_2$ to $\$400$ in response to the advertising campaign. What is the effect of this decision on the postcampaign price elasticity of demand for $X_1$? Compare this elasticity with the one calculated in part a when $P_2$ was left unchanged.

c. Can you make a general statement about the effects of firm advertising expenditures on "product loyalty"? Will this statement hold if rival firms increase advertising outlays in response to increases in the firm's own advertising outlays? Explain.

d. What effect do changes in $P_2$ have on (i) the "position" and (ii) the price elasticity of the demand for $X_1$?

4. Assume that market demand in a particular industry is given by $P = 500 - 2x$ and that there are two firms in this market with cost functions $C_1(x_1) = 931 + 3x_1^2$ and $C_2(x_2) = 870 + 2x_2^2$. Also assume management of firm one has learned through bitter experience that firm two has lower costs and for this reason has agreed to dividing up the market "fifty-fifty" and letting management of firm two set market price. Firm one quickly follows any price change on the part of firm two.

a. What price will be set under this arrangement? (Hint: The "market share" demand functions facing each firm are $P_i = 500 - 4x_i$, $i = 1, 2$.)

b. What price would firm one like to charge? Why doesn't it?

c. Calculate firm one profits. Firm two profits.

d. What is the total amount sold by the two firms under this agreement?

5. Two large corporations are the only producers of a certain product. The companies have attempted to differentiate their products but without much success. (Marketing studies show the products to be very close substitutes.) Call the two products $X$ and $Y$ and assume that the seller of $X$ has the demand function for $X$ estimated. The estimate is

$$x = 300 - 10{,}000P_X + 9{,}000P_Y + 24Z$$

where $Z$ represents consumer disposable income. At present, $Z = 100$, $P_X = \$1.30$, and $P_Y = \$1.20$. If variable production costs for $X$ are given by $D(x) = .92x$:

a. What price would the seller of $X$ like to charge?

b. Under what assumption is this the profit-maximizing price? Is this assumption likely to be met? Explain.

c. What additional information does the seller of $X$ need to determine its optimal price?

# Solutions

Following are solutions to problems in the text that have numerical answers.

## CHAPTER 1

2. (a) 4.66%; (b) $5500
3. .12
5. (a) −8; (b) 4.88

## CHAPTER 2

1. (a) −.13; −.2; (c) .5% increase; (d) 2.5%
2. (a) 503.09 million tons; (b) −.20; (c) −.17
3. (b) (i) $x_B$ will increase by .09%
       (ii) $x_B$ will increase by 1.05%
    (c) $x_B$ will increase by .32%
5. (b) 3.7%, $9.60, $103,714; (c) $9.84
11. (a) −.14, −0.36; (b) −.11, −.28
12. (a) it decreases; (b) −2.14 thousand tons, −71.3 thousand tons;
     (c) −.076, −2.55; (d) .336, 2.40

## CHAPTER 3

1. (e) 1.25, 1.00
2. (d) 1.4

3.

| $v_1$ | $\epsilon_1$ |
|-------|--------------|
| 1     |              |
| 2     | .47          |
| 3     | .49          |
| 4     | .48          |
| 5     | .47          |

Use average values of $v_1$ and $x$ to calculate $\epsilon_1$

## CHAPTER 4

4. (a) no, $v_1^0 = 3v_2^0$; (b) $\epsilon = 2$
6. (a) $v_1/3v_2$; (b) (3750, 2500); (c) (3000, 4000); (d) $\epsilon = 1$
9. (b) (4, 4); (c) $(8/\sqrt{3}, 3)$
10. Cost of producing 1100 units is $880 under the present technology and $1099.98 under the new technology. Stick with the current set-up.
11. (i) use only labor; (ii) use capital only; (iii) use that combination of labor and capital such that $RTS_{LK} = w_K/w_L$
12. $v_1^0 = 16$, $v_2^0 = 0$
15. (i) $a = 1/2$, $b = 1$; (ii) yes, if $w_2^0/w_1^0 < 1/2$
17. (a) Process III; (b) $920; (c) 1. Process III, 2. Process III, 3. Process IV
18. (a) 600 units in Process III, 400 units in Process IV (i.e., $k_3 = .6$, $k_4 = .4$); (b) $C = \$1052$
19. (a) $\$21.31 < w_1 < \$42.62$; (b) Processes II and III, $k_2 = k_3 = 10$
20. answer in text
22. $v_1^0 = 5$, $v_2^0 = 8.7$; only 744 units can be produced in this case for $89,600.

## CHAPTER 5

2. (a) $x_1^0 = 0$, $x_2^0 = 25$, $y_3^0 = \$.406$, $y_1^0 = y_2^0 = 0$, $L_1^0 = \$12.50$;
   (b) any mix from $x_1 = 10$, $x_2 = 20$ to $x_1 = 0$, $x_2 = 25$ yields $7500
3. (a) $x_1^0 = 10,909$, $x_2^0 = 27,272$; (b) $y_1^0 = y_2^0 = 0$, $y_3^0 = \$84.84$, $y_4^0 = \$10.61$; (c) $S_1^0 = 13,636.5$ hrs., $S_2^0 = 910$ hrs.; (d) $175; (e) no, if $X_2$ becomes more than 1.8 times as profitable as $X_1$; (f) $x_1^0 = 12,000$, $x_2^0 = 26,000$; (g) graph this constraint along with the previous constraints to answer this question.
4. (a) $x_1^0 = 333$, $x_2^0 = 400$; (b) $Z_2$ and $Z_3$ are being used to capacity;
   (c) $y_1^0 = 0$, $y_2^0 = \$1.33$, $y_3^0 = \$.39$; (d) to $37.50 or higher
5. (a) $x_1^0 = 6$, $x_2^0 = 20$, $x_3^0 = \$10$; (b) since $\partial x_1^0/\partial d_3 = .4$, output in sector one must be increased by $(.4)(\$2.5$ billion$) = $ one billion dollars

## CHAPTER 6

1. (a) yes; (b) $D(x) = 2.76\sqrt{x}$; (c) $D(x) = 3.06\sqrt{x}$;
   (d) $D(x) = 3.45\sqrt{x}$
2. $D(x) = 1.63x^{2/3}$
3. $D(x) = (2/\sqrt{5})x$
4. (a) $D(x) = .92x$
   (d) $D(x) = \begin{cases} .92x, & 0 \le x \le 900 \\ 2.24(x - 900) + 828, & 900 < x \le 1200 \\ 3.2(x - 1200) + 1500, & 1200 < x \le 1800 \end{cases}$
7. (a) $D(x) = 4.96x$; (b) $D(x) = 3.36x$; (c) $D(x) = 1.56x$

2. no
3. no
4. true
6. (c) no
8. $97.50

2. (a) $329 < x^0 < 375$
   (b) $x = \dfrac{P - 100}{2.4}$, $\quad P \ge \$100$
   $\quad x = 0, \quad P < \$100$
3. (a) $x = 20{,}000$; (b) $76,000
4. 9.5 million; zero
5. $x = 36{,}962$ units if 36,962 units can be sold at $149.50, otherwise the optimal volume is whatever buyers will buy at this price (see Fig. 16 in text)
7. (a) $x = 354$; (b) $x = 306$
8. (a) To somewhere between 56 and 63.3 cents per gallon, depending upon whether the shortage is 10%, 14%, or somewhere in between; (b) only 6.6% of the shortage could be eliminated; (c) they will be be lower.

## CHAPTER 9

2. yes
3. Lower price, the former price is 1.63 times higher than the new price.
5. $12.75
6. (b) yes, $P^0 = \$36$
7. (a) $P^0 = \$1.43$; (b) $D = 1.38x$ and $P^0 = \$1.67$
8. Solve by graphing marginal revenue and marginal cost functions:
   $x^0 = 900$; $P^0 = \$1.86$

9. (a) $5; (b) same decision as (a)
11. $x_1^0 = 1250$, $x_2^0 = 1875$ and $P^0 = \$6875$
12. (a) yes; (b) $98.13; (c) $\partial P^0/\partial Y = .3$; (d) $99.63, $102.63
13. no, $P^0 = \$44.66$

## CHAPTER 10

3. (a) $\eta_{11}$ increases from $-.96$ to $-.75$ due to the advertising effort;
   (b) $\eta_{11}$ decreases slightly to $-.77$
4. (a) $P = \$333.36$; (b) $357.14; (c) $\pi_1 = \$7750.11$, $\pi_2 = \$9546.66$;
   (d) 83.32
5. (a) $1.14

# Index

## A

Accounting profit, 78, 182, 216
Average cost
   geometry of, 142, 144
   long-run, 150
   shape of, 141
Average fixed cost, 141
Average product
   and average variable cost, 141-43
   defined, 63
   geometry of curves of, 64
   relation to total and marginal products, 64
Average revenue, 172
Average total cost, 141
Average variable cost, 141

## B

Barriers to entry, 202-3
Brand loyalty, 235
Breakeven analysis
   price maker, 210
   price taker, 197
Buyers, number of, 191

## C

Cartel
   defined, 227
   market sharing, 228
   profit maximization, 227, 229
Cobb-Douglas production function, 89

Collusion, 226
Competition, *see* Monopolistic competition
   *and* Pure competition
Complementary commodities, 3, 4, 6
Constant returns to scale, 67, 93, 153
Cost curves
   average products and, 142
   linear technology and, 143-44
      example, 145-50
   long-run
      average, 153
      theory of, 150-56
   marginal products and, 142
   short-run, 140-42
      average, 141-42
      average fixed, 141-42
      average variable, 141-42
      marginal, 141-42
      total, 141-42
Cost-plus pricing, 209
Cost of production
   alternative, 77-78
   derivation of, 139
   direct, 78
   estimation of, 156, 161
   long-run theory of, 150-56
   maximizing output for a given, 81, 89
      example, 85-88, 101-3
   minimizing when subject to given output, 83, 89, 97, 99
      examples, 85-88, 101-3
   opportunity, 77
   short-run theory of, 139-44
   total input, 78
   *See also* specific type of cost

## DATE DUE

| 4/ѵ3/76 | | | |
|---|---|---|---|
| | | | |
| | | | |
| | | | |
| | | | |
| | | | |
| | | | |
| | | | |
| | | | |
| | | | |
| | | | |
| | | | |
| | | | |
| | | | |
| | | | |
| | | | |
| | | | |
| | | | |
| GAYLORD | | | PRINTED IN U.S.A. |